AN ACT OF LOVE

&

MARIE FLEMING

WITH SUE LEONARD

HACHETTE
BOOKS
IRELAND

First published in 2014 by Hachette Books Ireland
First published in paperback in 2014 by Hachette Books Ireland
A division of Hachette UK Ltd

A CIP catalogue record for this title is available from the British Library.

ISBN 978 1 44479 122 8

Typeset and layout design by Bookends Publishing Services
Printed and bound by Clays Ltd, St Ives plc

Hachette Books Ireland
8 Castlecourt Centre, Castleknock, Dublin 15, Ireland

A division of Hachette UK Ltd
338 Euston Road, London NW1 3BH

www.hachette.ie

AN ACT OF LOVE

About the Author

Marie Fleming was born and raised in Donegal. She left school early and became a mother at just sixteen, before returning to college in her twenties where she later gained her MBA. In her mid-thirties she was diagnosed with MS, which led her to take a landmark case, years later in 2012, against the Irish state to lift the ban on assisted suicide. Although she lost her case, she gained a huge groundswell of public support and brought the 'right to die' issue into the forefront of public debate. Marie had two grown-up children and lived in Woodenbridge, County Wicklow, with her partner and carer, Tom. Marie died from MS in December 2013.

ΩΚΥ

About the Co-Author

Sue Leonard has made her living from freelance journalism for eighteen years. She writes interview-based features for the *Irish Independent*, the *Irish Examiner* and many other publications. A former columnist with the *Evening Herald*, she currently writes the 'Beginner's Pluck' book column for the *Irish Examiner*. Author of *Keys to the Cage* (New Island, 2010), Sue has previous experience as a ghost writer, having worked on three books, two for Penguin Ireland. A consultant for Inkwell Writers, she is ___ly in charge of manuscript assessments.

'In many ways the most remarkable witness which any member of this court has ever been privileged to encounter.'

High Court President Mr Nicholas Kearns

⁂

'It is many years since I first read Marie Fleming's account of growing up in Donegal, but her story stayed with me and it is with a pang of great pride I see it finally in print, along with all the joys and sorrows that followed. The heart of a true writer beats in these sentences, and a writer's hard work is seen on every page: tell it straight, keep it close, let people know.'

Anne Enright

To my grandchildren:

Jordan, Cormac, Aran, Evan, Lorcan, Aoife and Cara

CONTENTS

ઐᏧ

CONTENTS

FOREWORD

෩෨

It is a great honour that I have been asked to write this foreword for Marie's book, but it is with great sadness that I write it. As I sit here, my eyes welling with tears, I think back to the wonderful times Marie and I shared together. While trying to think of the right words to say, my attention is drawn to a tune on the radio. Dido's 'Thank You' sums up everything I feel, playing in this moment as if to provide inspiration. The number of times things like this have happened since Marie passed away two weeks ago, on the 20 December, is uncanny. Through the sadness and heartbreak I feel at the moment, I am so thankful to have shared part of my life with such an amazing person. Her strength and courage through very difficult times, when MS gradually took away more and more of her ability to live as she would have wanted, was a constant source of wonder and inspiration to me, and indeed to all who came to know her in the last few years. I often wished I could swap places with her, though I know that I could never have coped with things the way she did.

Marie began writing her memoir many years ago, when she still had the use of most of her body. She began writing into notebooks in longhand, continued by typing on her laptop and finished with dictating. The story of her early years in itself made worthy reading and, when coupled with the recounting of her journey through Multiple Sclerosis and the ensuing challenge to the Irish law on assisted suicide, truly reveals just what a wonderful person Marie was.

Our ambition was always to have it published and Marie was delighted when it became clear this would happen. We used to joke about me being able to go to a bookshop, buy a copy of her life story and bring it home to her. While that is sadly no longer possible, I can only hope that her words will provide the same inspiration and courage to others as they have to me.

My years with Marie were not always a bed of roses – although one of the many lovely things we shared was the planting of many roses, as well as lots of other additions, to the garden haven we developed and enjoyed together. When two strong-willed people come together, there will be the occasional disagreement, and we were no exception to this. Marie could be as strong-willed in making her point as she could in living her life but, like most people, we would eventually agree to differ, make up and get on with enjoying our life together. Life for Marie was not easy as the MS progressed and took away her physical capabilities. Despite this, I never heard her complain. I was both humbled and inspired by the way she faced everything that life threw at her, and never stopped thinking of other people and how they might be affected.

Her fame spread around the world as she went to the highest court in Ireland in an attempt to establish her right to take control away from the MS in determining the time and manner in which she died. To her, this was the ultimate fight against the beast that had taken so much from her. She was determined that the MS would not control her death as it did much of her life – and her concern was not just for herself but for others in similar situations to us. And, while she had the assurance from me that she could be in control at the end, the court case was an attempt to protect those who were prepared to help her. While she may have lost the case, she ultimately won in the end.

During the final years with Marie, so much time was spent on the subject of death, that it is lovely, though very sad, to be concentrating now on her incredible life, in celebrating the publication of her memoir.

Life without Marie will be very different. We will all miss her so much but I know that while her body is no longer with us, her heart, her courage and her spirit will be with me and all of us for a long time to come.

Tom Curran
January 2014

PROLOGUE

ജ്ഞ

M y last request on this earth is to be allowed to die at home in the arms of my partner, Tom, and with my two adult children, Corrinna and Simon, close by. I want to be held, hugged and whispered to as I pass on. To do this without fear of prosecution for Tom, I had to take the state to court.

Under the 1993 Criminal Law (Suicide) Act it is a criminal offence to assist anybody to die. Had we won the case, it would have allowed me the right to be assisted to drink a medication that would put me to sleep for ever – something that is done for sick animals as a matter of course. It is voluntary euthanasia, or assisted suicide, and it is the way I have chosen to end twenty-four years of immobility, incontinence and pain.

The law stopping me now is the only law on the statute

books where it is illegal to help somebody to do something that is legal. The case is based on Article 40 of the Constitution which specifically states that the law will protect the rights of the vulnerable, including the disabled. Suicide is not just perfectly legal, it is a right, and there are cases in the High Court and the Supreme Court where people were given the right to perform acts to take their own life.

People like me, who have a disability that removes the physical capability of taking their own life, also have their rights removed. They are not allowed to get assistance. This is why I took my case.

It was not an easy decision, or a quick one. When I made it, I could walk a little. I could move my hands, and I had the full power to swallow. Knowing what is ahead, I want to take my life at a time when my disability becomes unbearable. Six years ago, we considered Dignitas. It seemed the only option, and because my swallow was going, we would have to act quickly. I wasn't ready then.

I didn't want to go to Switzerland. And I was worried that, afterwards, Tom and the children would have to come home alone. And that, maybe, they would face prosecution. We talked about it, and Tom said, 'You don't have to go. I will help you die at home when the time is right.'

CHAPTER ONE

DAY IN THE LIFE

෨෬

When you have a disability like mine, it's not the large things in life that you miss. It's the tiny, tiny things that are so difficult to live without. When people approach me holding out their hand in a gesture of friendship, I can't reciprocate. I have to say, 'I'm sorry. You'll just have to touch my hand.' And when they do that, I don't usually feel their touch.

In simple terms, multiple sclerosis is a debilitating disease in which the myelin sheath running down the nerve is affected. It develops holes, so the brain sends the wrong signals to the muscles of the body. In the healthy body, the brain tells the hand to lift, and the legs to walk. In MS, scar tissue or plaque forms on the myelin sheath, around the nerve. So instead of the messages going directly from the brain, they get impeded by that bit of plaque. My brain has four plaques at the top of my spinal cord, and that means that all my motor functions are affected.

Some people with MS stumble, lose their balance, or find themselves unable to move one leg. Others have sight problems. Their eyes mist over, and they see an outline of someone, but not the whole person. Their hands might shake, so that they are unable to hold a glass, and they have to drink through a straw. My side-effects are now so severe that I cannot move my hands at all. When my nose itches I send constant signals from my brain to lift my right arm, so that I can put my hand up and scratch my nose, but nothing happens. This is, to me, a terrible problem.

My sense of hearing is still intact. Tom says I would hear the grass grow. It surprises him that I can hear, and recognise, all the cars that pass on the road outside. I know exactly who each one is. I tease Tom when I've heard his car turn into the drive. I listen out for how many attempts it takes him to reverse in a straight line. I hope I don't lose my senses, because without them, you are little more than a vegetable.

My feelings are heightened because of my MS. That can be hard. There are people around me who act as my arms and legs, but they can't really know how it feels to have fingers and toes that jangle, to have legs that jerk without your permission. Sometimes my scalp is so sensitive that my hair feels as if it is digging into my brain. That is a horrible sensation.

Since I have been unable to move, my days have taken on a pattern. When dark turns to light I hear the birds twittering outside. Then the alarm rings, and Tom turns to knock it off, before he goes to the bathroom for a shower. Then he walks through to the kitchen, and Scruffy, our dog, jumps up from his bed and follows him. A small terrier-type mongrel, he appeared in our garden one day a few years ago and refused to go away. He has been a loyal companion ever since. My day begins when Tom arrives at the side of the bed with the day's first set of medication. There's Zanaflex for spasms, Lyrica for pain, and so it continues. I have to take twenty-two tablets first thing; the pills are blue, brown and gold.

During the early stages of MS, I had a bedroom upstairs. But when I was cooped up there, in that poky cottage room, for three weeks during a particularly nasty chest infection, there was nothing to do, and nothing to see. I would hear horses in the field next door, but that just reinforced the isolation I felt.

I was unable to move, let alone get up or down the steep, winding stairs. It was like being in a prison cell. Worst of all, I had to pee in a commode, an indignity that proved to be the final straw. It was then that Tom and I decided that, as soon as money allowed, we would build a new downstairs bedroom. We've done that, and I now have a bedroom en suite. I love the room, with its warm buttermilk walls. I feel bathed in sunshine, even on grey, cloudy days.

Since then, the garden has been given a good facelift too. And now, when I wake, Tom draws back the curtains, so that I can watch the blue tits and finches fighting over the feeders. We have five feeders, strategically placed around the periphery of the Indian sandstone patio, so that I can watch the birds through the bedroom's French windows. It gives me such pleasure watching the birds flit from tree to tree, occasionally stopping to nibble on the peanuts trapped behind the feeders' green netting wire. I can see our water feature too; it's a waterfall with a roar as loud as the Atlantic Ocean.

My morning carer arrives at nine o'clock. She puts the sling on me, so that I can be hoisted off the bed and into my shower chair. I love being in the shower. When the hot water runs over my head I feel that I am standing there all by myself. It is when they start soaping and rinsing me down that my heart sinks. It took me two years to get the courage to allow someone to bathe me. I fought it all the way, but when your legs give out, and then your arms, you have no choice. The last thing I wanted was to turn into a smelly old woman.

After my carer has washed me and dried me off, I have a lovely perfumed cream rubbed all over my body. I've always looked after my skin. I think I inherited that from my beloved maternal grandmother. I remember, when I visited her as a child, I would stroke her arm; it was soft and smooth. I'd sit with her for hours.

After that, I might have an incontinence pad to contend with. I find that degrading, and I give a childish whimper now and again. My dignity has definitely suffered. When that's done, a decision has to be made about my clothes. Sometimes I decide on something outrageous. Perhaps purple shoes, with a red pair of trousers; or maybe a green Aran cardigan over a navy polo neck and matching trousers. That's my small rebellion.

The radio is my salvation. I listen to RTÉ Radio One all the time. I miss some of *The John Murray Show* between nine and ten o'clock because that's when I'm in the shower, but I catch most of the *Today* programme that follows. This brings me up to date with the latest problems facing Ireland in 2013 – and with our current economic crisis there are many. Often they discuss the government's ineffective use of resources.

As I write this, Tom and I have been in the news. It is so strange when I hear my illness discussed. I listen and I think, 'That poor woman!' It is hard to realise they are talking about me. I don't think I will ever get used to that.

Tom often takes some time off for himself in the mornings. He'll go out for a cup of coffee, or maybe he'll do the shopping. He is good at that. And he is an excellent cook too. He always was. I particularly like it when he cooks fish with a nice sauce, or a chicken stir-fry.

Once I am dressed, it's time for my second set of pills. Taking them can be a trial. The muscles in my throat are so weak now: some of them have atrophied and that can make me choke. This happens especially if I am getting over an infection. Usually I take the tablets with water, but when I'm weak I have them with a food supplement to help them down. Even this isn't foolproof. I might choke every time I'm given tablets. I'll have to be thumped on my back, and that is exhausting.

Once the tablets are down, it's time for breakfast. This might be porridge covered with seasonal fruits, and topped with maple syrup. The carer feeds me that. I have a rota of carers. They are all good, and are patient, but I loathe being fed. I hate it when food dribbles down my chin and has to be wiped away. It makes me feel like a baby. It can take a long time too. After breakfast, the morning routine is finished. It all takes two and a half hours; sometimes, by the time I'm ready for the day, current affairs have made way for *The Ronan Collins Show*.

By then I can be so tired. That is the terrible thing – how getting up can exhaust me. The fatigue is the worst thing about having MS. Well, the fatigue and the constant pain. I get tired and that's when I'm more likely to choke. And choking makes me even more exhausted. This morning, as soon as Margaret, today's carer, had me up and sitting in my chair, I was so tired I just wanted to go back to bed.

I have seven carers. Someone comes in every day to get me up. Margaret comes on Monday and Wednesday mornings; Anne comes in for three afternoons a week, arriving at one o'clock, and on two days she stays on to put me to bed too. It takes an hour to get me to bed. On Mondays and Thursdays Geraldine comes at 6 pm. When Anne puts me to bed I go at 5 pm. At the weekends, a carer comes in to get me up, and Tom puts me to bed. On bank holidays there are no carers. That is very tough on Tom.

All my carers are wonderful. Anne updates me on all the news from around the area. It's like having my own mini news programme. She amuses me. By the time she arrives, my chair will have been wheeled into the sitting room and I will be ready to have my lunch. Today I ask for melon and prosciutto, and Anne gently forks the food into my mouth, rather than spooning it in. I like that.

After lunch it's time for my third lot of tablets. Anne gives me those. My tablets are a mixture of ones to reduce the pain and others to stop my muscles from going into spasm. Even with the tablets, I feel pain all the time. I have pain in my shoulder and my neck. That's because my left arm is placed back a bit so that I can support my head. My neck is getting weaker by the day. The pain goes from the shoulder down to the tips of my fingers. My hands are very painful too, as are my feet.

If it's fine, I'll sit in the garden, but I have to be well wrapped up. MS works on the extremities. Your hands and your feet are always cold. I adore being out in the fresh air. I always loved my garden. It frustrates me that I now have to rely on Tom to keep it in order for us. I like nothing better than to watch him working there. He says I'm a hard taskmaster.

These days I rarely go out. The last time I left the house was three weeks ago, to have Sunday lunch with my daughter. We have a specially adapted car and my wheelchair goes straight in. But once we leave the house, the roads are so bad that by the time we get into Woodenbridge, I am in pain from being bounced around. Tom frequently has to stop the car to get me repositioned.

Before my health deteriorated in March 2013, we would regularly get out in the car. Sometimes we went to the Bridgewater Shopping Centre in Arklow. We would have a cup of coffee somewhere, and maybe a sandwich. Then we just wandered around the shops. That was good, because it didn't matter if it was cold and raining. We did think about moving to Arklow, instead of living in the middle of the country, but we decided against it. We love the cottage too much to leave it, and there is a great sense of community here.

I am in constant touch by phone with my children, Corrinna and Simon, and with my seven grandchildren. Simon, his wife Susan, and their children Evan and Jordan live in Waterford, so their visits are limited, but we see Corrinna regularly. When my health was better we sometimes met her for a coffee in the Avoca café in the Mount Usher Gardens because, with her living in Dalkey, that's roughly midway between us. When I was still in an ordinary wheelchair, Tom used to wheel me around the gardens. I loved that. That stopped when I graduated to this mechanised wheelchair, which is more comfortable but considerably less wieldy. Tom was frightened that, with the uneven paths, I might topple over and end up in the river.

On other days we met Corrinna in Dún Laoghaire for lunch. I liked that, but I made sure Tom found a corner table so that I could sit with my back to everyone. Then they couldn't see me eating. I hate people to see me being fed like a baby; I get very embarrassed. I would order pasta or fish, and normally a big dessert. I've always had a sweet tooth.

Sometimes we went to Corrinna's house in Dalkey for tea. When her five children heard the car turning into the drive they would all come running out of the house shouting, 'Granny! Granny!' The twins, Aran and Cormac, raced out – they're eleven now – and Lorcan, who is seven, wouldn't be far behind. He has my mother's eyes. We used to call my mother Juicy Eyes, and he has those same pools of black. I just adore him. Well, I adore them all. The nice thing is that I've been in a wheelchair since all the kids have been small, so they have known nothing else. It is normal to them.

I still see my grandchildren regularly, but now they come to the cottage. They jump into my wheelchair and give me big kisses on my lips. I love that. Aoife, who is five, climbs up into the wheelchair to offer me a drink. She will have the glass in her hand. It would break your heart. And Cara, who is only two, tried to give me a drink the last time I saw her. When she couldn't manage that, she gave me a grape. She just popped it into my mouth. I love seeing them, but I ache to touch them, to run my fingers through their hair and to give them a hug. It's those little things that I miss so much.

I am in touch with my family in Donegal too. They visit me when they can, and my sister Noeleen keeps in touch with me by telephone. That means a lot to me. I have other visitors too. Friends and neighbours often pop in and I love seeing them, even on the days when I am confined to bed. They tell me that I'm great company.

Most afternoons are quieter. Tom will be in and out, talking to me, giving me sips of water or moving my head when it slips to one side. And before I know it, the afternoon has gone and Joe Duffy and Derek Mooney have finished for the day on RTÉ Radio One. I love *Mooney*, especially on a Friday when they talk about nature on 'Mooney Goes Wild'.

All too soon it's time for bed. I dread the process. When I think how much I once loved dressing-up, how excited I'd feel, changing to go out in the evenings, it makes me sad. These days, the putting on and taking off of my clothes is so tiresome. I have to be hauled around, my limbs forced into various positions. All I want to do afterwards is sleep. That sounds ridiculous, but now that my illness has become terminal, I am sleeping more. I could lie in my bed for two days and still not feel rested.

I like being in bed but not asleep. I use this time to think and to process all the information I have. I think about my life and about the case I took in the High Court and then the Supreme Court. I plan stories, and the book I want to write. I love the night hours. It's the time when I can dream. When I can run ahead, walk up a mountain, and other exciting adventures. I am always running or cycling in my dreams. Or doing a James Bond jumping out of a helicopter, like Queen Elizabeth at the opening ceremony of the Olympic Games in London.

I make up stories for the grandchildren. Since they were babies, the twins used to say to me that they wanted stories out of my head, not out of the book. I had to sit for hours in a wheelchair entertaining my first grandchildren with stories of the ruby red dragon who lived in the mountain behind me. I managed to keep that going for three years, and used the same stories for Simon's son Evan, who is two years younger than the twins. Then Lorcan told me that I was imagining things. That knocked me off my high stool for ever.

I couldn't use the same stories for Aoife and Cara. I tried, but stories of jumping out of boats and going to a red and blue island didn't impress Aoife one bit. She kept telling me to shush, that she didn't want to hear boys' stories. So the pink princess won out and I have never told the boys' stories since.

Later on in the evening I watch some soaps on television from my bed; I love *Emmerdale* and *Coronation Street*, but I don't watch *EastEnders* because it's so violent. Soaps are good because they are not demanding. It's easy to concentrate. I love period dramas too. I adored *Downton Abbey* and recently I enjoyed *The Village*, even though that was quite dark. Tom doesn't watch any of those, but when a quiz is on he comes in and we watch together. We love *University Challenge*. We surprise ourselves with the questions we can answer. I think we are equal in our general knowledge.

At around 9pm Tom comes in and turns off the television and

the lights. Then I listen to the radio again and wait patiently for 11.30, when it's *Late Date* with Alf McCarthy. I love the radio, but sometimes I wish I could text a show. I hear someone on *The John Murray Show*, for example, saying something I don't agree with and I yearn to comment. It's the little things like that which can sometimes get me down.

It's tough for Tom too. We had an alarm. It was a comfort to Tom. It meant that he could go out somewhere local, and if something was wrong, I could alert him by pressing a button. But that disappeared because I can no longer press a button. We then tried voice recognition but that didn't work because my voice varies so much in strength.

Tom is such an integral part of my life. I would not have a life without him. He is everything to me, but on some days when I am feeling down I think I am unbearable to live with. I cry inside. And on those days I snipe at Tom. I can't help it. I'll shout at him. I will say, 'I love you really, but I can't stand you sometimes, because you are so irritating.' The really maddening thing is that Tom just walks away, mid-row. And of course I can't follow him. Sometimes we'll bicker for a few days. Then when I know I've pushed him too far we'll kiss and make up.

CHAPTER TWO
NOBODY ASKED

&?&?

When I lie in bed watching the birds and waiting for my first carer of the day to arrive, I think back over my life. It hasn't been an easy one, and the difficulty started in my childhood. When I think of that time I wonder if the stress I experienced in those early years contributed to the onset of my illness.

I wish I could say that my childhood was a happy one and that my parents loved each other, but I don't ever remember seeing them hug or kiss. From my earliest years the house was full of tension. My mother had married young; she was just sixteen to my father's thirty-two. I learned later that she was pregnant with me at the time of their marriage. She went on to have four more children: Noeleen, Shaun, Brian and Don. I didn't realise then that the marriage was a troubled one. As a child you just accept the way things are.

We lived in Lifford in south-east Donegal, near the border with Northern Ireland. I wasn't an easy child. I was too strong-minded for that. I wasn't an easy baby either. Daddy once told me that he had had to make a new rocker for my pram. He said I was always so restless that he would wake up in the morning with his hand on the handle of the pram. He would have dropped off over it while trying to rock me to sleep.

I remember that pram. It was a huge Swan one that Mammy's sister Mary, who lived in Birmingham, had arranged to have delivered. When I was a small child my mother took us for walks every single day in it. By the time there were five of us, that meant two children in the pram – one at the top and one at the bottom – and two dragging on Mammy's hand. As the eldest I had to dawdle along behind. If Daddy was there he always took my hand.

For three years we lived with my Granny Maxwell, my Mammy's mother. We were squashed into her back bedroom. I get a warm feeling inside when I think of that time and of the way Granny would cuddle me. I don't recall my mother ever doing that. Not even once. And perhaps as a result of that, I was always trying to please Mammy. Often I would help her roll her knitting wool into balls. I would hold out my arms to support the skeins of wool. I loved that, and I hoped my help pleased her. But she never said.

Daddy always singled me out and made me feel special. He

read me stories and sometimes we took a train together and went to visit my other grandmother, his mother. She lived about four miles away.

Eventually Mammy and Daddy got a house of their own. It was on the Coneyburrow estate in Lifford, and that's where they settled. After six years of marriage they were delighted to have a place of their own, a spanking new council house. It was a new beginning. They were a quiet couple at first, preferring to spend what free time they had with their children rather than in the pub.

They adored doing up the house. While Daddy spent time carefully painting, papering and tiling our new three-bedroomed house, Mammy saw to all the sewing. She made curtains and cushions and she revamped old frayed eiderdown quilts from remnants of material, and all with great style. Our place was the show house of the street.

I don't take after Mammy in many things, but I have inherited her ability to make a house look nice. It is almost a need in me. I love my security, and I like to be surrounded by nice things. In our sitting room in the cottage we have paintings of some of the grandchildren. And the house is full of furniture that I have collected at auctions over the years. That gives me great pleasure, and brings back memories of happy times.

Mammy was always making us clothes too. She would use cast-offs or hand-me-downs. Her hand-knitting was renowned in the locality; she knitted pullovers with fancy cable stitches, Aran cardigans with matching berets, and snug warm mittens. Even the leftover wool was put to good use when she made lots of outfits for our wee dolls.

I don't think Mammy really accepted Daddy as an equal. She seemed to look down on him and think he was inferior to her. She probably thought him dull. Being sixteen years older than she was, he was a lot more grounded. We all sensed Mammy's dissatisfaction. So did Daddy. I remember him saying that in her eyes everybody was better than him. I think she wanted us to lose respect for my father, but I never did.

Mammy was the most beautiful person I ever saw, except for Elizabeth Taylor. She was far and away the best-looking mammy in the street. She had waist-length chocolate chestnut hair and it was wavy, like ringlets. She was so beautiful, and my poor father, compared to her, looked haggard. But then, when we were young he was taking on multiple decorating jobs in an effort to keep Mammy in the style to which she had become accustomed. She wanted only the best, and she taught us to want the same. She was never happy with what she had, and that is another trait that I inherited. It's a shortcoming. When you're like me you don't always know what you want, but you can be sure it's something you don't have.

I think, looking back, that life must have been tough for Mammy. She was tied down to a man she didn't love, and had five children, and she craved a bit of fun. In a sense Mammy was rather immature. She wanted to go dancing, and possibly felt that by marrying so young she had missed out on the fun of youth.

Every Sunday Mammy dressed us up in our best clothes and inspected us before leading us for a family walk by the banks of the River Foyle. She looked a million dollars. I remember particularly her knee-length dogtooth check skirt with the split up the back. She had style, and somehow always managed to look good, even when she was doing the housework with curlers in her hair and an old apron on. So good that when the milkman or bread man came to the door for their money they would say, 'You're some looker, Annette.'

On those Sundays we would stop by the river to have a picnic. We had packets of crisps, minerals and occasionally bags of Emerald sweets. Then to round off our day we visited Granny Maxwell in her wee cottage. I loved that, because Granny was my favourite person in the world. She often baked treacle bread for us. I liked it best though when I visited Granny Maxwell on my own. She had a soft spot for me, and made me feel special.

Granny was a big soft dote. She had a soft, sleepy voice and her hair was white and fluffy like cotton wool. She wore it pulled loosely back into a bun, revealing a face full of love and understanding. I loved her so much that when I was eight years old I ran away from home to live with her. She sent me back when she realised Mammy didn't know where I was. She had discovered the loaf of bread and half pound of sausages Mammy needed for dinner, in the basket of my blue bike.

It makes me sad when I think of Granny Maxwell. I miss her still, but it's not just that. The memories bring home to me all the things that I can't do with my own grandchildren. I watch their development, the way that the smallest ones find their feet and learn to hold a spoon, and I can't help comparing their developing bodies with my deteriorating one. I find that so hard. What really hurts though is that I can't be the kind of grandmother I would like to be. I can't teach them to knit, and I'm unable to share my love of baking.

Granny lived in a two-up, two-down cottage with her daughter, Auntie Doreen, and Doreen's three adult sons, my uncles Tony, Eddie and Patsy. Granny's eldest son Willie lived there too. The house was always full of laughter, mischief and fun. It felt safe. I loved it when the 'boys' came in for their midday dinner. Especially Uncle Eddie, who was eighteen and had blond curly hair, big blue eyes and a smile that made me feel weak. He was learning his trade as a builder and told me that when he qualified he would build me a house, 'just like the one Red Riding Hood's granny has'. Before he got his coat off at dinnertime, Eddie would go over to the old Pye wireless and twiddle the knobs until he picked up Radio Luxembourg. Then, running a hand across his hair to give himself a quiff, and grabbing a spoon off the table, he would stand in front of Granny, legs wide apart and shaking, singing 'Hound Dog' or some other Elvis song.

'Will ye catch yeself on,' she'd tut, 'before ye rupture yeself.'

I loved the sleepy afternoons when the boys had all gone back to work. Granny and I would sit quietly by the fire looking for faces in the flames. Most days she dozed off. I would sit caressing the white porcelain skin on the back of her hands.

Nobody in my home appreciated books. I always loved them, but whenever I tried to read, I would be told to 'get your nose out of that book'. There was always something else Mammy and Daddy wanted me to do. I started to hide my library books in Granny's house. We had a secret place on her bedroom windowsill. They were piled high on the right-hand side, hidden by a net curtain. Granny always encouraged my love of reading.

When I was eleven Granny took to her bed. Mammy asked me to go and stay up there and help. I was to look after Granny while Auntie Doreen worked. It meant that I couldn't go to school. I loved being there, but it was tough seeing Granny get so weak. She slept more and more, and would doze off the minute I started reading to her. I would give her sips of water, or sometimes Lucozade. I liked that, because she let me have a slug of it too. Soon afterwards her health got worse. She asked to be taken into hospital, saying that she wanted to die with dignity. When she died, I felt I had lost my best friend in the world.

I felt guilty, as a child, for loving Granny Maxwell so much. Especially the times when I found Mammy hard to like. There were people in Lifford whom Mammy looked up to, people like Sergeant Fitzpatrick, and Doctor Coyne's wife. When we met them she would introduce my sister Noeleen as the good-looking one, then she would turn to me and be lost for words. But if she couldn't find words to describe me in public, she had no bother describing me within the four walls of our home.

'Ye good-for-nothing mad bitch,' she'd say. 'Ye remind me of yer Auntie Doreen.' I was afraid of Mammy at times. She'd give me a good skelp when her temper was up. Sometimes she used her hand, but mostly it was the birch rod that Daddy kept behind the sacred heart picture. That rod licked my legs nearly every day. When I showed Daddy the welts he'd say it was my own fault, and he had a point. Because I had a temper too. I could never stop myself from answering Mammy back during a row even though I knew she would take a lunge at me. She would pull on my ponytail, shouting, 'I hate the sight of ye. Why don't ye clear off and leave us in peace.'

I don't know if she saw me as the reason for her bad marriage or whether she just didn't like me. My feelings for her were complicated. I hated her, but I craved her love. I wanted to feel special, like an only child would. So though I loved my siblings, I also sometimes hated them. I couldn't stand watching her lavish attention on them while ignoring me. On family picnics I remember my siblings and our parents would sit on a rug, a happy family, and I would be sitting well away from them on my own, huddled up in my coat.

I didn't have my mother's love, but I do have some happy memories from those early days. I danced at the local feis. I loved that. I thought I was the best dancer in the place, whatever the reality. I was full of enthusiasm, but kept bumping into the other dancers. I never was well coordinated.

I had a lovely sit-up-and-beg bike back then, which I called Betsy. It had a basket at the front and a huge squashy seat. Daddy painted it bright blue, the same colour as our front door – and most of the other front doors in the area. I was laughed at after that when people saw me ride by. They said I must be going on my holidays because the bike was the colour of the sea. I didn't care. I loved cycling above everything. It gave me a sense of freedom.

After national school I was sent to the local vocational school. Master Sweeney, the headmaster, told me that I should sit the entrance exam for the Finn College, a more upmarket school, 'because you would have no bother getting in'. When I told Mammy this she just scoffed, and said the shirt factory in Lifford was crying out for workers.

Noeleen left school early and went to work in the factory. She loved it. She had already put in some hours there, as she had worked on Saturdays to earn some money. At just twelve she'd had to lie about her age, but that was no bother to her. She was beautiful, just like my mother, and she made the best of herself. She loved dressing up and going to dances. I was never like Noeleen. I didn't have her confidence and I wasn't good at the easy banter she enjoyed.

When I was fourteen, Noeleen twelve and my youngest brother Don barely two, my mother walked out of our lives. This was a Friday in May 1969. Mammy had a job at the Inter County Hotel. She worked there most nights and I joined her at weekends. She loved it, and got on well with all the staff and the guests. That night she was in charge of taking coats for a young farmers' hop; they had one at the Inter County most weeks. I was waiting tables.

The hotel was owned by one Senator Paddy McGowan. When he had first opened the hotel people thought he was mad. They said it was too grand for Lifford and would never do a good trade, but they were proved wrong. McGowan was well enough liked and was respected for the work he had done for the area since his election to Seanad Éireann in 1965.

I was setting the tables for breakfast when Mary, the head waitress, told me I was needed at the door. I found Daddy there, looking distraught.

'Marie, your Mammy's gone,' he said.

'What? She can't have.' I ran to the cloakroom expecting to see her charming all the customers as usual, but she wasn't there. And it turned out she had indeed fled, clearing the wardrobe of all her clothes. How could she have left my father and all of us children? How could any mother?

It spelt the end of my childhood. I had to leave school at the end of term. That hurt. I loved books and learning, and did really well in my Inter Certificate. When I was told that I had passed my exams with flying colours and that my name was up on the board at school, my father didn't seem particularly pleased. 'It doesn't matter, Marie,' he said. 'All that *does* matter is that you stay home and look after things while I work. Someone has to.'

And that's exactly what happened. At fourteen I looked after the whole Brolly family, becoming a companion to my forty-seven-year-old father Danny and a substitute mother to my siblings. That was hard, as they were inconsolable at her loss. Shaun was eleven back then. Brian was six and Don two.

It was hard getting them all off to school. They would beg to stay at home in case Mammy appeared while they were out. Don was too small to worry where his Mammy was. He would just follow me around the house dreamily, wanting to 'help' with the washing up by splashing dirty water all over the place. He called me Mammy Marie. It broke my heart.

I had already had a hand in their care. With Mammy's late hours at the hotel, she often stayed in bed in the mornings. So I was used to waking up all the gang and getting them to school. And when we came home for lunch she would give me some coins and send me to the shop to buy cream buns. Now, though, it was left to me to do all the shopping, the cooking, the cleaning and washing, as well as caring for them all.

Cooking meals was the real bugbear, because I didn't know how to set about it. I knew how to make tea and toast, but not dinner for six. I made many mistakes. I boiled the spuds dry; I produced gravy which was nothing but lumps; and my balls of mince were burnt on the outside, raw in the middle. When I did eventually master making beans, mince and gravy I gave it to the gang every night of the week. You can imagine the complaints.

I missed working at the hotel. It had been fun, as there had been a good gang of us up there. I had recently started going out with one of the part-time barmen, Johnny McNally, or Jumbo as he was known. He lived across the border in Strabane and I couldn't meet him now that I was needed at home day and night.

My father, meanwhile, spent the first few days after my mother's disappearance searching the neighbourhood. He reported her as a missing person to the gardaí but he worried that they weren't doing enough to find her. So, proclaiming that his wife had drowned, he took to walking the river bank. He still worked as a painter and decorator, but every spare minute was taken up with the search.

As the weeks went on I dreaded Mondays more and more. It was wash day and I didn't have a washing machine or a twin tub. And with all the upset, Shaun had a bed-wetting problem. I used to fill the bath with water. It would be full of sheets, of Daddy's shirts and socks, and of the boys' underwear. The water would be boiling hot so I'd leave everything soaking until it cooled enough for my hands to bear it. Then I'd get the washboard and a brush and set to scrubbing the clothes. I would then take Daddy's shirts again and give the collars another going over. After that I would haul everything out of the bath and take the sodden clothes outside. We had a mangle out there. I would squeeze everything through, taking care not to mangle my fingers; then I hung everything out on a big line that ran the length of the garden. It was tied round a sturdy tree trunk. There was a branch with a V in the top to hold up the line. All the while, little Don would be at my feet. I think he was scared that if he lost sight of me, I might disappear too.

Shaun was the most affected of all of us. There he was, with adolescence knocking at the door. Somebody should have seen what he was going through and tried to help him. It's only now I realise how deep the effect of Mammy's departure must have been for him. He had already suffered a terrible trauma: his best friend had recently drowned swimming in the river at the bottom of our road. Shaun possibly carried that hurt to his death, from suicide by drowning, years later. But things were never easy for him; he was always the troubled black sheep. When I complained to Daddy about Shaun's bad temper he just shrugged. 'For fuck sake, Marie, give me head space. I'll deal with it later,' he'd say, and stomp out to the refuge of his shed.

When Shaun turned twelve Noeleen managed to get him a job with her in the shirt factory. He was to keep the machinists going by to-ing and fro-ing with work for them from the cutting room. Twice a day, just before the morning tea break, he had to set off with a shopping list from the workers to buy crisps, sweets, fags, or sometimes, when it was hot, iced lollies. Noeleen reckoned he got a start there only because the manager felt sorry for us with Mammy gone. I didn't give a shite what the manager felt as long as they allowed Shaun to stay. I would have done anything to keep him out of my hair for a few hours every day.

As the days of Mammy's disappearance turned into weeks, Daddy began to confide in me. He said he thought Mammy had run off with the senator. She had been making curtains for the hotel and he felt she had stayed there long after she had put down the tape measure.

'I'm sorry she ever started to work for the wee baldy bastard,' Daddy said.

I tried to calm him, though deep down I suspected he was right. I knew Mammy liked the senator and the world of his hotel; it was such a contrast to the drudgery at home. I just wished Daddy would stop crying, and start helping me for a change. I didn't ask for much, but I got less. Take Shaun's bed-wetting. I frequently asked Daddy to wake him when he came up to bed and take him to the toilet. Yet most mornings I would be faced with more wet sheets to wash.

If a situation like ours had happened in Woodenbridge, County Wicklow, where Tom and I live now, I feel sure everyone would have rallied round to help. My neighbour Kitty Kilhoran would organise a rota to lend the family a hand; nobody likes to see a teenager turned into a skivvy. But I don't remember much support from neighbours back then. I was probably too proud to ask for it, and no doubt they were busy with their own young families.

Any time I showed my face outside the house, the neighbours would appear from nowhere and ask, 'Have you heard from yer mother yet?' They probably meant well but it felt like a rebuke. The kids in the street were the worst. Whenever the boys went out to play, they would start to sing that song 'Chirpy Chirpy Cheep Cheep': 'Where's your Mama gone, where's your Mama gone, little baby Don.'

Our wee Don always clapped and cheered when he heard it. He thought it was a song *for* him, not *about* him. Shaun had a different approach: he kicked out if he caught anybody even humming the tune. To Shaun's annoyance, Brian wouldn't lash out at the torturers. Instead, he always came home in tears.

Noeleen had to put up with the gossips in the shirt factory too. They would be more sneaky, though. Some of them would ask her if Mammy and Daddy were planning on going to the parish dinner dance. One asked Noeleen if she could make her an appointment with Mammy; she said she wanted her to make her a frock to wear to the dance.

Noeleen tried her best to hide the fact that Mammy was missing. She told a few of Mammy's auld cronies that she had gone to Dublin for a few weeks to make curtains for some big hotel there. It was only when she caught them laughing behind her back that she realised that everyone knew our mother had done a runner.

Without concrete news, rumours spread fast. Some said Mammy had run off to live with a commercial traveller in England. Others said that she was hiding in one of the bedrooms down in the hotel. Daddy was inconsolable. The only time he came alive was when someone thought they had spotted her. Every possible sighting was investigated eagerly, with weekends spent scouring the countryside in our blue Morris 1100.

As soon as we arrived in Donegal or Letterkenny, Noeleen would run off up and down the streets, convinced she would find Mammy standing around the next corner. Shaun would look in shops, fabric shops mainly, just in case. Daddy would show a photograph of her to all and sundry, begging and pleading with them to remember seeing her somewhere – anywhere. Me, well I just held Brian's and Don's hands and followed on.

For solace, Daddy turned to his religion. The locals would gather in our kitchen for the rosary to pray for Mammy's safe return. And he got the parish priest, Father Flanagan, to say a

Mass, 'for the safe return of Nett, the only woman I have ever loved'.

Looking back today, after all the recent scandals in the Catholic Church, it's easy to forget quite how powerful priests were back then. A big man with grey hair and a fierce expression, Father Flanagan was someone to reckon with. He mixed in the same circles as the doctor and the lawyer. If he went to the pub, he could be sure someone would buy him a pint. The town held him in awe.

At least all the adults did. Us children were terrified of him. It seems to me he was a very bitter man. I remember him coming into the national school to check on our progress. Or rather, to have a go at everyone for not doing well enough. I escaped his scorn because I was good at school, but I hated him for upsetting my friends.

After a few weeks, by which time we thought we would never see Mammy again, she came back. Pleased as I was to see her, it was a shock. She had changed towards us, and had lost any warmth she had felt. I had never found her easy, but now she was impossible. She was there, and yet she wasn't. We did everything we could to make her happy. We cleaned and cooked and did the messages, but nothing pleased her, and she would often scream at us or hit out.

And she had become so secretive. She didn't tell us where she had been, and she kept running across the street to make phone calls or wrote letters when she thought nobody was looking. She had even taken to driving the car alone at night – 'to get some peace and quiet,' she told Daddy when he asked if he could go along for the run. Her mood affected him badly. We'd hoped he would be back to his old self, playing with Don and telling us yarns from his childhood, but he was subdued. He just urged us to do whatever Mammy wanted.

'Don't be annoying her,' he'd say. 'Or she'll go away again.'

Life was one long round of 'dos' and 'don'ts' (two occasions of latter). Mainly 'don'ts'. At night I would lie in bed, listening for the sounds of lovemaking. All I heard was murmuring and sobbing. She stayed for a while, but just as we were getting used to having her back, she left again. It was heartbreaking.

I had heard rumours that Mammy was staying with McGowan in his other hotel in Dungloe, but I didn't tell Daddy. He was heartbroken as it was, but someone did mark his card and Daddy went to the hotel in Dungloe on a number of occasions. Staff there denied knowing Annette, and McGowan threatened Daddy with legal action if he showed his face there again.

Life had settled into some kind of routine, when Mammy appeared again. This time she was with Father Flanagan, who was contriving to act as a peacemaker. 'You need to stop thinking about yourselves for a moment,' he said, looking from Mammy to Daddy. 'Your children's welfare comes first.'

The weans were overjoyed to see her back, but all signs of life left our home that Saturday. There was no more laughing or crying, just explosive silence. We children didn't argue anymore. We just hung around the house, guarding Mammy in case she skedaddled again. The nights were the worst. Daddy's presence seemed to agitate Mammy, so half an hour before he was due home from work she would go to their bedroom – well, her bedroom really because Daddy didn't sleep there anymore; he would sit by the open fire downstairs and just smoke.

She spoke to no one but Noeleen. They were great chums and Mammy didn't allow anyone else into the bedroom. Noeleen carried her in the supper that I prepared every night, or the dinner that Daddy made at the weekends.

When Mammy left for the third time, I felt more alone than ever. When I went to bed I prayed that by the morning everything would be back to normal. Our family life before hadn't been perfect but at least there was some stability. I craved that now. Neighbours didn't call by. It felt as if nobody cared if we were alive or dead.

The only one who bothered about us was Mammy's eldest sister, Auntie Nellie. Every day she came trundling round the corner from her house to check on us. She would glide into the house, nodding in quiet contemplation, or maybe relief that I hadn't killed one of the weans during the night. Her being there made me feel safe.

The first Christmas without Mammy was terrible. Everyone was in bad form except Don, who, at three years of age, was irrepressible. He loved his blue Raleigh tricycle with the honky horn that Santa had left him under the tree. But it was a miserable day. Our Christmas dinner was memorable for all the wrong reasons. Noeleen and Daddy kept bursting into tears, and who could blame them after the dinner I'd served up? The turkey was dried out, the spuds were like rockets, and the gravy was my worst effort yet, so full of lumps that nobody would touch it.

The strain started to get to me. I was tired all the time and I had desperate pains in my head, but when I went to see our family doctor all he wanted to talk about was Daddy.

'Your father is going through a rough time now, Marie,' he

said. 'He needs all the support you can give him.' He handed me two envelopes of pills, but they weren't painkillers for me. 'Make sure you give him a white tablet first thing in the morning and a yellow one at night,' he said, explaining that Daddy was depressed and that the tablets would make him better. So I was to be his nurse now, on top of everything else. I left the surgery feeling more burdened than when I'd arrived.

When Daddy first handed me his pay packet – two pounds seven shillings and six – I hadn't wanted to take it. 'I'll never be able to manage it,' I told him.

'Sure ye will. Just do what yer Mammy does.'

'What's that?'

'Pay all the bills. Then, with whatever's left, get the food. Simple.'

It sounded easy enough. So I said I'd give it a go. The first couple of weeks were hard because I didn't know what bills needed paying but bit by bit it fell into place. Pay the bread man, milkman, coal man, rent man and insurance man first. Then settle with Harley's material shop in Strabane. What was left paid for the messages, but there was never enough money.

I started buying on tick, and that worked well until the shops started demanding money I didn't have. When after some months Ringer McGrane's the grocer's threatened me with the courts, Daddy heard about my debts and confronted me. There was all hell to pay.

By this time Daddy knew that Mammy had left to be with Senator Paddy McGowan. Everybody knew it. Yet there he was, a respected member of the community, married, with eight children. The worst of it was that he didn't give Mammy a good life. He left her in various bed and breakfast places around Dublin and saw her for a night or two a week when he visited the capital on Senate duty. However unhappy her marriage had seemed to her, she could surely not have been happy spending days on her own.

Mammy came back five times in all, and you can imagine all the pain that caused. We were up and then down; up when she first arrived, yet afraid to leave her even for a minute in case she was going to disappear again. We hung around doors. We sat on the steps inside the house. We played in the street outside the house, constantly running inside to check that she was still there.

We would start to worry more when she began running over to a neighbour to use the phone. Soon after, a van, sent by McGowan, would arrive to collect her. One time she walked out leaving the spuds cooking on the stove, and Don alone. I will never understand how she could do that. Anything could have happened. Auntie Nellie found him wandering the streets. I met them after that one day I worked in the shirt factory – the shortest job ever.

I didn't enjoy the factory, but at least it had got me out of the house. It had seemed like a chance to have a more normal life. And here I was, back to the washing, cooking and caring for the family again.

One time we all went to stay with Mammy in Dublin for a weekend. It was a disaster. She left us alone in this strange B&B while she went 'to work' at seven in the evening. She gave us the hugest bag of sweets you ever saw in an effort to keep us quiet. Noeleen and I kept watch half the night at the window, worrying that she would never come back for us. When she eventually appeared we noticed she stepped out of the senator's car, and when she got into bed beside Shaun her breath stank of booze.

She dragged us up and down O'Connell Street shopping for the three boys. She bought presents for Noeleen and me too. I got a chain belt, which was to prove extremely useful. I would leave the house wearing my skirt at a length Daddy could not object to, and as soon as the house was out of sight I'd use the belt to hitch the skirt up to my thighs.

On the Sunday we had a picnic in Saint Stephen's Green but that ended in a row because a park keeper yelled at Shaun and Brian, who were climbing the trees. It was the last straw for Shaun. 'Dublin's shite,' he said. The boys were restless. All they wanted to do in Dublin was go to the zoo; they kept on at Mammy to take us but she claimed that she didn't know where it was.

Daddy had let us visit Mammy only because Father Flanagan said that if he did allow us to go, maybe Mammy would come home with us. I was given the task of persuading her. That was hard, because although a part of me wanted her home, I knew if she came she would leave again, and the pain of that was slowly destroying us all. She came back with us on the bus, but anyone could see that she didn't want to. And that time she lasted for only a few days.

Father Flanagan made one last desperate attempt to persuade her to come home. He took Noeleen and me to Donegal Town to meet her. It was snowing, and the priest's grey Volkswagen slithered at a crawl over Barnesmore Gap. We were to meet her at the Central Hotel. Noeleen couldn't wait to see Mammy and she ran in ahead of us, but there was a message at reception telling

Father Flanagan to go to room number twelve alone. He ordered us some tea and ham sandwiches, but we were both too het up to eat. We waited anxiously. And waited. An hour or so had passed before Father Flanagan returned.

'Where's Mammy?' Noeleen asked, jumping to her feet.

'I'm sorry,' he said. 'She won't be coming home with us.'

'Why not?'

He didn't answer our question. He just kept repeating, 'I'm sorry. I can't do any more. I've done my best. I've done all I can.'

Noeleen asked if she could see Mammy. Father Flanagan looked agitated. 'Five minutes … no more,' he said. 'We have a hazardous journey in front of us.' Mammy looked wonderful when we entered her room. She was so gracious, so ladylike. It was as if she was meeting royalty, not two daughters whom she hadn't seen for nearly three months. Holding Noeleen to her, she told us not to cry.

'Why aren't ye coming home, Mammy?' I asked, wiping my eyes and my nose on the sleeve of my coat.

'Father Flanagan will tell yez later,' she said, and her eyes were soft with emotion. 'First he'll speak to yer father.'

The truth shook us all, but Daddy most of all. Mammy was pregnant. She was having the senator's baby.

'That's it,' said Daddy. 'We've lost her for good now.' And we had. Auntie Nellie always said she would never have left us at all if Granny Maxwell had still been alive. Maybe that's true.

CHAPTER THREE

FIRST LOVE

୨୦ଓଌ

Tom came in just now while my carer Margaret was sorting out my clothes for today. 'I have to go to Dublin later,' he said. 'Had you remembered?'

He has a meeting with The Carers Association. He is on the committee, and they are fighting the government because of the recent cuts to services. 'Corrinna is coming to keep an eye on you,' he said. 'She's bringing Cara with her too.'

'Oh yes,' I said, delighted that he had reminded me. I love Corrinna's visits. 'Margaret, you'd better put away that garish cardigan. If Corrinna sees me in that she'll tell me I look like an old woman.'

It hurts Corrinna to think that I no longer care what I wear, because she thinks of me as stylish, in an understated way. I always was, until this wretched body decided to let me down. Clothes have always mattered to me. It was one of the things my first boyfriend, Jumbo, said he liked about me. He was the one person in my life who stopped me from going stir-crazy in those months after Mammy left.

Jumbo, like me, was fourteen. He was tall, with piercing blue eyes and floppy fair hair. I thought he was beautiful. He played lead guitar in a group with some school friends. He was huge into Jimi Hendrix and Cream.

When I told Jumbo that I liked Brian Coll and the Buckaroos, he laughed like a drain.

'Only culchies like shit-kicking music,' he said. I was mortified, and decided he was a big-headed bastard. We avoided each other for months after that, but I was acutely aware of him, and his friends said he was mad for me.

I could see that he liked me. It was the way he'd look at me when he'd say, 'How's it goin' there?' I was flattered by the attention. Jumbo could have had any girl he wanted. When he asked me to go out with him, I wanted to say yes but I was scared. I was so innocent. Suppose he put his hand up my skirt, or tried to French kiss me? After sleeping on it, I got a friend to tell him 'yes' but only if we went somewhere public. We arranged to meet the next afternoon, Holy Thursday, at the hospital corner at four o'clock. I was on lunches that day so hadn't a chance to go home and change. I sprayed myself with a musk fragrance I had bought from the Avon catalogue and I secretly hoped that he *would* try to kiss me.

The weather was glorious: sunny with a soft, light breeze. It felt good to be alive. Jumbo was leaning against the hospital wall smoking a cigarette when I approached. He looked every inch the college boy in his duffle coat and striped scarf. We made small talk, but relaxed once we got to Kitty's Café where we drank Coke and shoved shillings into the juke box. We spent the afternoon walking, talking and laughing about my love of, and his hatred of, school, of our weekend jobs and the supervisor who made our lives a misery. Occasionally our hands brushed together, and we would jump apart as if hit by lightning.

On Good Friday we were allowed two hours off work to pray. Jumbo and I arranged to go to Mass together. We would meet in Strabane, we decided, in the last pew on the left-hand aisle. I nicked Mammy's black mantilla to wear as a disguise. I reckoned I could hide my face if I saw anyone from home.

Sitting beside Jumbo in the pew was pure agony. I could feel his body heat. And when his thigh brushed mine, I thought I was going to faint. And from fearing French kissing, it was, suddenly, all I wanted. The thought shocked yet thrilled me. But we didn't kiss, not until later that evening when we were both on duty at the hotel. I was in the storeroom when the door banged shut and he pulled me into his arms. After feeling his lips on mine though I began to cry. He pulled away and I whispered, 'I'm sorry. It's just that nobody has ever held me like that before.'

I had never felt so loved, or at least not since Granny Maxwell died. There was no keeping us apart after that. Working the odd shift in the hotel gave us a great excuse to meet. If anyone asked where I was going I'd say, 'I'm working every night this week,' even if I wasn't. And Jumbo would do the same. I was so happy. When we weren't going for walks or sitting in Kitty's Café chatting and listening to Dusty Springfield singing 'I Only Want To Be With You', we were dancing. Jumbo made me into a different person. I became more confident, and wanted to look good when I was around him.

Jumbo was different from all the other boys I knew. His family, like mine, were working class, but he was known to be clever; and his parents, who were proud of him, had sent him to Saint Columb's College in Derry. Great things were expected of Jumbo – but he hated the long bus journey every day and said that he simply didn't enjoy academia. Music was his passion.

Every Friday night after work I ran to the toilets with a change of clothes and my black-and-white Mary Quant make-up bag and I'd get ready for the Young Farmers' Dance in the hotel. It was the highlight of the week. The ballroom was such a happy place, and Jumbo and I would dance the night away. There was a revolving mirrored ball in the ceiling that turned your partner's face into a jigsaw of coloured pieces.

There would be lots of young people from across the border at those dances, mingling with us locals; they would be escaping from the Troubles and the worry about being shot or blown up. I shut my ears to all that gloomy talk and to the fear of civil war. I was scared Daddy would be sent off to fight. Suppose he got shellshock like Uncle Willie? He had never been the same since coming back from the Second World War. At least in the Free State we were safe. I did not read the papers but Jumbo said he couldn't forget all the killing. 'Not with them fucking B Specials stopping and searching me every night when I cross the border.'

One night Jumbo was out of sorts. He'd been grounded until

after his O levels. And that's when he said, 'I think I love ye, Marie.'

We danced. And, feeling his arms around me and his warm breath on my neck, I was pretty sure I loved him too. Why else did my insides go all gooey when I looked at him?

'No fuckin' way will they keep us apart,' he whispered, kissing my ear.

⁂

We had been going out together for eight weeks when Mammy upped and left for the first time. And though it became hard to see him, in one way my troubles drew us closer still. Once things settled down I would often sneak off to Strabane to see Jumbo in the evenings. Sometimes I'd take little Don with me. I loved mixing with all Jumbo's hip friends from the band. They practised nearly every night when they had a gig coming up. When his electric guitar, Brendan's drums and Phelim's bass kicked in, the place rocked and swayed to music that I had never heard before. I felt so good and so free that when they passed me a bottle of beer I took a big, long gulp.

'Easy on, Marie. I have to take ye home,' Jumbo said, removing the bottle from my hand.

One day I saw Jumbo on the street when I was in the car with Daddy. Anxious to talk to him, I asked Daddy to stop the car. When I got back in I thought he'd make some smart comment, but he surprised me by saying, 'Why don't ye bring him home?'

That made life a lot easier. Jumbo would come home with me often, and we'd sneak off to the bathroom to kiss and caress each other. One night Noeleen spied on us through the keyhole. She made my life hell after that. First she said she was going to tell Daddy. Then she changed her mind and said it was our secret. I could have kissed her I was so relieved. But now every time she wanted to go out somewhere and I started to complain, she'd just say 'bathroom' and I'd back down. Daddy really liked Jumbo and I didn't want that to change.

I don't know how I would have managed without Jumbo. He made sitting in with Daddy every night bearable. He talked to Daddy about music and to Brian about football, and he played hide-and-seek with Don. Shaun was never around. He was always out wandering the streets with his friends Fergal and Firebug. 'Getting up to no good,' Auntie Nellie tutted, on her daily visit to our house.

Noeleen only ever came home for her tea and a change of clothes. She spent most of her free time after work in her friend Emily's house. 'It's better craic down there,' she'd say, when I got annoyed with her for leaving me to look after Daddy and the boys for yet another night. As for Daddy, he started to devise ways to get back at McGowan. It was all he talked about and it cheered him up no end. Deciding to let the whole county know what the senator had done, he made posters out of cardboard boxes saying, 'Paddy McGowan is a wife steeler.' Seeing the bad spelling, Jumbo offered to change the 'e's to 'a's.

'I'll show that wee bastard up if it's the last thing I do,' Daddy said, sounding better than he had for the past seven months. Jumbo and I became Daddy's comrades in arms. Every night we drove to towns around Lifford looking for suitable trees to which to nail the posters. I didn't mind, because he was my Daddy and

I wanted to make him happy. And Jumbo was prepared to do it simply to please me.

'I wanna spend every minute of my life with ye,' he whispered one night when we were out helping Daddy. 'So I'd better keep yer old boy happy.'

Our romance continued throughout that winter and the following summer. When Mammy came home, Jumbo would lie low. We would conduct our love affair by walking aimlessly up and down Lifford High Street just holding hands, and occasionally ducking into hidden doorways to kiss. When the cold got to us we would run into Kitty's for a hot chocolate.

I lost my virginity – well, we both did – one cold January night soon after my sixteenth birthday. I would love to say it was a beautiful moment, but we were in the girls' shelter of the local national school. It was a convenient meeting place because it was directly opposite the Inter County Hotel, so Jumbo could sneak over there as soon as he'd finished his work. To avoid prying eyes, all us young couples would crowd together in the upper girls' shelter.

We would lie on a long wooden bench that ran the length of the shelter. We'd kiss, fumble and cuddle to keep warm. I used to look up at the once-white gable walls, which were now covered in squishy grey marks made by girls from third or fourth year, from throwing tennis balls against the wall in a complicated and competitive game of catch.

That night I was wearing a mini-skirt, topped by my camel coat, which, being only an inch longer than the skirt, didn't stop my legs from going blue with the cold. We rolled off the seat and, before I knew it, Jumbo was on top of me and my knickers and tights were in a tangle round my knees. Neither of us knew what to do. Penetration was quick and painful. My main memory is of the smell of pee rising from the cold concrete floor. I was terrified I would vomit before Jumbo had finished. I wondered what all the fuss to do with sex was about, but afterwards Jumbo said, 'That was great, Marie.' He gazed at me, but, saying nothing, I avoided his eye. 'It was fucking brilliant,' he said.

I avoided Jumbo for a while after that. I couldn't get my head around what we had done. I wondered if anybody could tell by looking at me that I'd 'done it'. Something had changed. My body didn't feel as if it belonged to me anymore. Jumbo pursued me, sending me notes through Sheila, a waitress in the hotel. He sent me chocolates too, begging me to meet him. Sheila asked me what was wrong between us, and, against my better judgement, I told her.

'But he's still fifteen,' she said, with all the superiority of her seventeen years. 'That's illegal. He could go to jail.'

I regretted telling her. When after a week or so Jumbo arrived at my front door, he said Sheila was blabbing to everyone that we had had it off. So my name was being dragged through the kitchen and bar of the Inter County Hotel. I was mortified. Terrified too. Suppose someone told Daddy? Or, perhaps worse, the senator would hear of it and tell Mammy. She had already warned me off Jumbo, saying I was too young to be going out with a boy.

It was a while before it dawned on me that something might be wrong. I woke one morning with a jolt, and realised that I hadn't had a period for a few months, and I was always regular.

But surely I couldn't be pregnant? Not after one bloody time. Not when I knew of girls who had had sex with everything in a pair of trousers and got away with it? When I told Jumbo I thought I was going to have a baby, he couldn't believe it. He gazed at my stomach and said, 'No. No, you can't be.' And I didn't show, it's true.

When another week had gone by and my period still hadn't arrived, I took a urine sample to a chemist in Strabane. They said the result would be ready in a day, but I was too scared to go back in – so I sent Jumbo instead. This was on a Wednesday afternoon. I waited down the street, biting my nails. And when he came out and walked down the street towards me I could sense his blind terror. He looked white with shock.

Jumbo didn't tell me the test was positive. He just put his hands on my shoulders, looked into my eyes, and said, 'What are we going to do?'

After that we didn't talk about it for months. I didn't look like I was expecting. I wasn't fat or anything and I could still get into my mini-skirts, so we didn't even think too much about it. And then the sickness arrived. I'd had a dose of the flu. It was going around, but I couldn't stop vomiting. I thought I was going to die. Daddy was reassuring. He said a man he knew from work had been as sick as me. 'I'll make ye some hot milk and pepper. That'll make ye better,' he said, feeling my forehead.

I didn't tell Daddy I was pregnant. I didn't tell anyone – and neither did Jumbo, but somehow it got around the town. The bigger I got, the more whispers I heard. Nobody confronted me, but Shaun had picked up something. He was thirteen, and said all the boys in the street were calling me the bicycle. I don't think he knew what that meant, but he knew it was bad. He kept taunting me with the word.

Daddy still didn't know, or if he did, he was in denial. And when I was about five months gone, an event happened that put my pregnancy into the back of my mind. Daddy took a court case against his enemy. He accused the senator of stealing his wife, and in the spring of 1970 we were all called to the High Court in Dublin.

AN ACT OF LOVE

CHAPTER FOUR
MY FATHER'S COURT CASE

80CB

My court case seems to have captured the public imagination. It keeps coming up in the media, on various current affairs shows on radio and television. This morning it was referred to on *Today with Seán O'Rourke*. The panel were talking about the case's ramifications. They expressed sorrow for me and my predicament. Then one of them said, 'Marie Fleming is so courageous. I admire her so much. She is terminally sick with MS, she can't move and has trouble with her speech, yet she went to the High Court and gave evidence. What's more, she was magnificent.'

Hearing those words, I couldn't help smiling. But the

panellist got it wrong. It wasn't courage that got me to the court in November last year. It was anger, determination, and a desire to protect Tom. It's simple. I want a dignified death, and I can't have that without Tom's help. Knowing he will assist me has made the thought of death bearable. He is prepared to help even though he may be prosecuted; he may go to jail. I have to do everything in my power to prevent that. I felt compelled to take the case.

Nobody wants to end up in the High Court. It's a forbidding place. I certainly didn't take my case lightly. It meant everything to me, and the same was true of Daddy. He was so desperate to get Mammy back, and he saw taking a case against the senator as a last resort. The poster campaign hadn't worked; the gardaí had put a stop to that one, visiting the house to give Daddy a talking to. He had then tried to shame the senator by storming into a meeting of Donegal County Council. He regaled us all with the story, painting himself as the hero. He had told the meeting that their chairman, Senator Paddy McGowan, was a wife stealer.

'He has left me without a wife, and my five weans without a mother,' Daddy had told the council. 'Ye could a heard a pin drop,' he said. 'Then all hell broke loose as McGowan tried to get out past me.' Daddy had then lost the head, and ended up attacking the senator with an iron bar. Furious, McGowan threatened to have him up for assault.

Left to his own devices, I doubt Daddy would have taken the case, but two local Fine Gael representatives started to call to our house in the evenings. I would put the kettle on and make the three of them a cup of tea, but I was never allowed to sit with them. Daddy would tell me to leave the room. These secret meetings went on all over Christmas and the New Year. Then Daddy spoke to me.

'Marie, I'm suing McGowan for taking yer Mammy away from us,' he said one night as he was eating the stew I had made for his dinner. 'I'll be late home tomorrow night. I'm meeting a solicitor in Letterkenny. Ye can heat up me dinner for me when I get home.'

Soon after that, Noeleen, Shaun and I were called in to see the solicitor, Mr McCloughan, to give our side of the story. I was nervous going into his office, but his questions were straightforward enough. He wanted to know whether, when I had worked in the hotel, I had seen Mammy and McGowan together. And of course I had. I told him Mammy had loved her job in the hotel and that sometimes McGowan would join her, the manager and the head receptionist for a drink. I remembered how fed up I used to get waiting for her to finish her vodka and white lemonade so that we could go home.

McGowan, I remembered, had commanded respect in the hotel. He used to mingle with the staff but made it clear that he was doing them a favour by doing so. He insisted they call him Senator McGowan and never 'Mister'. And he would command the head barman to fetch and carry for him, collecting his leather briefcase and holdall from the grey Mercedes. He had so many lackeys, yes-men and -women running after him that, as Jumbo often remarked, 'it's a wonder he can clean his own arse.'

When the day of the court case arrived, my biggest worry was hiding my pregnancy bump from everyone. Well, everyone except Mammy. I wouldn't have minded if she had noticed. In fact I wanted her to. I was feeling so very alone, and decided that the moment I saw her I would tell her my news. She would know what to do. Because I certainly didn't, and Jumbo wouldn't talk to me about it, at least not in any practical way. He was as scared as I was.

Father Flanagan was to accompany us to the big city. He was being called as a witness for the prosecution. He called the night before to say the rosary for a safe journey and a speedy resolution to the case. Before he left he handed Daddy an envelope which contained £100 from the Saint Vincent de Paul fund, to help us pay for the petrol and a bed and breakfast for the night.

I thought I knew what a court looked like, because I had seen various courts on television. I loved watching *Perry Mason*. But the Four Courts building, with its six imposing pillars, scared me rigid. It looked like the sort of place you went into only to disappear, never to be heard of again. The eight of us piled up the steps, Don dragging on my hand. Daddy and his solicitor huddled together in deep conversation, cigarette smoke swirling above their heads, as they waited for the barrister to arrive.

Three middle-aged men with white curly wigs walked up with two younger men in brown suits. These underlings, as Mr McCloughan called them, carried big thick books, and dog-eared folders full of sheets of paper.

'Good morning, Mr Wood,' boomed Daddy's solicitor, bending and touching his forelock to a very tall, good-looking man with luscious brown eyes. It was clear from the way everyone kowtowed to him that Mr E.M. Wood was chief of the operation. He introduced the other members of Senior Counsels, Mr McKenna and Mr McWilliams. Daddy became suddenly shy, hiding behind his solicitor, just nodding when someone spoke to him. Father Flanagan, in contrast, spoke to the barristers with ease, as if he had known them all his life.

Nobody so much as looked at us weans. It was as if we didn't exist. Wasn't this case supposed to be about us and our welfare? We weren't introduced to the barristers, and nobody asked how we felt about Mammy leaving, or what we thought about the court case. I wondered what we were doing there.

Before the case got started, McGowan's barrister applied to have it held in camera. Our side nearly had a fit. The amount of running to and fro between Judge Teevan and the senior counsels was something to see. I didn't know what 'in camera' meant, but a kindly junior counsel explained that McGowan wanted the case to be heard in private so that it wouldn't get reported in the newspapers. Daddy was not pleased.

'Over me fuckin' dead body,' he said. 'I haven't come all this way for nobody to hear about it.' After an hour of legal submissions he got his way, and we were asked to take our seats in court number three. I sat at the back on a wooden pew, between Shaun and Father Flanagan; Daddy and his solicitor were beside him. Noeleen, meanwhile, had taken Brian and Don to the cafeteria. She had volunteered because, being close to Mammy, she didn't want to be asked to take the stand.

That courtroom was the most intimidating place I had ever been in. I was terrified of making a noise, because the slightest sound reverberated around the room. And when my stomach started rumbling, Father Flanagan shushed me, looking angry. Then, seeing my anguished expression, he handed me a packet of Polo mints. The jury of five men and seven women looked as lost and uncomfortable as I felt.

It was then that I saw Mammy. She was sitting with McGowan in a front-row seat just to the left of us. I ached to run to her, to throw my arms around her and tell her I was going to have a baby and needed her help; but when she turned around and saw me, she stared through me as if she didn't know who I was.

Mr Wood set out our case, saying that Daddy was claiming damages against Senator Patrick McGowan, hotelier, member of Seanad Éireann, father of eight children, from Knock, Ballybofey, County Donegal, for alleged criminal conversation with Danny Brolly's thirty-four-year-old wife and for enticing her away from his house and society. 'Mr Brolly also claims that the senator, on a date in May 1969, and since, debauched and carnally knew his wife. And on numerous occasions and for considerable periods since May, unlawfully enticed and procured his wife, against his will, while harbouring and detaining her at Lifford, Dungloe, Bundoran, Rossnowlagh and other places in County Donegal, Sligo and Dublin.

'The senator is living with the plaintiff's wife openly. He has made the plaintiff's wife his captive woman, whereby he has refused to send Mrs Brolly back to her husband when requested to do so by him and others. The only way to deal with a man like that,' he shouted, pointing at McGowan, 'is to bring him into court and castigate him in public so that he and his like may be warned about the consequences when the big man rides roughshod over the little one.' There were murmurs of 'Aye, aye' from the gallery, where reporters mingled with the public.

Mr Wood rambled on, then addressed the jury. 'You have the power to assess damages on three bases,' he said. 'There could be contemptuous minimal damages; you could find for compensatory damages, which would recompense the plaintiff adequately for the loss and damage done to him; or the damages could be punitive, meaning the defendant had acted with wilful disregard for the rights of another.

'Mr Brolly has been deprived of the society and services of his wife,' he continued quietly. 'Their family rights have been violated, and the constitution and authority of his family have been destroyed for ever. Danny,' he said, turning to look at Daddy, 'has suffered and is still suffering great mental distress. In fact, his health may be affected permanently. If ever there was a case for punitive damages, this is it.' Mr Wood sat down.

That sounded impressive, but I hadn't a clue what any of it really meant. I waited to see if Vincent Landy, senior counsel for the defence, or McGowan's lackey as Daddy called him, would make any more sense to me. But he said McGowan denied everything. He claimed he had never 'debauched or carnally known' Mammy ever. He said he had not enticed her away or encouraged her to remain from the family home. If she had been away, but he wasn't admitting anything, it was her own choice.

Landy then heaped praise on McGowan. 'The senator has worked tirelessly for the people in his constituency, providing badly needed employment for the inhabitants of Lifford in his hotel,' he said. 'He is a good father to his children and he loves his wife dearly.'

Then he turned to Daddy, and claimed that Mammy had become pregnant before they were married.

'Mrs Brolly – or Miss Maxwell, as she was then – was an innocent girl of sixteen who didn't know the facts of life,' he said. 'She never ever wanted to be married to Danny Brolly.' He kept saying this over and over again, as he stabbed the air with his gold pen. Turning to the jury, he said that Mammy was never happy in her sixteen-year marriage.

'What about us?' I wanted to shout. 'Wasn't she happy with us either? Did we mean nothing to her?'

Landy then talked about the poster campaign, alleging that Daddy's only aim was to put McGowan out of public office. 'To sum up,' he said, 'Senator McGowan denies harbouring, detaining or refusing to bring or send Mrs Brolly home. In fact, the senator denies he was ever requested to do so by Mr Brolly or anyone else.' Pushing his glasses further up the bridge of his nose, Mr Landy said, 'Senator McGowan further pleads that any act of default of his caused Mr Brolly no mental distress or injury to his health. This, Your Worship, is the case for the defence.'

Well, I knew a lie when I heard one. I had specifically gone to the hotel one night soon after Mammy had left, to see McGowan. I remember how scared I had been, waiting to speak to him. I didn't want to be there at all, but if it could help get Mammy home to us, then it was worth a try. I had waited over an hour in reception and then finally was told to go up to his room. I had pleaded with him to send Mammy home, but after handing me a hanky to wipe my tears he said, 'I've absolutely no idea what you are talking about, Marie.'

છજાજી

Daddy took the stand, and Mr Wood started the questioning. He asked him to confirm where he had met Mammy, and to explain the type of relationship they had had up to now. Daddy answered him in a very low, shaky voice. He told Mr Wood that he had married Mammy on Easter Monday, 6 April 1953. She was sixteen years younger than him and up to 1968 their marriage was a happy one. He talked about her work in the Inter County Hotel, staying out late and coming home drunk most weekends, 'since startin' to work in that den of iniquity'.

He spoke of the first time that she had left home, after a row over his suspicions that she was involved with the senator, and of his subsequent meeting with McGowan to see if he knew where Mammy was. As he talked about Mammy's five departures and homecomings, Daddy's voice broke down. Then a document was handed to him. He identified it as a birth certificate. It stated that a daughter had been born in May 1970 to Annette Brolly and Patrick McGowan, of Knock, Ballybofey.

Mr Wood thanked Daddy and sat down. I breathed a sigh of relief. That hadn't been so bad. But then Judge Teevan told Daddy not to leave the stand, because Mr Landy had to cross-examine him. And that's when the real shocks began. His first question sounded innocuous. He asked Daddy if he had met Mammy's mother, who would have had to sign a consent for the marriage, Mammy having been under eighteen at the time. Daddy's answer confused me. He sounded evasive, and said that he'd met her but that it wasn't relevant.

'My wife was raised by her grandmother,' he said, 'and *she* welcomed the marriage.' What could he mean? Was he saying that Granny Maxwell wasn't really my grandmother at all? That she was actually my great-grandmother? And if so, then who was Mammy's mother? Who was my real granny?

Then I remembered something. Occasionally, Mammy had gone on holiday to visit a woman called Gracie in Limerick. Gracie had stayed at our house too. And Daddy had sometimes referred to her as 'Annette's mad Mammy'. When Mammy first disappeared he had thought for a while that she might have gone there, 'now that she's decided she's not good enough for the likes of us'. I hadn't taken much notice at the time. But could Gracie be my granny?

Mr Landy suggested that Mammy had always been unhappy and had never intended to stay with him anyway.

'She stayed for nearly sixteen years until she met that bastard,' shouted Daddy, waving a fist at McGowan. 'Fit him better if he hadda stayed at home with his own wife and weans.'

'Mr Brolly, please restrain yourself,' Judge Teevan said, hitting his desk with a gavel.

'I'm sorry, Yer Worship,' mumbled Daddy. 'It won't happen again.'

'Please call me Your Lordship.'

'All right. Right, Yer Lordship.'

I was worried about Daddy. The questions were making him jittery.

'I see you have a very quick temper, Mr Brolly.' Mr Landy turned to the jury. 'Are you prone to violence often?'

'I don't know what ye mean.'

'Oh come, come now,' said Mr Landy, rubbing his double chin. 'Did you not injure the senator with an iron bar to the head?'

'Unfortunately, not fatally,' Mr Wood whispered, from his seat on the bench. Those near enough to hear erupted into laughter.

Landy didn't find it funny. He glared at Mr Wood.

'You don't *really* love your wife, do you, Mr Brolly? Otherwise you wouldn't have gone to a council chamber in front of other members and say, "Senator McGowan is the man who has had a child by my wife." Now would you?' He turned and looked up at the public gallery. 'I put it to you, Mr Brolly, that your objective in going to the council chamber was revenge, and not loss or love of a wife.'

'How can ye say I don't love Nett?' Daddy looked close to tears as he pointed at McGowan. 'That man broke up me good decent home with his big ideas, jewellery and fur coats.'

Ignoring Daddy's interjection, Landy said, 'Is it not also true that your wife found living with you intolerable? You knew that she was unhappy, didn't you? That's why she left home. Not because of any inducement by Senator McGowan.'

I couldn't take this. I put up my hand, wanting to tell Landy that he had it all wrong. Father Flanagan restrained me, saying, 'Shush, shush, child.'

'But it's all lies. Daddy's not like that.' I was sobbing. I wanted the judge to know how gentle and funny Daddy was, how he had always made my life bearable, and how it was Mammy who was difficult to live with, Mammy who had reduced me to tears time and time again.

I couldn't believe that the allegations were true. But even if they were, the judge needed to know the Daddy I knew, the one who had entertained us all with jokes and stories, the one who gathered all his children in front of the fire and told us tales of his childhood. My father was gentle, loving and kind. How could anyone say otherwise? As the court stopped for a mid-morning break I could see it was all getting to Daddy; he was pale as he got into a huddle with his legal team, leaving Shaun and me to discuss all that we had heard so far.

'Marie, do ye think Mammy will ever come home to us again?'

I shook my head. 'Not after everything that was said in there this morning.'

'Do ye think she loves us then?' Shaun said, as he bent to tie his shoelace.

'I don't know.'

Not ready to fully confront that one, let alone share it with my thirteen-year-old brother, I rushed off to the ladies' toilets, telling him I felt sick. Sitting in the cubicle, I peeled off the two roll-ons that were holding in my growing belly. I wondered how long I would get away with hiding the bump – and half-hoped someone would guess, so I could end the charade.

I didn't want to go back into the courtroom, worried at what else would be dredged up about Mammy or Daddy, but it was Father Flanagan's turn on the stand and he was on our side. He said he knew our parents well and had always considered theirs to be a happy enough marriage.

He told Mr Seamus McKenna, Daddy's senior counsel, that Mammy was a good homemaker who kept her children clean and well dressed and who helped out in the community; she would sew something for the local bazaar every year. He said he was shocked and surprised when Danny Brolly told him Annette had run off and later alleged that she was having an affair with Senator McGowan. He had approached the senator for Daddy, but Paddy McGowan had denied knowing anything about the matter.

'However, since that first unproductive visit, both Mrs Brolly and Senator McGowan have admitted to an affair,' the priest said. He told the court that he had done all he could to dissuade both parties from prolonging the liaison, outlining various meetings he had had with them to try to get them to return to their respective families. 'Some failed, some were successful in that Annette returned home for short stays.' He still hoped that the affair would finish.

I was due to go into the witness box in the afternoon but I really didn't want to, and had decided I would simply refuse. But as it turned out, there was no need. During the lunchtime break there was news: McGowan wanted to settle outside court. Daddy was delighted. I asked him what that meant.

'It means that bastard McGowan is feared he's gonna lose.'

'So we've won, then?'

Daddy looked confused. 'Maybe. I'm not rightly sure,' he said.

Then, as if there hadn't already been enough drama in the day, a man in a tweed jacket approached us. He introduced himself as David Fitzgerald.

'I'm Gracie's son,' he said to Daddy. 'Gracie, your wife's mother?' Wringing his hands in excited agitation, he said, 'I never knew Annette was my sister, well, half-sister. I always thought she was my aunt.' And that's when everything clicked into place.

I thought back to those times when Mammy returned from her holidays in Limerick. She would talk about the stud farm, the hunt balls, the gals going out riding before breakfast, and about this young man, David. She said he was a cousin. And when Gracie visited Mammy at home I always felt she was looking down on us and making Mammy do the same. I hated her. And she *was* my real granny? Making *me* related to those snobby bastards? I didn't think I could take any more, and Daddy looked as if he would explode.

'Aye, right,' he said, shaking David's hand limply. 'And what does Gracie want?'

'No, you don't understand,' said David, and gave his long explanation. It had all been one big coincidence. An undergraduate student of law, David had been advised to attend Daddy's case because the prosecution were using an old nineteenth-century law which hadn't been invoked in Ireland for over 100 years. He had been astonished that the case centred on a sister he didn't know he had. He was close to tears.

'I met Annette when she visited the house in Limerick,' he said. 'Everyone said she was my mother's younger sister from Donegal. I had no idea who she really was. Mother never talked about that early part of her life. I wish I'd known.'

'Like mother, like daughter. That's all I have to say on the subject.' Then turning to walk away, Daddy said, 'Now. If ye'll excuse me, young fella, I have to see a man about a dog.'

I later learned that Gracie had become pregnant with Mammy at sixteen, and she was sent away to Dublin to have her baby, which was returned to her family in Donegal. Gracie went on to meet and marry a barrister whom she met in Dublin, and she moved to his stud farm in Limerick, where she made a new life with this big, horsey family.

୨୦୦୪

After all that drama, it was an anticlimax when the case ended. Just two hours into the afternoon session Daddy accepted an offer of £3,800, including costs. Everyone on our side was delighted.

When we left the court we were besieged by a crowd of reporters, cameras clicking. Thrusting microphones under Daddy's nose, they shouted out their questions.

'Danny, how do you feel now that the case is over?'

'Have you anything more you want to say to the senator and your wife?'

I got my share of attention too. 'Marie, look this way.' Click, click went the cameras.

'Run, Marie. Just keep running,' Father Flanagan said, his hand pressing into the small of my back. 'And keep your head down.'

Daddy stayed calm. His solicitor urged the reporters to leave us alone, and luckily Noeleen and the weans had already made their escape and were well down the street.

There was no great chat about the court case when we got home. Auntie Nellie told me that the neighbours didn't need to ask any questions since they had spent nearly a week reading all the juicy bits in the daily newspapers.

'Have ye kept any of the newspapers?' I asked, walking her to the front door. 'Jumbo said that our photos were all over the front pages.'

'Indeed I have not,' she said. 'You wouldn't catch me with rubbish like that in the house.' I asked her what the papers had said that was so bad, but she was tight-lipped, merely saying that I was too young to hear it.

'But Shaun and me were in the courtroom,' I said. 'We heard it all.'

'Sweet merciful Jesus,' she muttered, and blessed herself.

CHAPTER FIVE

INCARCERATED

∞⟨⟩∞

I didn't see so much of Jumbo after the case. He would tease me about my fat tummy, but otherwise he ignored my pregnancy. I was scared he had gone off me. With nobody else to talk to, I told Noeleen about the baby.

'Does Daddy know?' she said, sympathising. It was then that I cried. She persuaded me to tell Auntie Doreen, who now lived in Granny's old cottage, so the next time I saw her, I did. She said, 'Yer mother needs to know this.' That wasn't a lot of help, because I didn't know where Mammy was, but it turned out Noeleen did know. Mammy had talked to her after the case at the High Court, when Shaun and I were dodging the photographers.

'She's livin' in Dungloe,' Noeleen said. 'She's in a mobile home near the sea, and she's goin' to ask Daddy if we can all go there for a holiday. She said she misses us.'

Auntie Doreen said she would fix it for me to visit Mammy, and, true to her word, she went to see McGowan at the Inter County Hotel and arranged it all with him. He was to pick me up at two o'clock and drive me down to Dungloe. Auntie Doreen said she would invent an excuse to tell Daddy. Noeleen was coming along for the ride. We didn't tell McGowan, but we had a vague plan to live with Mammy there so I wouldn't have to face telling Daddy my news.

It was a two-hour journey. I sat in the back seat because I didn't want to talk to McGowan. He caught my eye now and then in the rear-view mirror. I glared at him, mouthing 'home wrecker'.

'What was that, Marie? Do you need the toilet?' I shook my head. 'I thought someone in your condition always wanted to pee,' he said, and I cursed Auntie Doreen for letting him in on my secret.

'Well, here it is,' he said, turning into a field which led to the shore. 'Isn't that a beautiful sight?' He stopped the car at a rather battered-looking caravan. 'There's nobody else around for miles.' He sounded so happy about that, but how could Mammy manage there when he was working?

'Where are the shops?' Noeleen asked.

'What do you need shops for when you can have fresh air and a breathtaking sea view like this?' he said, and I wondered, not for the first time, if the man lived in the real world. Then the caravan door burst open and Mammy jumped down the step and made a beeline for Noeleen. From the malevolent glance she flashed at me over Noeleen's head I could tell at once that she knew. I started to tell her, but she said, 'I can see for meself. That fuckin' waster has got ye pregnant, hasn't he?'

'Jumbo is not a waster.'

'He'll be off. You'll see.' Then glancing at McGowan, she said, 'And I'm too young to be a granny.'

If I had expected that Mammy would be helpful, I couldn't have been more wrong. The way she ranted and raved, you'd have thought that she herself was as chaste as a nun. McGowan let her continue her tirade for a while. Then he interrupted her and said to me, 'Marie, you have to fess up to your father. Or else he'll be taking me to court for kidnapping.' He spluttered with laughter, almost choking over his tea. Then Mammy's new baby started to roar, and the pressure, finally, was off me.

I was hoping we would have a civilised evening and talk through how I would cope with *my* baby, but the minute the baby was asleep, Mammy and McGowan said they were off. They were going to McGowan's hotel in Dungloe and said they'd be back soon with some sheets and pillows, but they didn't return until the small hours.

The caravan was a kip. The toilet was a bucket jammed into a press; there was no bathroom. McGowan said they washed in the sea. And there was only one electric light that worked. How could McGowan expect Mammy to live there with a small baby, and why did Mammy prefer this kip with him to home with Daddy and her other children?

I did my best with the baby but she wouldn't stop whingeing. I fed her and changed her twice, but it took ages for her to settle.

Mammy still wasn't home, so I spent the time writing to Jumbo. I asked him to check on Brian and Don; I was worried how they'd cope without me there. I worried about Daddy too. Would he have to stay home from work? I felt guilty for leaving him and hoped Auntie Doreen had set his mind at ease.

Noleen and I went to bed finally, but woke with a start. Mammy and McGowan were back, clearly the worse for drink. Mammy was giggling as they found themselves somewhere to sleep. 'We should've slept in the hotel like I told you,' she said. And I wondered again why this successful man made the woman he said he loved live like this, cramped, uncomfortable, and miles from civilisation.

The next day was worse. Mammy called me a stupid bitch for letting 'that bastard from Strabane' have his way with me. As for the senator, he worried only about the fallout from my pregnancy on himself. 'And I'm in politics,' he kept saying, as if we weren't all well aware of the fact. It was a relief when he stormed off to his car, saying he was needed at the hotel and would see us all later. I then snuck off to the nearest village to post my letter. It was a long walk but I didn't care. It was good to get away from the stifling caravan and from Mammy's ill-humour.

We were still there three days later when Jumbo appeared, walking down the corkscrew lane towards the caravan. I was thrilled to see him, but Mammy went crazy. 'That bastard is not allowed in here,' she shouted. And she meant it. She wouldn't let him through the door. She wouldn't even talk to him, let alone give him a cup of tea. We sat together on a sand dune looking out to sea, sharing a Mars bar.

'My mam read yer letter,' he said. 'She knows about ye. About ye expecting and all.'

I blanched. 'What did she say?'

'That I was a stupid bastard. And that her and me da have never been able to trust me to do anything right.' He took a slow drag on his cigarette. 'The usual. What are we gonna do?'

I hadn't an answer, but I knew I couldn't stay in that caravan any longer. I waved him off to the bus stop and the next morning I cadged a lift from the senator, who had a meeting in Lifford. Mammy looked relieved, but was pleased when Noeleen said she'd stay behind with her.

I hoped the journey would pass in silence, but the senator was full of chat. 'Marie, me and your mother really love each other,' he said. 'And it hasn't been easy this past year, you know. What with that bloody court case and the newspapers chasing us all over the place.'

I didn't answer. I couldn't. I was scared I would start to cry.

'Your mother didn't want to leave you lot behind, you know. It was your father she didn't love, not youse.' He reached for my hand but I pulled it away sharply. 'Look, Marie, I've lost count of the number of nights she has cried herself to sleep over youse.'

'Oh yeah?'

'We didn't mean for this to happen. All this unhappiness. Annette and myself never set out to hurt anybody. We just fell in love, that's all.' He was silent then, until we reached Stranorlar. Then he showed me a half-finished bungalow, saying it was for him and my mother to live in. 'She'll be out of the caravan before the bad weather sets in,' he said.

By the time we reached Lifford, I felt sick with nerves. How could I tell Daddy my news and when I did, what would he say? But the senator drove past our street, and I realised he was taking me to Father Flanagan. He dropped me at the presbytery and drove off. When the priest opened the door I could tell he had been expecting me and that he knew my news. But he made me say it.

'I'm havin' a baby, Father.'

'Are ye indeed?' He drummed his fingers on the new oak door. 'You'd better come in, then.'

It was the middle of July, but the living room was freezing. We sat on chairs facing each other, and I started to cry. 'I didn't mean it to happen.'

'Oh I'm sure you didn't. Most girls like you don't expect to get caught, do they?' His face was like thunder, and I started to tremble.

'We only did it once.'

'You shouldn't have done it at all.' His calm voice chilled me. 'Haven't you heard about staying in a state of grace until you receive the sacrament of marriage?'

'Jumbo and I love each other.'

'And will he marry you?'

'Yes. We plan to marry,' I said, hoping it was true. We had talked about it, vaguely, a number of times. I just prayed that Jumbo would actually commit.

'And what has your father to say about that?'

'I haven't told him yet.'

'You should have known better. You've seen what your mother put him through with her recent pregnancy. And now you've done the same thing.'

Getting up, he told me to wait where I was, and he left, slamming the door behind him. I sat alone for three hours, shivering in front of the empty grate. I heard Daddy before I saw him. He was in full flow, roaring at me.

'You're nothing but a whore,' he shouted. 'Just like yer mother.' Then he broke down crying, and that was worse. Father Flanagan suggested that I leave the room so that they could decide what to do with me.

I felt helpless. Why would nobody listen to me? I wanted my baby. I'd known I wanted it from the moment I was pregnant, and I loved Jumbo. We wanted to get married. After I had told Daddy the news, I rang Jumbo. And he said of course he would marry me. Daddy then invited Jumbo's parents to our house to discuss what they all called 'the wee problem'. Daddy nearly lost his head, but Jumbo's parents, Mr and Mrs McNally, were calmer. They weren't happy, though. They said, 'Jumbo has no money, no job, no prospects, nothing.'

In their opinion it would be better if Jumbo went off to join the Royal Ulster Constabulary cadets, to try and make something of himself before settling down. After all, wouldn't it be a great opportunity for him to go to England and see a bit of the world? 'Then he can come back, settle into a good pensionable job with the police, buy a nice wee bungalow in a good area in the North, and then, if you both still wanted to, get married.'

After they had gone, Daddy kept going on about Jumbo. How he had no job and no prospects, and how we would ruin our lives if we had a baby. 'It'll have a better chance if it's adopted,' he said. 'And after it's over, ye can come home as if nothing ever happened.' I told him I would *never* agree to that, and I never would.

Jumbo felt as badly about that plan as I did, but what could we do?

⋙⋘

Six days later, on a Sunday, Father Flanagan arrived at our home in Lifford before nine o'clock Mass. He had arranged for me to go to the Saint Anne's Good Shepherd mother and baby home on the Ormeau Road in Belfast. They were expecting me before one o'clock. This came as a terrible shock.

When I first told that story to a teenage Corrinna, she simply could not believe it. 'Why would Granda put you in a home?' she asked, sounding bewildered. And from the perspective of today, it does of course sound totally mad. But back then any girl who became pregnant brought disgrace on her family. She was regarded as a sinner and a fallen woman. The mother and baby homes were seen as a welcome refuge for girls with nowhere else to go. I don't think Daddy felt he had any other choice. He was so used to doing whatever Father Flanagan suggested he should do.

I was due to see Jumbo at two, so Noeleen went out and rang him for me. He rushed over, and came with us to Belfast, sitting in the back seat with Noeleen. Brian and Don wanted to come along for the ride but Auntie Nellie said she'd keep an eye on them, so it was just the four of us. Jumbo kept groping for my hand, and when I turned around he mouthed the words 'I love you.'

The Good Shepherd institution was massive. There were

three large buildings, but only the middle was the mother and baby home. It was a large Victorian sandstone building with ivy creeping up its walls. The front door was huge, with a gleaming brass doorknocker, a letterbox and a bell.

We rang the big brass bell, and heard the sound echoing inside. I was shaking with nerves and wanted to turn and run. Jumbo squeezed my hand and whispered, 'Why don't we go to Gretna Green?' It seemed like a great idea, but then the door swung open and a young novice beckoned us into the front hall. She introduced herself as Sister Catherine.

'Sister Mary Agnes will be with you soon,' she said, leaving us there on the quarry-tiled floor, looking up at a sweeping staircase. When Sister Mary Agnes appeared, Daddy genuflected. He was always like that with anyone from the church. Ignoring him, she turned to me, her eyes resting on my bump.

'And when, may I ask, is the baby due?'

'In September,' I said. Auntie Doreen had helped me work out my dates.

'And you, I presume, are the father,' she said, glancing at Jumbo as if he was dirt.

Then, sweeping towards her office, she beckoned to Daddy and said over her shoulder, 'That is all they do now. Have sex.' I followed Daddy, but she shut the door in my face. And when a few long minutes later the door opened again, she called me in, but said Jumbo and Noeleen must remain outside.

'Marie, you will be staying here until your baby is born. And then, if your father allows it, you may go home.' She glanced at him and added, 'If he doesn't want you back, we can find employment for you here.' This was news to me.

'Here?'

'In a local factory.'

'What about my baby?'

She and my father exchanged glances.

'We will find a home for your child,' she said, looking at Daddy and not at me. 'And don't worry. It will be a good Catholic home, with a mother and a father. Then your child will be brought up properly.'

'I'm not staying here,' I said, panicked. 'Not for a single night. I'm not. I'm going home with Daddy.' I looked over at him, pleading, but he wouldn't meet my eye.

'Give it a try here, Marie,' he said. And I could see he had made up his mind. Daddy had always been in awe of the church. I kissed him, Noeleen and Jumbo goodbye.

'Get me out of here,' I whispered to Jumbo. He shrugged, helplessly.

Sister Catherine said she would show me to my room, so I dragged the battered blue suitcase up the stairs to this tiny cubicle, measuring just six foot by eight. The door wouldn't open fully because a sink was in the way. There was a single bed and a wardrobe. That was it.

That first night was the loneliest and the scariest night of my life. I cried for my younger siblings and I cried for myself. I watched the night sky over Belfast turn an orangey-red; this was 1970, nearing the height of the Troubles, with constant bombs and gunfire. I wondered if a bullet would somehow find its way into my room. Feeling my baby kick, I stroked my stomach gently. I whispered to my unborn baby, telling it that, somehow, I would keep it. We would get through this.

It was all so unfair. I knew many girls who had had a few one-night stands and had never been caught out. Jumbo and I had only 'done it' once, but we were different. We loved each other and wanted to get married. Why couldn't our parents understand that? Why did they keep saying we were too young and didn't know what love was? Wasn't Mammy sixteen when she got married?

I woke the next morning to my new life of discipline. Here we all were, fourteen of us, old enough to have a baby yet not old enough to think for ourselves. There were signs everywhere saying, 'No Entry', 'No Smoking', 'No Talking', 'No Congregating in Each Other's Rooms', 'No Music' and 'No Phoning'. It all added up to no living.

Each day we rose to the boom of the gong at 6.15 am. It sounded again fifteen minutes later, summoning us to morning prayer, and it punctuated our days. I had realised, it being a convent, that we would be expected to pray, but I hadn't realised that they would want us to work as well. And when I reported to the recreation room at eight o'clock I assumed I would be able to while away my morning reading a book. I had brought *Tess of the D'Urbervilles* with me, and couldn't wait to start it.

The recreation room was large, yet welcoming. A floral-covered sofa and matching armchairs were arranged around a marble fireplace, and there was a television at one end and a mahogany table with a mismatch of chairs at the other. The windows looked onto a garden, with steps down to a newly mown striped lawn.

I was about to settle into an armchair when Sister Catherine pointed to an old Singer sewing machine in the corner, the type with foot pedals. 'That, MB, is your place of work,' she said. 'You will sit there sewing from eight in the morning until six in the evening from Monday to Friday.'

'What? Sew? All day?'

'You will have adequate breaks for coffee, lunch and tea, of course, MB.'

'My name is Marie.'

Sister Catherine pursed her lips. 'We use initials here. Confidentiality is called for.'

She then read out a list of things that I could, or in most cases could not, do. As she talked, six girls wandered in, taking up positions around the table. Then Sister Mary Agnes appeared carrying a cardboard box. She emptied the contents with a clatter. Out spilled scissors, thread, green satin, braid, and an assortment of pincushions and needles. There was also a cheap plastic doll with a spooky grin and shocking pink toenails and fingernails.

Mother Superior, it transpired, had found these dolls in a penny shop on the Falls Road. The plan was for us to transform these ugly creatures into Colleen dolls to sell to American tourists. She said they loved anything Irish. I wondered what tourists she meant. With all the bombing and shooting going on in Belfast, the only people visiting Northern Ireland were the journalists who were covering the Troubles. And the only mementos *they* would want, I imagined, were interviews with masked men holding guns, or photographs of some poor unfortunate family scrabbling among the rubble of their burnt-out home in an effort to save a wee part of their lives, or perhaps close-ups of children setting fire to cars or throwing stones. That was what their editors would want, not stupid dolls.

But it wasn't for us to question Sister Mary Agnes's logic. We had a production schedule to stick to and daily targets to reach; and we all had our specific roles. TC, nicknamed Tom Cat, cut out the costume, which comprised a skirt, a top, a shawl and an apron. We were supposed to make knickers too, but they were too fiddly so we gave up.

With my initials, MB, it was perhaps inevitable that I would get called Mad Bitch by the other girls. I didn't mind. But I wasn't keen on my job, which was to sew the skirts and the blouses. In fact I hated it. It was almost impossible to get the armholes to match, and the skirts to meet the tops. I spent most of my time ripping the stitching apart and starting again.

DO'R, or Plank as she became known, had the best job. She painted black T-bar shoes on all the dolls. She was very artistic and creative. Now and again a doll would end up with one ankle and one knee-length boot. We would all laugh like drains when she'd hold one up by the hair to show us the latest in fashion boots.

'What foot do ye think this jazzy bastard kicks with? Taig or Prod?'

Plank's creative ability came to the fore two weeks into the job and a day after she received a letter from her boyfriend telling her it was all over. Apparently he had met someone else and, he said, he had never really loved her. That day Plank decided to give some of the dolls pubic hair. First she'd paint a little black triangle between their legs, then she reckoned that some of them would have enough for a beard, so she'd paint one halfway down their thighs.

Soon after that, the reverend mother realised the scheme

wasn't going to work. She thought about getting us to knit Aran sweaters for the dolls, then realised *that* plan wouldn't work either. And that's when we were put to work as the nuns' slaves doing domestic work, 'tailored to meet our physical needs'. I had the job of scrubbing and polishing the hall floor twice a week, alongside Plank. It was a desperate job. The nuns' shoes left black marks which only steel wool would shift. We would then apply a thick layer of Mansion polish, but when we paused to let it dry, Sister Mary Agnes would flap her arms at us and tell us to keep going.

'You'll never get fit if you keep stopping,' she said. 'And you know how important this exercise is for your pelvic, leg and stomach muscles.'

'Fit my arse,' muttered Plank. 'They only say that because they want skivvies.'

Of the fourteen girls in the home, I got on best with Tom Cat. At eighteen, she was the eldest. She made the most of her lot. She worked in the gardens and had a real feel for gardening, weeding around the roses and tending them with care.

I snuck into her room one night and we chatted until past midnight. She told me about Raymond, the boyfriend she was due to marry, about how they met and had fallen in love. She had become pregnant a month after their engagement but hadn't dared tell her mother. She had told her she was working at a hotel in Belfast to pay for the big day. I couldn't understand it. She was eighteen. Why didn't they just get married and keep the baby?

'The shame would have killed Mammy,' she said. 'She could never have faced the priest.' Instead they planned to go to Gretna

Green, get married, then go home to Enniskillen and start having children.

'What about the one you're having now?'

'The nuns said it'll go to a good home. They promised me,' she said, picking at the edge of the green candlewick bedspread. 'They said it could be lucky and go to a doctor or a solicitor even. Anyway, it will only go to somebody who's rich and can give it all the things I can't.'

The nuns were constantly telling us that our babies would be better off if we gave them away. Plank reckoned they would tell us anything just to get us to sign the adoption papers, yet she had agreed readily enough to hand over her baby. I don't think any of us really thought it through. We were so innocent, and had been brought up to believe in the goodness of the nuns. We certainly didn't know that Irish babies could end up in America. That 2,000 of them did during those decades so didn't become public knowledge until the late 1980s.

It seems extraordinary that we weren't aware of the Magdalene laundry. It turned out to be one of the other buildings in the complex, the third being the reverend mother's house. And, I now believe, when we were told we could stay after our babies had been born, the factory job they had promised us would actually have been a place in the laundry. I shudder when I think of it. When the news of the Magdalene women broke, I thanked God, Daddy, and Jumbo that I hadn't been subjected to that fate.

The Magdalene women have been on the news a lot of late. Since the scandal of their incarceration came to the fore some years ago now, many of them have told their stories of abuse, but ultimate survival. In February 2013 the Taoiseach Enda Kenny apologised to them in the Dáil. He made an extremely emotional speech and looked close to tears.

Tom and I were watching his speech on the news. And after the Supreme Court judgement when, in summary, the judge suggested that the government could change the legislation to grant me my rights, we remembered it. If Enda Kenny was so sympathetic to the Magdalene women, offering them a package, surely he would look kindly on our case too. It gave us such hope.

When the Independent TD for Waterford John Halligan approached Tom and said he wanted to get involved in our case and was willing to ask a question in the Dáil on the right to die issue, we were both delighted.

This took place late in May; Tom and Corrinna were there and we prayed for a favourable response. But the Taoiseach said that the matter was out of his hands.

Enda Kenny tried to soften his words. He said he had compassion for me, but as Tom said afterwards, what use are words? Tom was magnificent. He found the right words for the press, as, somehow, he always does. He said, 'Words of compassion are very easy, but it's compassion in action we want to see. We feel abandoned and, more importantly, dismissed as if we're dirt on their shoe.' And that is absolutely my sentiment.

We did see the laundry girls when we were in the mother and baby home – but only when we got taken to Mass. It was the only time we ever got out of our prison. We were taken through an underground tunnel to the chapel and sat in pews on the right-hand side. Our section was curtained off so that the God-fearing general public, the good Catholics, would not be contaminated by the sight of us sinners. We always wondered who the girls were who had shorn heads.

Much as I liked going to Mass to get a break from the routine, I couldn't say my prayers. I felt that God had let me down. He had given the nuns and Father Flanagan the power to punish me for the crime of loving Jumbo and getting pregnant. I felt annoyed with Christ for forgiving Mary Magdalene but not me. I kept thinking about Jesus letting her wash his feet, and her a prostitute. I would think of the many men she must have had. And there was me: done it once, and I end up in the club. It wasn't fair.

One morning we realised Tom Cat wasn't around and wondered if she had gone into labour. We asked Sister Mary Agnes where she was and she said she was in the sick room, as a precaution. We waited for news of her baby but it didn't come. We never saw Tom Cat again. Rumour had it that she had almost died from blood poisoning. The doctors saved her, but her baby died. The news sent us all into a state of gloom.

The worst thing was that the nuns refused to talk about her. They wouldn't answer any of our questions, walking away when anyone broached the subject. When it was obvious that we would keep asking until someone told us something, a statement was posted on a noticeboard saying, 'A certain person, who shall remain nameless, is safely back at home, in the bosom of her family. Thanks be to God.' I've often wondered what became of Tom Cat. Did she marry Raymond and have more children?

Soon I felt buried under a black cloud. I took to my bed, refusing to get up. I would stare at the walls for hours and days. The nuns came to visit. They talked to me, cajoled and threatened me, but I wouldn't listen to anyone. I stopped eating. They called, finally, for Daddy. He came with Noeleen, and when he saw the state of me he asked if he could take me home.

There was a big fuss about that. The reverend mother said I had to stay and claimed that Father Flanagan agreed with her. I worked on Daddy, and he got Jumbo's parents involved. It wasn't until Jumbo signed a document swearing that he would marry me that Sister Mary Agnes reluctantly let me go.

CHAPTER SIX
FIGHTING FATHER FLANAGAN

೫つ෮

When I woke up this morning, rain was streaming down
the windows, and I felt gloomy. I hoped this wasn't
going to be a bad day. One of the most debilitating side-effects
of MS is depression. You can start by just feeling down, and
you are convinced that by tomorrow it will be better. Tomorrow
arrives and you don't want to get up out of bed. All of a sudden
everything is bleak. When you look out your window all you can
see is grey. Grey sky, grey trees, grey shrubs, everything. Even
people appear to you in a shade of grey. At these times I think I
must be unbearable to live with.

I cry, and when I have no tears left, I cry inside. Tears don't come into my eyes – instead they seep into my chest, and go straight to my heart. These are the days when Tom and I bicker. I can't stand him to look at me. This sniping can last all day and doesn't stop until I go to bed. There are arguments over nothing.

It was a bit like that when I returned home from the mother and baby home in Belfast. It was great to be home, at first. But I soon realised that I had brought my dark cloud with me. I didn't miss those nuns, but it was hard having nobody to talk to or nobody who understood how I was feeling.

When I looked in the mirror I didn't recognise my body; it was strange and hideous. My stomach was stretched to breaking point and there was this faint blue line running down from my belly button. My breasts had grown heavy and my nipples were large and dark. They leaked a thick yellowish fluid that disgusted me. Surely that wasn't normal? I worried that perhaps I had cancer.

My siblings were all busy with their own lives, and the only one who seemed interested that I was home was little Don. He would jump on my bed each morning and force my eyes apart. He'd say, 'Mammy Marie, up, up, up. The lights are on in the sky.'

No friends visited. My best friend from the road, a girl I had always been close to, refused to speak to me now. And Jumbo had just left for Hendon, near London, training for the RUC. He had done extraordinarily well to get chosen; only five boys were sent for training and for once his parents were proud. But it hadn't made him popular in the area. He was called a turncoat. People whom he had considered friends, who were sympathetic to the republican cause, called him a defector, a traitor and a rat.

I was worried about him, but as the days passed I became more worried that he hadn't written to me.

Auntie Nellie, now sixty, was my saviour. She would come round every afternoon and keep me company. She accompanied me to my first antenatal appointment. I was booked into a hospital in Strabane; Daddy had agreed to pay for me to go to a doctor there. Anything rather than go to Lifford, where I was known and would be sure to be looked down on.

I thought I would get to ask questions at the hospital and to find out what to expect, but I was wrong. I waited for hours to see the doctor, and when I finally saw him the consultant was too busy giving out to me for being pregnant to listen to any of my worries.

'A girl of sixteen isn't physically or mentally capable of giving birth,' he said, muttering on about my cervix, as he felt it with his rubber-gloved hand. Then he talked about contraception, suggesting that I should get a prescription for the birth-control pill from my doctor. Then, realising I was from across the border in the 'Free State', he said, 'Oh, sorry. The pill isn't allowed there. Your government won't legislate for it.' Gathering up his notes, and stuffing them into a buff folder, he added, 'More to the point, the Catholic Church would declare war on them if they dared to try,' and I remembered what Plank had to say on that matter. 'Those highfalutin dog collars would rather us girls had babies who were adopted, abandoned, killed, neglected or who lived in some home run by nuns than allow us to swallow a wee tablet.'

It saddens me now to remember how impersonal my antenatal care was. Things are so different for mothers today. When Corrinna was pregnant with the twins I accompanied her to some of her appointments in London. I will never forget the excitement of that first scan. There was such joy in the room. She looked forward to each visit, and so did I. It was a wonderful way to meet each new grandchild.

There was no such excitement about my baby, and the pregnancy continued to drag me down. One night, when Don and Brian were in bed and I was all on my own, I ran a deep, hot bath and lay in it, worrying that I still hadn't heard from Jumbo. I had nightmares about the Provos taking him to a remote barn. I imagined him being questioned at length about the RUC's plans for the North. Then when he wouldn't pass on vital information he would be tarred and feathered and tied to a lamp-post near his home as a reminder that all Catholics should tow the line. What if he wasn't there to marry me, even if he still wanted to? How would I manage to keep my baby then?

I felt tired after my bath, and wanted to go to sleep and never wake up. I ached with loneliness and couldn't imagine my life ever changing for the better. There were some sleeping pills in the bathroom cupboard and I swallowed a handful. Then I walked aimlessly round and round the kitchen before falling into the nearest armchair and dropping off to sleep.

Daddy discovered me two hours later. I was gurgling and dribbling frothy spittle. It scared him to hell. He was convinced that I was going to die. Panicked, he slapped me about the face to try to wake me up. When that didn't work, he half-carried, half-dragged me out to his car.

The doctor at the local hospital decided that since I was drifting in and out of consciousness, he had better pump out my stomach. This, he told Daddy, was the safest thing to do because they didn't know how many sleeping tablets I had taken. Daddy told me all this later. I do remember some of it, though. I vividly recall trying to raise my hand to my head when I heard a 'nee naw, nee naw' sound in the distance. But it wasn't until I had been transferred from Lifford Hospital to Letterkenny General Hospital that I woke up properly. Bringing me my morning tea, a nurse said, 'A nice man is coming to talk to you.'

'Why?'

'To help you with your wee problem.'

The nice man came, but he wasn't nice. He had glassy eyes that stared at me blankly. He talked to me several times over two days. He told me that I had scared Daddy and that I had traumatised the weans so much that a younger brother was now wetting the bed. And I thought, so what's new? The man talked but he didn't listen. He didn't ask me why I was feeling so bad or how I felt about the baby, about Jumbo. Instead, he used threats.

'If you try anything like that again, I'll have you committed to the psychiatric unit across the road in Saint Conal's,' he said. When he saw he had my attention, he added, 'And you'll stay there for good. You can be sure of that.'

His threats hit home. For the rest of the day I lay there imagining the life I would have in that madhouse, away from everybody. I swore to myself that if I ever felt that low again I'd make damn sure nobody would find me. I would get it right.

සටඔ

Close to the time my baby was due, Auntie Nellie gave me some castor oil. She spooned loads of the disgusting stuff down my throat, saying it would get me started. Then she poured me a deep, hot bath and helped me get into it. And sure enough the pains began. They were so bad they had me doubled over, and Auntie Nellie called an ambulance to take me to the hospital in Strabane.

I had never felt pain like it. I thought I would die, but after the nurses had shocked me by first shaving off my pubic hair and then sticking a tube up my bum and pouring in loads of water, a procedure they called an enema (which they said was quite routine), the pains abruptly stopped. And I was sent home. The young doctor said I had probably been suffering from constipation all along. 'Being bunged up does sometimes feel like being in labour,' he said.

A week later the pains came again. This time I decided I wouldn't let Auntie Nellie anywhere near me, for fear of what she might make me swallow. I walked around holding my stomach, crying with the pain. Then I squatted at the top of the stairs, unable to move. Noeleen tried to help. Rubbing my back, she cried with me.

'I wish Mammy was here,' I said. At that, Noeleen ran downstairs, shouting, 'Get Auntie Nellie,' and I was in too much pain to care. Daddy was worried that if I went in to hospital I would be sent home again in disgrace, like the last time.

'Give her a cup of tea,' Auntie Nellie said. 'If she can't drink it down she's definitely in labour.'

The very thought of tea made me want to throw up. I thought, I can't even stand up – how will I manage? Daddy and Noeleen half-carried me down to the car and took me back to Strabane. I begged Noeleen to stay with me and hung on to her hand for dear life, but the nurses sent her and Daddy away. They wheeled me into a ward with six beds, but no other patients. They probably didn't want me corrupting the nice married mothers. So I had no contact with anyone who was pregnant, and no comfort, or information from staff about what was going on. I was convinced that the baby was about to come. It had to be, or what was all this pain for? But a nice blonde nurse from Sligo told me that I had at least twelve hours to go.

'You're in the first stage of labour,' she said. 'Your cervix is two centimetres dilated. It has to get to ten centimetres before the second stage starts.'

That wasn't encouraging. She tucked me tightly into the bed and left me alone, telling me to sleep. I'd left for the hospital at eight in the evening and my labour went on for twenty-four hours. The pain was excruciating; I thought it would tear me apart. I was terrified. Was I dying? I wanted someone with me all the time, just to hold my hand and listen. I wanted Mammy. Thinking of her made me cry hot tears.

I shouted and roared, and the nurses would come in and tell me there was nothing they could do. I would just have to wait. During the afternoon I was lying there wondering if the baby would ever be born, and the sun was shining through a patch of window. When I looked at the wall opposite the window, the image was like a cross, and I could see an outline of myself pinned onto it. And I thought, that is exactly how I feel. I feel crucified.

Soon after that the nurses examined me and said I was making good progress. They wheeled me into the delivery room. There was another pregnant woman there and she was moaning and letting out an occasional scream. We were separated by a screen but I could see her through it – not her head, just her lower half. As she panted, gasping for air, I saw how her baby's head was stretching her to breaking point. Was that what was going to happen to me? Watching in horror, I felt that my baby was coming too. I screamed out in pain and fear, and yelled for the midwives to come to me.

'You're not ready yet,' one shouted from across the room. 'Just wait. We'll be with you soon.'

I felt a sudden desperate need to go to the loo. So I slithered off the bed, shuffled painfully to the toilets, and locked the cubicle. There was a sudden gush of water. It was like a waterfall, tumbling unchecked down a ravine. The nurses, hearing me, hammered on the door, telling me to open it and come out. But each time I tried to get up and let them in, another gush escaped. It went on for what seemed like minutes, and then I was hit by such a sharp pain that I screamed and crumpled to the floor.

The blonde nurse, the one I liked best, went into the cubicle next door, climbed up, and threw her leg over the partition. She lowered herself carefully, swearing to herself as she did do. As she unlocked the door and helped me get to my feet, she yelled at the others, 'She's started. She's started.'

She and the bossy staff nurse helped me back to the delivery room. I could feel the bulge between my legs as they eased me onto the bed. I pushed with all my might. They told me to stop and to push only when they told me to, but the urge was too great. I pushed and pushed and they said they could see the head. But try as I might, I couldn't push my baby out. Finally, at two minutes to eight in the evening on Thursday 17 September, my baby was pulled into the world by forceps delivery.

My baby was rushed out of the delivery room before I had time to catch my breath. I thought, my baby must be deformed. It must be so bad that they can't let me see. Then I decided the baby must be dead. Maybe by taking it away they were trying to save me more pain. But my arms ached to hold it. I asked the blonde nurse but she turned away and wouldn't talk to me. I couldn't understand it. They called the doctor to stitch me up. As he was finishing, he said, 'Your baby's head must have been some size.'

'I don't know. Have ye seen it?' I pulled at the sleeve of his pristine white coat.

'Dr McCabe doesn't have time for small talk,' the staff nurse muttered, glaring at the doctor.

Looking abashed, he kept quiet for a few minutes. Then, taking a deep breath, he said, 'This is an abomination.' He glared at the staff nurse. 'Tell the girl what she's had.'

'We're under strict instructions not to,' said the staff nurse, glowering back at him.

He swore under his breath.

Two hours later the blonde nurse wheeled me back to the empty six-bedded ward. 'You have a beautiful baby girl,' she whispered, settling me into the bed.

'Is she all right?'

'She's perfect. Just perfect.' She gave me a thumbs up: then, looking round at the door, said, 'Shush.'

I lay in bed, feeling light and airy. I wanted to dance around the room. I had a baby girl. A wee baby girl. And she was alive and healthy. And beautiful. I wanted to tell the world. But first I wanted to see my baby. I sat up and swung my legs over the side of the bed, then realised I wasn't able to walk, let alone dance.

'Get back into bed this instant.' Just my luck that the staff nurse was passing my door.

'Then bring me my baby.'

'We can't do that,' she said, in a sing-song voice.

'Why not?'

'The hospital has instructed us not to.'

'Why?'

'The matron will speak to you in the morning,' she said, turning her back on me.

I wept. And then when I heard babies crying down the corridor, I began to scream. I eased myself out of bed, shuffled painfully out to the corridor, directed to the nursery by the cry of the newborns. I opened the door and saw this row of box-like grey cribs with Perspex sides. I thought I would know my baby instantly and began to walk down the first row.

'*What* are you doing?' It was the night staff nurse. Pulling me roughly, she said, 'Get back to bed.'

'Where's my baby? I want to see my baby.'

'You've been told. You can't. We're under instruction from the hospital.'

'Why? Who said?'

'I don't know. Only the matron knows.'

'I have to see my baby.' I started yelling as she pulled me down the corridor. I screamed louder, and then some of the mothers, rudely awoken, started to mutter, asking what was wrong and shouting to the nurses to shut me up. I was still roaring when she escorted me firmly back to bed. And then I started hiccupping.

'I *have* … hic … to see … hic … my baby.' I swung my legs off the bed again.

'Don't you *dare*.'

'Then bring me my baby.'

Sighing, the staff nurse said, 'Keep quiet, and I'll ring Matron for ye. If,' she added, 'you're a good girl and try to sleep now. We can't have those nice mothers disturbed, can we? None of this is their fault.' She looked daggers at me, making it clear that she considered me either a sinner or plain stupid.

I tried to settle, and I must have dozed off because the next thing I remember is Matron softly pushing my damp hair off my face.

'What's this all about, Marie?' she asked.

'I just want to see my baby,' I said, fresh tears running down my face. She smiled, left the room, and a few minutes later wheeled in a crib – like the ones I had seen in the nursery. It was midnight, four hours since I had given birth. And through the clear Perspex sides I saw my baby girl. She *was* beautiful. She had a thatch of blue-black hair, and when she felt me gently stroke her head the sticky eyelids parted, revealing Atlantic-blue eyes. We gazed at each other and I thought she was perfect. She had the prettiest bow mouth. She seemed to be listening to me as I hummed Bob Dylan's song 'Corrina, Corrina'. I reached out to take her in my arms, but Matron stopped me.

'I'm sorry, Marie. Father Flanagan said you can only see her … not hold her.'

'What?'

'He thinks it would be easier for you not to get too close to her, in the circumstances.'

'What circumstances?' I was shouting now, and I could feel my heartbeat rising in panic.

'The adoption.' Looking at my face, she said, 'You do know your baby is going for adoption, sure you do. Father Flanagan and your father are agreed on it. It's for the best.'

'I never agreed,' I said, fighting her for possession of my baby. 'Never. And you can't take her from me. She's mine.' I took my baby into my bed with me and cuddled her close. Sighing, Matron looked down at me.

'I had no option but to agree to do what he asked,' she said. 'Father Flanagan is a priest after all. He said you wanted the baby adopted.'

'That is a big, fat lie. I've always wanted my baby.' It was the truth. I had bonded with the lump in my belly from day one. I spoke to it. I had told everyone I wanted to keep my baby. I had said it over and over when I came home from Belfast. I knew Father Flanagan wasn't happy with my decision. He was always saying to me, 'Marie, you have sinned against God.' He talked about Mary Magdalene and said, 'Women like you don't deserve to have a child. And there are thousands of people, good Catholic people, who can give your baby a wonderful home.' I had listened to him because I had no choice. How could he say I had agreed to what he was proposing?

'Well, you'd better tell him that again, Marie. Because he plans to collect the baby first thing in the morning.'

I refused to let go of my baby. I held her all night but didn't sleep, for fear someone would come and take her. I tried to breastfeed her but either I had it wrong or she did. I knew I should ring the buzzer for help or to get a bottle of formula, but I was scared the nurses would spirit my baby away. It was a strange night. I loved my baby but I felt useless, sore and very, very alone.

I don't know if Matron contacted Father Flanagan and told him not to come to the hospital or whether the news hadn't travelled to him yet, but he didn't come in the morning, much to my relief.

My first day as a mother was hectic. There was so much to do and to remember. The day started with the nurses teaching me how to feed and to burp the baby. That didn't go well. The baby would *not* take my nipple in her mouth. It didn't help that she was sleepy and I was tense, watching the door for Father Flanagan, convinced that he would appear at any second.

The bathing didn't go any better. I felt under huge pressure, made worse when the staff nurse on duty, wheeling in a trolley with a basin perched on top, said, 'You'd better get this washing business right, my girl, or they'll take the baby from you for sure.'

Biting my lip, I held my baby tightly as we lowered her into the sweetly smelling water. The staff nurse showed me how to hold her with one arm, leaving the other hand free to soap her and splash water over her. It looked easy enough, but the minute I took over, the baby wriggled and I almost let go. She was so slippery.

'You hold her. I'll wash her, just for today,' said the nurse, making me feel a failure.

'I'll never be able to do all that by meself.'

'Ach, I'm sure yer mammy will be able to give ye a hand,' she said. Then, glancing at me, added, 'Hey, why the tears? It gets easier, ye know.'

I was surprised at how much I missed Mammy; how much I needed her there, to be the proud granny. And I thought: surely when she hears the baby has arrived, she'll be here, to take a look for herself? But inside I knew better than to expect that.

I vowed right then that I would do better. And when each of my grandchildren was born I have made sure to be there, supervising that first bath. I was worried when Lorcan arrived because I could no longer manage the stairs. But Corrinna brought the baby bath downstairs and placed it on the dining-room table. It is such a bonding time.

The first person to burst through the ward door to see my baby at visiting time was Noeleen. She was hyper with excitement and made a beeline for the plastic crib. 'Where is she?' she asked. 'Where's the baby? I didn't sleep a wink last night, I was so happy for you. And worried.' She frowned. Then, noticing the baby in my arms, she pulled back the blanket she was wrapped in and said, 'Aw, she's like a wee doll.'

By now Daddy had arrived in the ward with Auntie Nellie in his wake but he didn't look in the least excited. He was uncomfortable and seemed surprised that the baby was with me. His eyes roamed the room, looking everywhere except at me and the baby.

'Who do you think she looks like?' asked Auntie Nellie, flopping down in a chair. 'Marie, put the wee baby in the cot so we can get a good look.' I gently laid her down and held my breath as Daddy took a sidelong glance into the cot.

'Nobody in our family,' he said shortly. My heart sank.

'She's got Marie's nose,' said Noeleen.

'She's the spittin' image of her father, Jumbo,' Nellie said, rising to her feet to make her way around to the cot. 'Just look at them big fat cheeks.'

'Right enough,' Noeleen said, looking at Daddy. 'They are pudgy, so they are.'

'She looks like nobody but herself,' I said quietly, a big lump rising in my throat.

'She looks a bit like me mother, so she does,' Daddy said, slowly moving from the end of the bed to get a good look at his first granddaughter.

'Def-in-ite-ly. It's the mouth,' Noeleen agreed. And I smiled to myself, because she, I knew, barely remembered Granny Brolly. 'Then again, Daddy, you know, she looks a wee bit like you.'

'Do ye think so?' Daddy stood taller, puffing out his chest.

'Aw, aye. No doubt about it,' Noeleen said, winking at me.

At that, Daddy moved closer, put his hand into the cot and began to rub the baby's face. Tears of joy bubbled inside me as I looked at the man who only the day before was insisting that I give up my baby for adoption. And now he was murmuring, 'Coochie coochie coo.'

And then my darling sister of just fourteen and a half, who had given me so much grief over my pregnancy, came into her own.

'She'll be no bother to rear, ye know,' she said, gently picking up the baby and rocking her like a pro. 'I'll help Marie, so I will.' Walking over to Daddy, she held the baby up and said, 'Look how beautiful she is. Look at that wee face. How could we even *think* of giving her away.'

It was probably just a few seconds before Daddy spoke. But it felt to me like hours.

'There'll be no giving her away,' he said. 'I'll see to that. She's coming home to where she belongs.'

'What about Father Flanagan?' I asked, and Daddy went slightly pale.

'Don't worry,' he said. 'I'll see to him.'

I knew that wouldn't be easy for him. Daddy hated going against the advice of the church. But I could see from the way he gazed at my baby that he meant it.

'Thank you, Daddy,' I said.

They left in a flurry of excitement. Daddy said he'd look out for the cot and the pram last used for Don, and Noeleen said she would go shopping for lots of lovely pink frocks. And Auntie Nellie, chewing on her false teeth, said, 'There will be plenty of time for style, Noeleen. We need to buy some nappies, and vests and nightgowns.' Noeleen raised her eyebrows.

That wasn't quite the end of it, though. I still had social workers buzzing around trying to persuade me that adoption would be best. They flashed the forms at me asking me to sign, but I told them they would have to break my arm and then pull it off if they wanted a signature.

I felt drained when my visitors had left. All I wanted to do was to sleep, but a young nurse came into the ward and told me I had to feed the baby.

'Aw, look,' she said, picking her up from the cot. 'The wee mite is ravenous. She's eating the fist off herself.'

She passed the baby to me and I unbuttoned my new pink nightdress. The baby's mouth moved instinctively towards my breast but she *still* wouldn't take my nipple in her mouth. The nurse tried to help me; she showed me how to put a finger in the corner of her mouth and how to guide the nipple in, but it was no good. The baby grizzled, sounding as frustrated as I felt.

'I'm sorry, Marie. She won't suckle.'

I cried then. 'I'm just useless. I canny do anything right.'

'Look, it's not you,' said the nurse, rubbing my baby's jet-black head. 'A lot of newborn babies are just like her. They can be a bit finicky. Shall I get ye a bottle?'

I nodded. And she laughed and said, 'Anyway it'll be better for ye in the long run. Ye'll be able to go out to dances and somebody else will be able to give her the bottle.'

'I think my dancing days are over,' I said. 'For a while at least.'

'What? You've just had a baby – you've not had your legs off.'

'Who's going to want to dance with me after this?'

'What about the baby's Daddy. Is he still around?'

'Sort of,' I said, wishing I knew for sure. I was worried. When I'd last seen Jumbo, before he left for London, he had sworn he still loved me. He had said he'd do anything for me. So why had I not had a letter? I was terrified he had found someone else. Why wouldn't he? He was a catch. I had always been surprised that he'd settled for me.

Seeing the doubt on my face, the nurse said, 'Marie, there are plenty of good fellas around who'd be only too willing to take ye on.'

'Ay, sure,' I said bitterly. 'There's plenty that will think I'm easy.'

One thing the nurses didn't have to teach me was how to love my baby. As I lay there I cuddled her close and hummed tuneless tunes to her. I talked to her too, telling her stories about her new family. I told her all about her Daddy who had been sent away from us. I almost burst with joy when her tiny pink fist curled around my finger. Shoving it into her mouth, I cooed, 'Why can't ye suck my breast like that, ye wee rascal?'

I felt loved, and wanted. I loved her newborn smell as I undid the top button of her soft cotton nightgown to give her little kisses around her neck and chest. I felt such love, and wondered if Mammy had felt like this when I was born. I held the baby tighter.

'I will *never* leave ye. Never ever,' I whispered in her ear. And she gazed up at me solemnly.

I felt peckish, and rummaged in the bag Noeleen had left me. And there, among the grapes and the magazines, I found a letter. Seeing the English postmark and the once-familiar handwriting, my heart beat faster. It was from Jumbo.

CHAPTER SEVEN
A BAPTISM AND A WEDDING

ॐ

When I watch Corrinna handle her growing family of five, I can't help but admire her. She has put her career on one side and is a quite wonderful mother. I admire her quiet confidence with each baby as it comes along. It is such a contrast to the way I felt when I left hospital with her, my first-born, all those years ago.

'But it was different for you,' she will say, trying to make me feel better. 'Daddy wasn't around. And there was nobody to support you financially.'

And of course she is right. Her husband Richard is always there for her, a constant support. When I first left the hospital with my baby I felt lost, with no home of my own to go to. I felt old too, and not just because I could barely walk after the twenty-one stitches I had had. I was still sixteen – my birthday wasn't for another three months, yet I felt all the burden of adulthood. I wished Jumbo could be there waiting for me in our own home, but in his letter he had said he would be away until at least December, so it was back home to Daddy and the weans.

The boys were delighted with the new addition to the family. They would do anything to help – running to fetch clean nappies and sticky cream for the baby's bum. Daddy helped too. He showed Noeleen and me how to make up her bottles. 'Be sure ye test it on the inside of yer wrist before ye give it to her, otherwise ye'll burn the mouth off the wee dote,' he said.

Our neighbours kept their distance, but you couldn't keep the children from the street away. 'I wish we had a baby in our house like her,' cooed ten-year-old Siobhan Lynch from next door. Noeleen said Mammy had promised to visit, and soon, but I didn't hold out much hope. Wouldn't any normal mother have been there to help her daughter through the trial of giving birth and to coo over her first grandchild?

Having the baby made me brood more about Mammy, about the way she had abandoned us for love. Noeleen and I had fierce rows over it. Taking Mammy's side, she said Mammy had been unhappy, so why shouldn't she go?

For all the shouting, I had to hand it to Noeleen; she could not have done more for me since I had got home from hospital. And she seemed happy about it – singing as she washed nappies, humming as she fed the baby her bottle, and pacing the floor to settle her when she cried. She even took her turn at the night feed, and all without complaint. She spent her money on the baby too, buying her pretty little dresses and tiny cardigans and bootees. It did me good, seeing how much she loved her. Daddy was the same. He would make a beeline for the wicker basket when he came home from work, and he would talk to her, telling her she was the most beautiful wee dote that ever lived.

I had expected a visit from Jumbo's family but they had not even acknowledged their granddaughter's birth. Yet Auntie Nellie had met Jumbo's elder sister, Anne, at bingo one night, and had told her the good news. Could they be staying away because of the scandal? I knew the neighbours were talking, and I could imagine the whispers. 'Only sixteen, not married, but sure what could you expect from the daughter of the woman who had run off with the senator?'

I was out pushing the pram one day when I saw my one-time best friend, a girl I had known almost all my life. I smiled and raised my hand in greeting but she crossed to the other side of the street. She wouldn't even look at my beautiful baby. I couldn't believe it.

In those early days I could never quite relax. Daddy might have given up on all thoughts of adoption but Father Flanagan had not. He came to visit several times to have a go at me, and to tell me how selfish I was in keeping my baby. Don became my early warning system. He would be out playing in the garden, and the minute Father Flanagan's Volkswagen drew up he would rush inside saying, 'Hide Corrinna. Hide Corrinna. That big bastard is coming.'

I needed to see Jumbo. I needed to hear him say out loud that he loved me and our beautiful baby daughter. He had said it in his letter and said he couldn't wait to marry me just as soon as circumstances allowed, but I felt more than ever that his parents would much rather that he didn't. Daddy didn't like Jumbo anymore. He thought he should have stayed around for the birth in spite of his parents' wishes. He no longer trusted him, and hoped I would forget 'that waster from Strabane'. If nothing else, that would keep me at home helping him with the weans.

I cheered up a little when a large brown envelope arrived for me containing not just a letter from Jumbo but a picture too. Wearing his RUC uniform of dark green with a cap sitting on his blond head, he looked so handsome. He had written on the back, 'To Corrinna from her Daddy.' I held the photo up to the baby every morning as I counted the days until the two would finally meet. I told her stories about him too, and I swear she took it all in as she looked at me with those trusting blue eyes.

I had called the baby Corrinna from the start. It was after the Bob Dylan song that Jumbo and I loved so much, the one I had sung to her when she was first born. But my family, horrified, refused to acknowledge the name. Auntie Nellie said it was ungodly and that the least I could do for my baby was to give her a nice saint's name. Daddy wanted me to call her Catherine after *his* mother, and Noeleen insisted on calling her Naomi. I'm not sure why. I was keen to get the baby christened before she became confused. I asked Father Flanagan and he said he would perform the ceremony on a Saturday afternoon.

'Why not Sunday morning after Mass?' I asked. 'Isn't that when all the babies are christened?'

'It's not appropriate,' he said.

'What's not?'

'Saturday is better,' he said. 'It's to save you any further embarrassment.' He glared at me until I looked away.

'I'm not ashamed of my baby.'

'Nobody said anything about shame. Your baby is a child of God's regardless of how she was conceived.'

'Then why ...?' I saw red. I shouted at Father Flanagan, telling him I would never forgive him for trying to take my baby away from me in the hospital and afterwards.

'I was only thinking of the baby,' he said. 'I thought she would be better off with proper parents, parents that could give her a good life. That's all.'

'That's all? I mightn't have a big fancy house or money but I have a big warm feeling in the pit of my stomach when I hold my baby. I love her, Father, so I do. No stranger could *ever* love her as much as I do.' I thought that would end the discussion. But, as usual, Father Flanagan had to have the last word.

'The one thing strangers have, and can give your baby, is something you cannot,' he said, turning to leave. 'And that's a stable home environment.'

The christening took place in early October 1970. The godparents were Daddy and Noeleen. I had wanted Uncle Eddie but Father Flanagan overruled me. So it was just the family gathered at the baptismal font. I was so flustered when Father Flanagan asked me what my daughter's name was to be that I said, 'Naomi.' Then, blushing, I corrected myself, 'No. Not that. I'm calling her Corrinna.'

'That's not a saint's name.' Father Flanagan and Daddy spoke in unison.

'I'm calling her Majella as well,' I said. 'After Saint Gerard.'

Now it was Shaun's turn to interrupt. 'Ye told me ye were calling her Jinny after Granny Maxwell,' he said.

'I am.'

'What?'

'I am as well. Not Jinny. Jane. Granny's real name. Corrinna Jane Majella.'

'Three names?'

'Four,' said Noeleen. 'Naomi too.'

Sighing, Father Flanagan told me to sit and think about it. And then he would perform the ceremony. I pretended to think about it, but my mind was made up.

Corrinna Jane Majella was as good as any baby could be, even though Father Flanagan nearly drowned her with water. Afterwards the priest told me to leave Corrinna with Noeleen and follow him to the front of the chapel to be 'churched'. I hadn't a clue what he was talking about but I followed him anyway. I knelt at his feet and, looking up at Jesus hanging on the cross, I blessed myself and asked God to make everything right for Corrinna and me. Then Father Flanagan laid his hand on my head and began to pray.

I expected him to share in my prayers for Corrinna and was alarmed when he spoke about exorcising demons from my soul. Did he think I was in cahoots with the devil? He muttered on about cleansing my soul so that I'd be acceptable again to the Catholic Church. I wanted to cry. I wondered if Mammy had had to go through this churching palaver when the weans were baptised or was it designed to make girls like me feel like lepers?

Later, standing outside the chapel hugging Corrinna and smiling into the box camera for Shaun, I wanted to cry again.

The whole process had made me feel dirty. Was it really so wrong that I had given birth to my beautiful baby without having a ring on my finger?

∞

Mammy came to visit when Corrinna was two months old. Or, in Daddy's words, two months after 'God sent us an angel'. Before she was even in the door she muttered that she couldn't stay long. 'Paddy and meself are moving into a new house in Bundoran,' she said, kissing Don on the top of his head.

'Lucky for some, to have no worries,' I muttered.

'I see motherhood hasn't tamed yer tongue.' She took off her fur coat and curled herself into Daddy's chair by the fire. I was so angry with her. Angry that she had left us, that she was happy, and that as yet she had barely given Corrinna a second glance. Yet as I watched her gather Don into her arms, handing him some boiled sweets, my heart ached.

Mammy was so beautiful, more beautiful than I remembered. Her porcelain skin glowed and her big juicy eyes danced with happiness. She had given birth to her baby just five months earlier yet her figure was perfect – so slim and shapely. I felt ugly sitting across from her in my blue nylon overall and Dr Scholl sandals. I knew I looked terrible; I could see it every morning in the mirror. My hair was lank and ratty. I had spots on my forehead and chin. But then, why would I bother looking good? Corrinna loved me anyway and I didn't see anyone else.

'Ye need to get yerself into shape, Marie,' said Mammy, lighting a cigarette. 'Or ye'll never get a man.'

'I don't need a man.'

'Every woman should have a good man on her arm.'

'A good man? Then what are ye doing with the senator?'

Her smile faded. 'At least he's not an auld woman like some I could mention.'

'Daddy's a good man. He would've done anything for ye.'

'My life with him were all work, no play.' She shuddered.

'And what about me? I want a life of me own but I'm not getting that until *your* weans grow up and leave home. Well, am I?'

'Yer father could get himself a housekeeper to look after ye all, so he could. He got nearly £4,000 for me leaving him when he sued poor Paddy in the High Court.' She sucked on her cigarette.

'He doesn't want just anyone looking after them. *He* loves them,' I said.

'Ye need yer head looked at. But if ye want to turn yerself into a skivvy, then go ahead. But I'm telling you, my girl, ye'll get no thanks.'

Don had run off by now, not wanting to be cuddled by the Mammy he barely remembered. That annoyed her. When a horn sounded outside she jumped up saying that she couldn't stay longer. 'Give the weans a big kiss from me and tell them I'll see them soon.'

'But Brian will be in from school in a minute.'

'Paddy's waiting.'

'Stay a wee bit longer. Ye haven't held Corrinna. And I need to talk to ye.' I walked after her but I was wasting my breath. The front door banged shut.

I cried when she had gone. I hated her, yet loved her. If she had shown me any affection I would have told her how scared I was looking after my new baby. I would have said I couldn't cope anymore with Daddy and the weans. I wanted to tell her that I felt bad, that I had to drag myself out of bed in the mornings.

That visit has stayed with me through the years. It still makes me cry. Why did she not feel close to Corrinna? How could she bear to leave without hugging her? How could any grandmother? There is nothing nicer than meeting a new grandchild. I remember particularly when Aran and Cormac, who were born premature, were in the special care unit, I sat with them through the night. And we beat a path to Waterford the minute we heard of Evan's birth.

I had been mooching around the house for weeks. I would listen to the wireless but that did not always cheer me. When Dusty Springfield came on singing 'You Don't Have To Say You Love Me' I would lie on the sofa and bawl. Daddy said I was wasting my life. And when one night Noeleen asked me to go to a dance with her and her friend Emily, I agreed just to keep him off my back.

I was almost excited as I got dressed in a purple hot-pants jumpsuit and white PVC knee boots, but as we walked into the hall I noticed groups of girls pointing at me and sniggering. Inside, the place was a cattle market. Us girls stood on one side and the boys walked up and down looking at us from top to toe. When I refused to dance with a neighbour, who was too old in any case for a hop like this, he got red in the face. 'Who the fuck do ye think ye are?' he slurred. 'Sure everyone here knows ye are nothin' but a big ride.' That was it. Grabbing my coat, I made for the door.

Jumbo was due home on 12 December. The closer the date got, the more excited I became. Excited, yet very, very nervous. Suppose he didn't fancy me anymore? In a panic I had my hair cut trendily short but I hated it, and Shaun said I looked like a boy. I was scared he was right. My breasts had shrunk from a 36B to a miserable 30AA. 'They're just fried eggs,' said Noeleen.

The big reunion was to be in Auntie Nellie's house at eight o'clock. I spent weeks debating what to wear and settled on a long lamb's wool midi-dress with boots and a wide belt. The dress clung nicely but hid my bony hips. I applied pan stick and black eyeliner, then rubbed it off again. Daddy didn't know where I was going. I was so worried he would stop me that I waited until I could sneak past him. It was 8.30 before, having managed it, I arrived at Auntie Nellie's house with Corrinna in my arms. I banged on the front door.

'We didn't think you were coming,' she said, and I looked past her to see if Jumbo was there. 'He's here,' she said. 'He's been looking out the window for the past hour.' That's when the nerves really got to me. Handing Corrinna to Auntie Nellie, I rushed for the loo. And when finally I walked into the kitchen I saw Jumbo holding a huge teddy bear out to Corrinna as she lay in Auntie Nellie's arms.

'She's beautiful, Marie,' he said, smiling at me. 'Just like you.'

'Ach, no. Everyone says she's the spitting image of you.'

'They do? Poor wean.' He laughed.

My insides were melting with desire. But I held myself off until Auntie Nellie said she had promised to visit her grandchildren around the corner. Then we fell into each other's arms, almost crushing our baby. 'I love ye, love ye, love ye.' We said it in unison. Then I handed Jumbo his baby. He held her awkwardly, as if scared she would break.

'She's strong, ye know,' I said. 'When ye lie her down on her stomach she tries to lift her head up.'

'Was it sore having her?'

I nodded.

'I'm sorry about all that's happened to ye. I promise I'll make it up to ye both. I love ye, and I won't let anyone keep us apart.' He handed me Corrinna then and, going down on bended knee, asked her to marry him. 'Of course, ye'll have to bring yer Mammy with yer,' he said.

He left when Auntie Nellie came back. He wanted to walk us home but I told him, 'No.' Suppose Daddy was looking out the window? I got in without him asking me any questions. I felt light with happiness and relief. My feller loved me and was going to marry me. We decided to keep news of our engagement to ourselves for now. First Jumbo had to tell his parents that he planned to leave the RUC. And he knew *that* would go down like a lead balloon.

He was right. They simply would *not* agree to it, and especially not when 'our news' leaked out. For one thing, Jumbo's mother didn't think much of me or my family. Well, she wasn't alone there. We had decided to get married on 27 December 1971, two days before my eighteenth birthday. At least I had decided. Jumbo wanted to wait until May when he would be eighteen. He said it would be simpler all round, meaning that then there was nothing anyone could do to stop us. But I didn't want to put up with the work and disharmony in our house five minutes longer than I needed to, let alone five months.

In the end his parents agreed. But only if he returned to London to finish his training with the police cadets. 'It was an honour to be chosen,' his father reminded him. 'Only a handful of ye were. Remember? Ye owe it to the RUC, and to yeself.'

I hated it when Jumbo left. But I decided to visit his parents every Wednesday so they could get to know me and their granddaughter before the wedding. His father, Jim, was nice to me but his mother, Kathleen, was trickier. I was determined that she would like me, but it was a losing battle. She blamed me for her son's fall from grace. They had hoped he would become a teacher; he had the brains for it, and they seemed convinced that it was *my* fault he had not done better in school.

For all that, I loved spending time with them. Kathleen was a great cook. She would make fancy dinners like pork chops with apple sauce and there would always be a pudding. More important still, to me, was the happy atmosphere. The house was full of laughter and song. Kathleen adored singing, especially in public. She and Jim were the Sonny and Cher of Strabane. She would take Corrinna on her knee at the piano and sing especially for her, making the baby laugh and gurgle with delight. Jim was more reserved, but he loved dancing. Swooping Corrinna into his arms, he would sway around the living room to Engelbert Humperdinck.

Meanwhile, I was trying to organise my wedding. Daddy did not want me to get married. He said he was worried about me – about the marriage and how we would survive when Jumbo left the RUC. But the real reason he was unhappy about it, I reckoned, was that Jumbo and I had found ourselves a flat nearby. That meant he would lose a housekeeper and substitute mother for the weans. He had agreed to pay for the reception; he saw it as a way of inviting all his cronies, while leaving Mammy's family out altogether. But that was the least of my problems. Father Flanagan didn't want to marry us, and worse still, we hadn't the money to pay for a dress, a ring or somewhere to live.

'I'll have ten pounds when I finish with the cadets. That'll help,' said Jumbo. I'd hoped his father might stump up something but Jumbo said there was no way he would even ask. I managed to gather the money for some cheap white material and a pattern for my wedding dress, but when I showed it proudly to Kathleen she said, 'But ye can't wear this.'

'I know it's not great, but it was reduced and was a real bargain.'

'But it's white.'

'Yes?'

'And yer not a virgin.' She lit a cigarette and said, 'I've seen a nice blue costume in that new boutique on Main Street. That'll do ye nicely.'

ഇറോ

When the wedding car left for the church I glanced back at our house and sighed with relief that my life there had come to an end. I was excited at the thought of married life. Daddy warned me that without money my marriage hadn't a hope, but I knew he was wrong. We loved each other so how could we be anything but happy?

I was wearing my white dress; I had never considered giving

in to Kathleen and wearing blue. But I made one concession: I didn't wear a veil. I didn't like them anyway. Instead I wore a big floppy lilac hat. She wasn't happy, and gave out yards to me in front of all our guests.

All through the wedding I kept thinking of what was to come. For months I had been dreaming of being alone with Jumbo, of lying in his arms on our wedding night. We would be in our new double bed with crisp white sheets and our lovemaking would be tender and slow. It would be the first time we had seen each other properly naked. But it didn't work out like that at all.

We left the reception with Teddy and Margaret, friends of Jumbo's who lived in the bedsit two floors down from us. Jumbo invited them to our flat and the three of them demolished the half bottle of vodka Jumbo had bought for New Year. I left them arguing about the Hare Krishna movement and fell into bed at 4 am, alone.

I was woken the following morning by noisy knocking. Leaving Jumbo lying on his back snoring, I opened the door. Noeleen stormed in carrying two bulging plastic bags and headed for the kitchen saying she would put on the kettle and make a cup of tea. Brian, who was now eight, was in her wake.

'What the fuck ...?'

'We've run away,' said Brian.

'You've what?' I wrapped my dressing gown tighter so that he wouldn't notice I was naked underneath. 'Run where?'

'Here, stupid.' Brian pushed past me and threw down another two plastic bags.

'But why?'

'We'd nowhere else to go.' Noeleen said that they couldn't live with Daddy for one minute longer. He was in a foul humour because the sherry bill for the wedding had been so huge. He had shaken her awake first thing, to rant and roar.

When I got back upstairs, Jumbo was awake. Smiling, he pulled me towards him. When I told him who was in the kitchen he wasn't one bit amused, and he turned the air blue. 'Just get rid of them,' he said. But the runaways refused to go home. They stayed for four days. Frustrated, Jumbo and I locked ourselves in the shed at the back of the flats. Hardly ideal, but at least it was private. We sneaked down there a few times to make love. It wasn't the way I had imagined.

We had three days as a family of three, and then Mammy turned up with her baby. The senator had dumped her. I wasn't surprised. After all his grand talk he had never moved Mammy into the bungalow he had supposedly built for her. She came to us straight from that godforsaken caravan. I didn't see how I could turn her away.

'It's only for a couple of days, just until she gets herself a flat or something,' I told Jumbo. But I crossed my fingers behind my back because I realised Mammy wasn't great at organising things for herself. Hadn't she always been looked after?

'But why the fuck had she to come here?' Jumbo picked up his guitar and started strumming. 'We've no room for her. It would fit her far better if she went home to her husband and her four weans.'

'Like that would happen.'

He played a discord. 'Nah. She'd rather sit here giving out about yer father and how hard her life was with him. And where will she sleep when we've only the one bed? She won't be happy on the sofa like yer sister and brother now, will she?'

'Couldn't she sleep with me – in our bed?'

'Fucking families,' he said through gritted teeth. 'I thought that once ye went to the bother of getting married ye slept with yer wife … in a bed. Not curled up by yerself on a two-seater sofa.'

I couldn't believe I was defending Mammy against Jumbo. But I felt sorry for her. She was distraught at having lost another man, and her pride was hurt too. I loved my family. But I hated the way they complicated my new life. Daddy hated me trying to help Mammy. As revenge, he made me give him my carpet sweeper and four glasses, and all because I'd used his Green Shield Stamps to get them. Mammy laughed when I told her. 'Miserable bastard,' she said. 'Now ye know what I had to put up with for all those years.'

With just the dole coming in, money was extremely tight. And when Jumbo spent two and six on guitar strings and a plectrum for his guitar I screamed at him, furious. Corrinna was crying with misery because she was cutting her baby teeth at the time, and if she wasn't crying, Mammy's baby was screaming with a tantrum. I ended up crying along with them. When Kathleen popped in to see Jumbo I shut myself in the bedroom. I hadn't forgiven her for giving out to me on what should have been the best day of my life. But the worst thing was the continuing lack of privacy. I was married, so why should I feel embarrassed when Mammy caught me kissing my new husband in the bathroom?

The very day I paid a month's rent in advance we struck lucky and were allocated a council house. I explained the situation to our landlord but he refused to give me back my money. I felt so frustrated that I smashed two teacups from my lovely new tea set.

Moving to the Ballycolman estate in Strabane took all of three hours. Jumbo carried most of the furniture in relays with his friend Teddy. We only had a sofa, two chairs, a bed, a cot and a few boxes containing cups, plates, cutlery and saucepans. Mammy and me followed on behind, pushing prams with our babies, along with bags of blankets and clothes.

'We look like the gypsies,' said Mammy. 'Could ye not have got a lend of a car?'

'I'm not speaking to Jumbo's mother,' I said. 'I wouldn't let him ask his father for help.'

Mammy gave me a sharp look. 'Pride will be the fall of ye one of these days, Marie. Ye mark my words.'

It was Jumbo who saved the day. He found Mammy a bedsit and gave her the name of the manager of the local shirt factory. 'They're always looking for women in that place,' he said, tucking into a plate of cabbage and bacon. 'There are no jobs for men in this town but plenty if ye wear a skirt and can sew a straight line.'

I threw my arms around him and kissed him when he gave us the news. 'Jesus, that's great,' I said to Mammy.

'What about furniture?'

I couldn't believe this. Could the woman do nothing for herself?

'It's fully furnished,' said Jumbo. 'All ye need is a couple of blankets, and cups.'

It took us two days to get Mammy moved out; she kept

insisting that she could not afford to live alone. It wasn't until Noeleen had handed her half her week's wages and given her a bag full of food that she had bought, on tick, on Daddy's account from Ringer McGrane's shop in Lifford that we finally got her through the door. The rent on the bedsit was already covered for the month because our old landlord, Mr Cassoni, owned this bedsit too. And he agreed to transfer the sum I had paid in advance. We closed the door on her, smiled at each other and fell into one another's arms. Finally we could settle down to family life with our baby daughter.

At first we were happy. I loved looking after Jumbo and I took great pleasure in decorating our new house. With the orange and purple hall, the beige and brown living room, the three mustard bedrooms and the lime-green bathroom it was the height of fashion for 1973. Jumbo had found himself a safe, pensionable job with the Department of Social Services. He was a benefits officer, and I now worked in the local shirt factory. I had to. We needed all the money we could get.

I hated my job, though, and the life that went with it. I felt like crying as I faced another day of having to drag Corrinna to a baby-minder before getting myself to a dirty, noisy factory. I would spend the eight hours there inspecting silk pyjamas and smoking jackets for Harrods in London.

Jumbo was lucky. He loved his job. He visited people in their homes and decided whether they were entitled to the dole. He hated turning people down but sometimes he had to because they had been caught working and signing on at the same time. 'Everyone has the right to live,' he said one night, tucking into his stew. 'If that means fiddling the state, then why not?' Secretly

I agreed with him. There were times I would love to have been able to fiddle someone, because both our wages were tied up paying off our debt.

I wanted the best and, sick of all the cast-offs we had been given, bought new furniture. I splurged on a cream tweed three-piece suite, a pure wool carpet, a glass-topped coffee table, a wall of teak bookshelves and a drinks cabinet that we used for keeping the debt letters in. We had furnished the bedrooms with white Formica and had acquired Venetian blinds for all the windows. The new loan was with the Provident Credit Company.

We might have managed had we not been feeding what Jumbo called the five thousand. But every night my father and all my siblings would arrive expecting their dinner. It drove Jumbo mad. 'Tell yer father if he wants his dinner made for him then he has to pay for it.'

'But he's promised to paint the kitchen. That's payment in kind.'

'He has been saying that for months,' said Jumbo, moodily strumming his guitar. 'It would end up cheaper to get someone in.'

'Maybe. But I don't want to hurt his feelings.'

'That's yer problem, Marie. Ye try to please everybody but end up pleasing nobody.' I had a horrible feeling he might be right. And it something I've carried throughout my life.

I tried dropping hints to Daddy but he never took me up on it. When he complimented me, saying, 'That was a nice plate of stew, Marie. Just what a man needs after a hard day's work,' I'd say, 'I'm afraid ye'll have to do with spuds and butter tomorrow night because I've no money left to buy mince.'

But he didn't get it. 'Nothing better than potatoes and butter for a body,' he'd say, opening the middle button of his paint-splattered overalls. 'Sure wasn't I reared on it and it didn't do me any harm.'

It was so unfair. Unfair on both me and Jumbo. Our debts increased when we had to buy a car on tick. We needed one because Jumbo's new job was in Derry and he wasn't able to get around all the housing estates by bus. That Hillman Imp caused nothing but bother from the day he bought it. There were times we ended up pushing it up a hill. The strain of it all soon showed on our relationship.

I hated the way our lives were going. I had imagined that marriage would be heaven. We would be all lovey-dovey, but Jumbo and I fought most of the time. Tired from working, we needed space to relax together and that didn't happen. Jumbo would retreat into a corner with his guitar, and the strain on me became unbearable.

A good social life would have helped, but our main outing was the weekly shop to Wellworths. And that would end in a row when the checkout girl tallied my bill and I realised I had only seven shillings and sixpence left to pay for all the bread and milk for the week. The strain got me down. It came to a head on the day of Princess Anne's wedding to Mark Phillips. Listening on the radio at the factory and dreaming of the romance of it made me realise just how unhappy I had become. I went to the doctor and told him how I felt. 'I can't stop shouting at Jumbo,' I said. 'I don't mean to do it, but I'm dead on my feet. Yet however tired I am, I go to bed and I can't sleep. I keep crying too.' At this I dissolved into tears and he told me to stop mothering everybody and start mothering myself. Then he prescribed the sedative Valium for me.

The Valium calmed me. I cried less, but the problems didn't go away. Sex, instead of being a pleasure, was becoming another job I had to do. 'We don't need to do it every night,' I said to Jumbo as I was picking his clothes off the floor. 'Wouldn't every other night be better?'

'Better for who?'

'I don't know. For a change, maybe?'

'Ye are joking! I need my conjugal rights.'

I was now relying on the Valium. I'd take one to get me to work, one in the afternoon to stop me stressing about all I had to do once I got home, one at teatime to help me cope with the gang and one at bedtime to ease the guilt for spoiling everyone's evening.

I thought, surely life will soon get better. But it didn't. It just got more complicated. First, Brian came to live with us. Daddy had thrown him out, saying he had been caught drinking at school. Then Shaun, at fifteen, said he was getting married. His seventeen-year-old girlfriend was pregnant. Daddy saw that as *my* problem. He came around saying, 'Ye'll have to do something about that boy, Marie.' Did he think I could perform a miracle?

Then Jumbo started asking friends around every night. I wouldn't mind, but these friends were the same age as Daddy. They called every evening at seven for a cup of tea and a chat about how life had let them down. They would smoke and splutter, and I'd think my lovely room was nothing but God's waiting room.

That, or the café at Donegal Town railway station. There

were so many comings and goings. I'd feed Daddy, the boys and Noeleen at six thirty. Jumbo's friends Tommy and Ambrose would arrive at seven and hang around until nine. Then Brian and his friend Busty would burst in, hungry after their football training, wanting banana sandwiches. They'd put a Bay City Rollers record on Jumbo's precious player and blast us out, while Jumbo fussed around.

At least I had Corrinna. She was such a good little girl, with her happy smile. She would give me lots of hugs and kisses, and she toddled around the house, helping me to clean up. I was determined, whatever else, that Corrinna was going to have a good life. I read to her constantly. 'Little Nell' was her favourite. She would sit on my knee enraptured, grabbing for the pages. I knew this child, like me, would have a love of reading.

CHAPTER EIGHT
MOVING ON

෨෬

I have never hidden my difficult past from my two children. I told them all about their nana, even though the stories could be distressing. I think that knowing it all has made them understand me a little better. Nothing in my life has ever been as bad as the day my mother left. It led to all kinds of sadness and stress, but it made me strong too. All my life since then I have been fighting to be independent. If I have taught Corrinna and Simon anything, it is that you must keep the fight and remain strong. To me, nothing else matters.

The children knew their nana. They loved her, but Corrinna has said she could never tell what was going on in her head. She was a closed individual, it's true. Now that time has passed I can understand her a little better. I think she was a product of all that had happened to her when *she* was growing up. If your mother has abandoned you for a better life, it must make you believe that it is acceptable to do the same.

Mammy had such a strange upbringing. When Gracie abandoned her in Lifford she was brought up as a sibling to her aunts and uncles, yet there was always money being sent from Limerick to make sure she had the best. She had been sent to a grammar school in Strabane. She learned French at a time when people in the South barely went to secondary school.

It must have been hard for her being tied down with all of us at such an early stage. And once I was married with responsibilities, I understood her a little better. I had to, really. Because in spite of all the love I had for Jumbo, my marriage to him didn't last. Looking back, I don't think it ever had a chance. There was no time for us to develop our relationship. I have very happy memories of holidays on the Ring of Kerry and of family outings, but it was *never* just me, Jumbo and Corrinna. Daddy was always there, and Brian and Don, or some combination of them.

One time, Jumbo, Brian, Corrinna and I went on holiday to Limerick to see Gracie, my real grandmother. Gracie was this larger than life glamorous person who adored her life of luxury. She was like an old-world film star. She always smelt of powder and perfume. The house was massive, like a stately home. There was this huge dining room with a highly polished mahogany table. We stayed in a room with a double bed and two single ones. Corrinna said it was like the house in *Goldilocks and the Three Bears*. It was a good holiday. There was a pony there, and

Corrinna was put on it, bareback. She loved that. It made her squeal with happiness.

Jumbo and I went out to Limerick one day, leaving Brian and Corrinna with this maid Patricia, who had a wonky eye. When we got back, Corrinna complained that she hadn't been allowed into the house. 'When I needed to wee I asked Patricia to take me inside but she led me to this outside loo in the yard,' she said, sounding shocked. That made me smile. Because I was well used to an outside toilet. There was one in Granny Maxwell's cottage where Mammy was brought up.

I often wonder why Gracie didn't reclaim her child after her marriage. In fact she did try having Mammy with her for a while. This was when she was eleven or twelve, but it didn't work out.

Gracie came to stay with Jumbo and me once. She sunbathed in the garden of our council house in her underwear. One of the neighbours, four doors down, couldn't believe his luck at the sight of this half-dressed voluptuous woman. He couldn't take his eyes off her.

Brian was still living with us, and Noeleen stayed from time to time. She was mad about Corrinna and she lavished gifts on her. She would come bursting into the house shouting for Corrinna. 'Look what I've got you,' she'd say, handing over a fancy outfit she'd bought from a French shop.

Corrinna adored Noeleen too. She loved watching her aunt getting ready to go out, fascinated by all the eye shadows, brushes and lipsticks. She would put Noeleen's rings on her fingers and have a squirt of her perfume. It was tough sometimes watching the fun Noeleen had, when Jumbo and I were short of money. Sometimes I felt like Cinderella.

Jumbo and I loved each other. We always had. Jumbo told me that he was smitten the minute he saw me. He said I was the most beautiful thing he had ever seen, and I was crazily in love with him. We were good together. If things had been different, if our romance had been able to take its natural course, I think we might still be together. But we had taken on so much so young. I don't think our marriage stood a chance.

Jumbo went off the rails a bit in his early twenties. It was drink, and other women and writing off cars. Daddy was always giving out about him. One time, when Jumbo had crashed a car and I was worried because he had been injured and was in hospital, his father stood there in our council house, pontificating. Jumbo, he said, was feckless and not to be trusted. 'And he hasn't even paid off the last car.'

He was right, of course. Jumbo and I always had money worries and it was me who had to sort things out, but that didn't make his interference any more welcome. I was worried about Jumbo. He had been injured in the crash and was in hospital.

Our problems started when Jumbo got his job in the civil service. He got into the habit of going to the pub with his workmates and he discovered vodka. Home was no fun for him when it was full of his in-laws, and he began to rebel. The problem is that he had too much responsibility too young. I don't feel any venom towards him; I'm fond of him still, but he really put me through the wringer. He would be away, and women would ring from around the county claiming that Jumbo was 'seeing' them. It was torture.

When Corrinna was four or five, Jumbo went missing for a whole week. He had taken the money that I had put aside for the rent and the electricity bill. I was frantic but I tried to hide it from Corrinna. We were one of the first families to get a house in the estate in Strabane so it was a safe place to play. I remember Corrinna going for a cycle with one of the boys who lived there. His name was John Lynch and he was a few years older than her. A while later Corrinna burst in saying, 'I think I know where Daddy is.' She tugged at my sleeve. 'John says he's probably in the tree on the green with the hollow trunk. Can we go and see?' she asked. 'It's a great place to hide.' I didn't know whether to laugh or cry.

My friend Eileen took Corrinna down to a house in Dunfanaghy. They stayed there for a few days. I was beginning to wonder whether I would ever see my husband again, but one afternoon his orange Volkswagen Beetle pulled in and Jumbo got out. We drove straight to Dunfanaghy to collect Corrinna. She ran into his arms and never asked any questions. But I did. I was furious with him. He had no excuses. He had been on the tear from work. In the end I forgave him, as I always did. Jumbo has such charm; he has always been a lovable rogue. He has said to me since that he knows he was a bastard. He is sorry for the way he treated me. He says he admires me as an intelligent and talented woman. And I have to admit that the marriage breakdown wasn't all his fault. I am not always the easiest to live with. I have a temper. When I see my life spiralling out of control, shouting is sometimes my way of venting frustration.

I will never forget the day Jumbo left for good. He came in, packed a bag and walked out. Corrinna was out playing on the front step. He didn't kiss her. He didn't even say goodbye. He just stepped over her and drove away. She was inconsolable. I was so worried that she would be affected by that all her life. But she doesn't remember it. Not at all. She has just blanked it out of her mind.

After his abrupt departure, Corrinna, Brian and I were on our own for about three years. It was a sad time. I was working hard in the shirt factory in Strabane as an examiner. I had to stand at the back and check everyone's work.

I wasn't a machinist at work, as Noeleen was, but I loved sewing at home. In that, I took after my mother. I was taught, by her example, that you should put your best foot forward and I made sure that Corrinna always looked good when we were out. It meant that I could hold my head up high. Corrinna wasn't mad about my sewing. She complained that the minute she got home from school I would start on the torture of sticking pins into her.

I did all the sewing from our council house too. I made all the curtains and all the upholstery. Every Friday I visited the market to buy material. I made everything – from cushions, to Corrinna's communion dress.

Keeping up standards was vitally important to me because I felt judged. Corrinna was at school with a whole glut of girls whose birthdays were near hers in September. Their mothers would have been in the same hospital as me at the same time and they were all much older than me. They were in their twenties back then and they knew I had been sixteen and unmarried when I had Corrinna. I felt that everyone looked down on me, especially now that Jumbo had left.

I was determined to give Corrinna the sort of magical childhood I would have liked for myself. I know I indulged her, especially at Christmas. I was haunted by the Christmases of my childhood, when all my siblings had presents and I had to buy my own. I gave Corrinna anything she wanted. Well, almost anything.

When she was six years old, she was desperate for a Colleen doll. 'Everyone at school has one,' she said. I tried to deflect her and to persuade her that, no, she really did not want one of those ugly things. And eventually the craze passed and she stopped asking. The truth of course is that since I was forced to sew clothes for the dolls in the mother and baby home, I couldn't face the sight of them. Years later I told Corrinna the whole story, and she was horrified.

Jumbo's parents were very good to me when Jumbo left. They took my side because they could see what their son had put me through. They adored Corrinna, their first grandchild, and she idolised them, especially her grandfather, Jim. She called him Bim, and it caught on. He was called Bim by the family until he died. She stayed over with them now and again. Jim was a good man. He did the wages for the city council. Corrinna thought that he must be so important because he went to work in a suit.

At his eightieth birthday party, when he was a bit infirm having had a stroke, he came into the room and Jumbo's sister said, 'Wait until he realises Corrinna is here.' The moment he saw her his eyes lit up.

I didn't have many girlfriends in those days. After my pregnancy my early friendships had perished, and afterwards I found it hard to trust people. It was difficult to shake off the stigma of being a young lone mother. But one night in 1977 Noeleen's friends persuaded me to go out with them. Noeleen was working in

Jersey at the time, and I was reluctant to go; it was only a month or so after my divorce from Jumbo had become finalised. To my surprise I had a great time. I got chatting to the disc jockey and he asked me out. His name was Alan Fleming.

We got on extremely well but I was careful not to let him meet Corrinna; I didn't want to confuse her, and wanted to see how the relationship would pan out. Brian was still living with us. I'd pay him a pound and ask him to take Corrinna to karate with him, to get her out of the way. After a year we both felt that the relationship would be permanent. I remember the day Corrinna met Alan. She took to him immediately. Before I knew it they were out playing ball together. That made me so happy.

Noeleen had her independence by then. She used to go off to the Isle of Man in the summer to work for the season, and Brian had a girlfriend, Mandy, so he was often out. That meant that Alan and I had the time and space to get to know each other properly.

I couldn't believe my luck when Alan and I moved in together. He gave me the kind of stability I had always craved. I was aware of the neighbours' gossip. I didn't mind that I was 'living in sin' but there were others who considered it scandalous. I didn't go to Mass regularly. I believed in God, but my experiences around Corrinna's birth had been enough to put me off being active in the church. So I was surprised when the parish priest appeared at my door. He had come to tell me that if I appeared at his altar he would not give me communion. I was both furious and upset.

Alan believed in me. He told me that I was a highly intelligent woman – the first time ever anyone had said that to me, except perhaps Granny Maxwell all those years ago. Knowing how I hated working in that factory, he encouraged me to go back to education. He made me see I was capable of so much more. I will always be grateful to him for that. I went to the technical college in Strabane for two years at night, then I did a further course full time, as a mature student. Brian's girlfriend Mandy and I would drive in together.

Life changed for the better with Alan around. One year he had work in North Carolina and I got a trip out there with him. It was shortly before Christmas and I couldn't believe how amazing the shops in America were. I went mad. That year there were more toys for Corrinna under the tree than ever. It gave me such pleasure watching her excitement.

When Corrinna was eight, Alan thought it would be nice to give her a pet. It was a toss up between a puppy and a pony – and the pony won. Looking back, that was insane. Corrinna hadn't been horse riding and had never shown any great desire to do so. There was a picture of her in pigtails on a pony from that holiday with Gracie but I don't think she had ridden since.

I don't know who was more excited that Christmas, Corrinna or me. To build up the tension I had put a bridle over the chair in the sitting room. She was confused when she opened that. When she opened the next parcel and found a saddle, she began to smile. The next one was a Sindy doll, and the next a horse for the doll. I couldn't help laughing. Then we got into the car and drove up to a farm a few miles away, and there in the field was the pony.

'Happy Christmas,' said Alan, beaming. Corrinna's face said it all. She said, 'This is the best thing *ever*.' She called the pony Mac.

Later we moved him nearer to home, to a field backing onto the cottage where my Granny Maxwell used to live. Corrinna was thrilled, but we were all so naive.

One time, early on, Corrinna was riding Mac in the field and he took off and jumped the fence into the next field with her still on his back. There was a mare in that field and he was trying to get to it. It turned out that he was a stallion, and he had never been broken in. We tried to train him ourselves. Alan and Corrinna took him out on the road with training ropes but Alan ended up having to employ a man to show him what to do. Alan spent endless Saturdays with Corrinna breaking the pony in. It was a good way for the two of them to get to know one another better. I was pleased that they had this common interest.

Then Alan organised riding lessons for Corrinna. The stables were up the road; it was a fiver for an hour. She loved it. Alan would go with her and hang around, then he began to have lessons too.

Not long after that, Mac had an accident. He got trapped in barbed wire and he suffered a nasty infection. He was taken in by the vet. We went down to see him every day. Then the vet told me he needed an operation and we wouldn't be able to see him for a while. I was worried. A week or so later the vet rang to say that Mac had died. I was devastated. I couldn't imagine how I was going to tell Corrinna.

I wanted to protect her. So Alan and I spent weeks scouring the country for a pony to replace Mac. We found one that looked approximately the same, but then I worried he wouldn't respond to his name. So I taught him. Three weeks later I took Corrinna to the vet's field again and she saw that Mac was back. She called his name and he came over to her and ate a sugar lump off her palm. She threw her arms around his neck, delighted that he was well again.

There was an awkward moment when she was stroking him on his nose. 'Look,' she said. 'He's grown a white flash.'

Thinking on my feet, I said, 'It probably grew during the operation.' Thank goodness she accepted that and didn't ask any more about it.

When she was twenty-one she came on a business trip with me to Bulgaria. We were having one of those mother–daughter conversations where you tell your secrets, saying, 'I bet you never knew this.' I told her that the original Mac had died. She was so shocked.

'It never entered my head,' she said, laughing. 'Though, now I think about it, I did wonder if Mac had shrunk a little.'

The second Mac was a success. Corrinna went trekking out on the roads. She spent a lot of time with her cousin Emmet, Eddie's son, who was pony mad. They would put up jumps in a field. They always had fun.

When Alan asked me to marry him, I felt that life could get no better. After years of being made to feel like a fallen woman, I had gained respectability. We were married in April 1981; it was a wonderful, happy day. Corrinna was eleven, and Noeleen and she were bridesmaids. I made my own dress – I thought it was absolutely gorgeous. It was very eighties and lacy, but beautiful. I got my hair done in Lifford. I had a lovely bob with a plum hue for the occasion; normally my hair was chestnut, thanks to a Harmony shampoo rinse I bought from the pharmacy. Noeleen and Corrinna wore plum velvet pedal pushers and white high-collared Lady Diana blouses. That style wasn't exactly conventional but I like to be a bit different. This was just before Lady Diana married. I remember being obsessed with the Royal wedding – it seemed such a fairytale – but then everyone was.

Our wedding was low-key but happy. It took place in a registry office in the Guildhall in Derry. When we arrived, we were ushered into a side room. 'Where's Alan?' I asked. And when I was told he hadn't arrived, I said, 'I will bloody kill him.' It turned out that he was in the pub next door having a pint with his best man. I think it was nerves, nothing sinister. After the formalities we went to the Kildrum Country Club, which was a popular place for dinner dances out of town.

All the talk was about Mammy and Daddy and how they would both be there, and how would we keep them separated when they should both be on the top table. And would they manage to be civil to one another for a change? That discussion came up every time there was a family occasion. It turned out to be a harmonious and happy day.

Alan and I both worked hard but we had fun too. One day he came home with a caravan. I was in the kitchen cooking supper and he burst in, full of it, saying what a wonderful bargain it had been. But when he showed it to me and I saw the inside I nearly died. 'It's just a shell,' I said.

'Now it's a shell. But imagine how it will look with some partitions, doors and fittings.'

'Yes,' I said, trying to envisage its transformation. 'We could make it into a trendy mobile home, with louvre doors. And I can make curtains and do all the upholstery.'

'And we can spend all summer in it,' said Corrinna, who by this time was jumping up and down with excitement.

While we worked on it, the caravan was parked outside our council house. Alan was worried that someone might torch it, this being the Troubles. For a while he would bring a baseball bat up to bed. I teased him about that but I didn't blame him. That caravan was our pride and joy.

We found a site in Kerrykeel, a beautiful part of County Donegal. The site had tennis courts, and horse riding was available too. That was vital for Corrinna, who was now pony mad. We transported the caravan down and were lucky enough to secure a corner site with a view straight out onto Mulroy Bay. We took bikes, and lots of board games for the rainy days, and we had this wonderful, idyllic summer.

I had worried that I was taking Corrinna away from her friends, but soon after we arrived she went out on her blue Grifter bike. She loved that bike. They were all the rage back then, and when she met a girl her own age who was riding a red Grifter bike, the two started talking at once. Laura, it turned out, lived in a house overlooking the bay. Her father owned the local garage and her sister had a pony. From then on the two were inseparable. It was such a happy time.

We were looking forward to more carefree summers there but it wasn't to be. The following winter a terrible storm hit Donegal, and Kerrykeel bore the brunt of it. Laura's mother rang to tell us that our poor caravan had been blown to smithereens. 'Your possessions are ruined, I'm afraid,' she said. I was so upset that I cried. And the worst thing was that Alan and I had not insured the caravan. So that was the end of that.

The following year we moved to Derry. Alan was brought up there and he wanted to get back to his roots. It was only fourteen miles from Strabane but, perhaps stupidly, I was homesick. I was so used to being near my family and seeing them all the time that I really missed them. Brian stayed in Strabane. He took over the lease of the council house.

We went back to Strabane every weekend to see Mammy and Daddy in their separate houses. There was always a drama with Mammy. After a while I got used to living in Derry. I couldn't be so involved in their lives and perhaps that was good for me. It meant I could concentrate on my new family better.

Corrinna went to the primary school for a few months before moving on to the grammar school. She settled quickly. It helped that Mac the pony moved with us. We kept him in a field in front of the house. It was rented from the Orange Order; they used it for celebrations every four years. Having the pony there was every child's dream. Corrinna was so happy. She got up without having to be nagged and she went out to feed Mac before breakfast. Then she set off across the fields to catch the school bus. The minute she got home she would go out and catch Mac. She would groom him until he shone and then she would saddle up and go for a ride.

I was worried she would soon get lonely riding on her own, but as luck would have it Corrinna met Gillian, a girl from the Protestant School who needed a field in which to keep Charlie, her pony. Charlie came to join Mac, and the two girls rode together and spent hours setting up jumps at the bottom of the field. Meanwhile, Corrinna had remained friends with Laura. She would go up there and stay for the odd weekend, and she spent a whole summer there after the fiasco with the caravan. They even let her take Mac to Kerrykeel with her and she was able to ride on the beach. I was so glad for her. It was really important to me that she should have the sort of childhood I had craved.

As for me, I had a job. I worked in a youth scheme at a community workshop. They were trying to get people off the dole at the time and needed someone to teach industrial sewing. I was well qualified to do that and I taught sixteen-year-olds from deprived backgrounds. I loved it. I especially loved the business side of it and I was good at it too. I gained in confidence. I felt I was making a difference to those girls, and that was really important to me. After my own upbringing and lack of education I was always keen to promote adult education. Everyone deserves a second chance.

In 1983 a vacancy arose in Magee College in Derry – that's a branch of the University of Ulster. They were looking for an administration officer, which was basically an advanced secretary in administration. I didn't think I had a hope of getting the job but I decided to go for it anyway. To my surprise and delight I got to the second round of selection. I didn't get the job but I was runner-up. It was disappointing to have got so far and then to have missed out. I was just settling down and accepting my bad luck when the university contacted me again and said the job was mine. I couldn't believe my luck. I was over the moon.

There was just one problem. The very week the job offer came, I realised that I was pregnant. Thrilled as I was to be expecting Alan's baby, I was frightened too. Corrinna's birth had not been easy and I worried about going through the whole process again.

The real problem though was that the job at the university did not include a maternity-leave package. That bothered me, but I wasn't going to let the job go. I took it anyway.

I didn't take it just because I wanted to. Since we had moved into the new house, money was tight. I don't think we would have managed were it not for my salary. Alan was hard-working and ambitious, yet somehow money was often scarce. When we first met he was working in a factory as a manager. In Derry he was managing a leisure centre. He saw that as a step-up.

I was a little worried about telling Corrinna. She had been an only child for so long; she was now in second year at school. One Friday when she came in I made her French toast, sat her down and said, 'I've got something to tell you. We're going to have a baby.'

Her face lit up and she threw her arms around me. 'That's wonderful,' she said. 'I've always wanted a baby brother or sister.'

The next day, I remember, Brian and his girlfriend Mandy came down. We were watching Wimbledon on a black-and-white set Alan had wired up in the garden, and we had also set up a game of cricket. It was a very happy time.

My next task was to tell the university my news. I didn't imagine they would be as pleased as Corrinna had been. But their attitude was, if it didn't affect my work with them they didn't mind. So now I just had to find a way to cope with a full-time job, a teenager and a pregnancy.

I worked up until my due date and then I took just three weeks off to have the baby. The pregnancy was stressful. It was really hard fitting my job around my home life but in many ways I enjoyed being pregnant. I looked back with horror to the way I had slopped around the house when I was pregnant with Corrinna. This time, as a respectable married woman, I would do it with style. I wore these Princess Diana-inspired pinafore dresses, with silk blouses underneath incorporating a bow tie. I had my tights and shoes dyed to match the blouse. I found it easier to cope when I knew I looked good.

During that pregnancy I had an absolute craving for tomatoes. One day when I got in from work Corrinna had made a beautiful tomato salad for me. That was so thoughtful, but it wasn't what I wanted. I liked to eat my tomatoes whole, like eating an apple. I would eat a whole bag in one sitting. It became a family joke. We began to name the bump Tomato.

Alan was working hard too. He would come in from work, grab some dinner, and three nights a week would rush out again. He was working as a DJ to earn extra money. He was never afraid of hard work. I liked that about him. The problem was, that meant he wasn't around to help me in the house. And that's where my sister came in handy.

Noeleen said she was willing to lend me a hand. She was married by that stage, to a nice man called Dave. They had a one-year-old daughter called Sophie. She came to stay, and was there the day my pains started. I had been dreading that day but it could not have been a more different labour from that first one. I had a surge of energy and spent the day painting cupboards, stopping when a contraction hit.

Noeleen and Corrinna looked increasingly nervous as the pains took hold. They felt I should go to hospital, but Noeleen couldn't drive. Besides, I wanted to wait for Alan to get home from work and, after the first time, I didn't expect this baby to arrive anytime soon. It was a night for Alan to be a DJ and he did not get home until two in the morning. The contractions were very strong by this stage. Alan looked terrified. We sped in. The midwives took one look at me, put me on a trolley and rushed me into the labour ward. And before 3 am my beautiful baby boy arrived.

Alan went home to have a shower, to find Noeleen and Corrinna still up. They had been too nervous to go to bed and had been hoovering and cleaning the house all night. He brought them up to the hospital as soon as visitors were allowed. Corrinna took one look at her brother and said, 'He's beautiful. But look – there's a hint of red in his hair.'

'It shows he's a Maxwell,' I said.

'Or it could be because of the tomatoes,' said Corrinna, laughing, as she stroked his head gently.

Right from the start Corrinna was wonderful with baby Simon. At fourteen she was always there to help look after him and never complained, even if that meant sometimes that she couldn't hang out with her friends or ride Mac as often as she wanted. And that was a relief, because it wasn't easy leaving such a small baby when I had to return to work.

We were blessed with Simon. The day before I was due to go back to work, he slept right through the night for the first time ever, the pet. We were all so proud of him. We were very lucky in our childcare. I would have hated to leave Simon with strangers, and we didn't have to because Alan's sister offered to care for him.

For all that, it was an exhausting time. It was especially hard keeping the house looking nice and clean. I would rush around tidying up the minute I got home from work but it was frustrating not having enough time to do all the things to the house that I wanted. Corrinna used to watch me with bemusement. 'Won't you at least take off your coat before you start cleaning,' she'd say. But when you are house proud, that is really hard to do.

Life became a little more hectic when Simon became mobile. He was a little ball of energy. It was as if, being born so fast, he was in a rush to grow up and take on the world. When he was just nine months old he was in a baby walker in the kitchen. The door was open for just a minute and Simon made a beeline for it. Rushing through the gap, he went down a step, toppled and landed on his head. Luckily, no harm was done.

I wasn't going to let my busy schedule hold me back. So when Simon was a year old I decided to take a business degree. I didn't give up my job. I was still enjoying it, and besides, we had the mortgage to pay. I found a BA in business that I could take part-time on a day release scheme. I enjoyed studying again. Corrinna had started her GCSE course at the grammar school by then. She was doing really well at school; great things were expected of her. She helped me with my degree. I remember specifically she helped explain statistics to me. I think that gave her a bit of a buzz.

After a while it all became too much. I was feeling tired all the time, struggling to fit in all the different elements of my life. I felt generally unwell, and my limbs were heavy and a bit numb. I imagined it was to do with all the stress of juggling work with an increasingly active toddler. I tried not to worry, but I thought it could do no harm to have a check-up with the local GP. I might have known it would be a waste of time. I remember getting home, fuming. I flung off my coat and wondered where to start with the housework.

'Now tell me. How am I supposed to rest?'

I was talking to myself really, but Corrinna, finishing her homework in the kitchen, had been anxious to know how I had got on. 'I'm sorry, Mum,' she said. 'But what exactly are you talking about?'

'That stupid man. He says there's nothing wrong with me that a few early nights won't sort out.'

'What about the numbness?'

'It's all the after-effects of flu, he says.' I sat down and sighed. 'And I'm sure he's right. But if anyone can tell me how to take things easy when there's a typhoon of a toddler in the house … well, I'll give them the Nobel prize. It's impossible.'

CHAPTER NINE

TURBULENCE

8OC8

I recovered soon enough and threw myself, body and soul, into my career. Alan, though, wasn't getting fulfilled. He had left the leisure centre and had gone to work for a company in Dungannon, which was more than an hour and a half's drive away. He was manager in a factory again and he always seemed to be stressed. He became increasingly unsettled, and when Corrinna was in fifth year at school he came home and said that he had applied for a job in Chester. He didn't get it, but after that he kept applying for jobs all over the place. It was a difficult time for all of us.

That September, in 1987, Alan had booked a family holiday

in Gran Canaria. We all needed a rest. We took Corrinna out of school; it was the start of her A-level course and we felt she would catch up with the work very fast. My now not so little brother Don was coming along too, with his girlfriend. We were all looking forward to the break.

The day before we were due to leave, I was shopping in Derry when I had this strange dizzy spell. As the day went on I felt worse. Alan took me to Accident and Emergency and I spent half the night there. I felt woozy and dizzy. I kept drifting in and out of consciousness. It frightened me.

I assumed the attack would pass and we decided to go on the holiday anyway. We all needed it. But that turned out to be a mistake, for me at least. Getting there was a real struggle, and it didn't get any easier. I was sick every single day of that holiday. The bright light hurt my eyes and made my head throb. The heat bothered me too.

That was bad enough, but there were other symptoms too. I felt disorientated. I confused my left with my right and I couldn't focus properly. I tried to keep all this to myself so as not to worry everyone else, but I think they were as scared by it as I was. I lay in a dark room for the whole two weeks.

Alan called a doctor but his English wasn't the best. He kept saying, 'The head, the head, the head.' I think he meant I had a problem with my nervous system. That worried me terribly and I could tell Corrinna was frantic with worry. Alan tried to make the best of it for Simon's sake. He kept saying, 'Come on. Let's enjoy ourselves.'

Simon was the sweetest child. He had flaxen-blond hair, which I kept cut in a pudding-bowl style. At three years old all he wanted to do was play in the pool, kick a ball around and enjoy some rough and tumble. Alan was good with him; so were the others, but Simon could not understand why I would not join in. It upset me that I was not able to participate.

Mealtimes were hard too. I ate very little, because, along with all my other symptoms, I felt nauseous. I would lie in bed listening to Alan and Corrinna trying to persuade Simon to eat. He had very weird eating habits back then. He insisted on having each different food in a separate bowl. One bowl would have plain pasta in it, another just sauce. And it wasn't just a fad about savoury food. He needed two bowls to eat jelly and ice-cream too.

We stayed in Gran Canaria for the whole planned fortnight, and the minute we got home I was admitted to the Royal Belfast Hospital, which is a two-hour drive from Derry. They kept me in for three weeks, during which time they prodded and poked me and asked me all kinds of questions about my symptoms. I lost count of the number of tests they performed, but at the end of it nobody was any closer to knowing what was wrong with me. My symptoms gradually eased, however, and I was able to go back to work.

We were under a lot of stress at the time. Alan had himself tied in financial knots. He had bought some land halfway between Strabane and Derry and was hoping to build a house there. He had taken out a bridging loan but then he didn't get planning permission. It turned out to be on the green belt. His job at Dungannon was in a dicey state; he was terrified he would be let go, and the bank was hounding him. They sent letters threatening to call in the bailiffs, but luckily the house was in our joint names. I refused point-blank to sign my half over. It meant that they couldn't touch us, but the strain was making me extremely nervous. I was terrified we would lose our lovely home, the first house I had ever owned.

Then Alan *did* lose his job. He found another, but it was in Swansea in south Wales. Reluctantly I agreed we should move there. There didn't really seem to be any choice, but the timing could not have been worse. I was thirty-four. I had a job I loved. I was finishing my business degree and I had had this strange illness which was undiagnosed.

It was terrible timing for Corrinna too. She was starting her A-levels in Derry. She was settled at school, with teachers she liked and who predicted she would get straight 'A' grades. The last thing I wanted to do was disrupt her by moving her to Wales.

'I could live with Nana and Bim,' said Corrinna, talking of her grandparents, Jumbo's Mum and Dad. 'I could get the bus from Strabane every day.'

It wasn't ideal, but it seemed like a good solution. She would be happy there, and I knew she would be more than welcome in their house.

Alan had to start his job almost immediately so we decided it would be better if he went over to Wales ahead of the rest of us. He would find us a house, and Corrinna and I would clear the house in Derry and pack it up. So Alan started his job, working in Wales all week and coming back to Derry for the weekends.

Life without Alan was hectic. Had it not been for Corrinna I really do not know how I would have coped. Between the two of us we worked out a pretty good system. I dropped Simon off at Alan's sister on my way to work. When Corrinna got home from school she tidied the house and put the dinner on. I would leave her a list of instructions each morning. And I picked Simon up on my way back from work. I then took over the household duties while Corrinna played with Simon, then we all ate dinner. After we had eaten, Corrinna would go upstairs and do her homework while I put Simon to bed. It worked well enough. Corrinna never complained, although it must have been hard for her at times.

We were congratulating ourselves on coping well when Alan rang to say he had found a house to rent in Swansea and we had to start packing up. That became a strain. And, to make matters worse still, the hospital picked that time to call me in for a lumbar puncture. I didn't think anything of it; it was just another test, but it flattened me. For a few days afterwards I lay in bed unable to move. I began to wonder how on earth I would manage the move to Wales.

Meanwhile, Simon was playing with his cars in the corridor and Corrinna was packing up the house around me. One afternoon Valerie, a friend of mine from the university, came to see me. Corrinna made us both a cup of tea and brought it up the stairs to us. Then she went downstairs and continued packing up all the *Encyclopaedia Britannica* volumes into boxes. The doorbell rang and I shouted down, asking Corrinna to answer it. I heard her talking in the hall, then she came upstairs carrying a brown envelope. 'It was the GP,' she said. 'He wouldn't come in. But he asked me to make sure you get this. He says it's important.'

She handed over the letter and, noticing that there was a note attached to the envelope, I read it.

'What is it?' asked Corrinna.

'Just a referral.'

'A referral?'

'Telling me to go and see a GP the minute I get to Swansea.' I looked up and realised with a stab of understanding just how distressed my daughter was. 'It's okay, pet,' I said. 'There's no need to look so worried.'

The minute she left the room I picked up a biro and, carefully rolling it around the seal of the envelope, gently opened the letter. And I gasped.

'What is it?' asked Valerie.

Putting my finger to my mouth to shush her, I whispered, 'It says "suspected multiple sclerosis".'

Although I read the words, I could not take them in. It was too much. I suppose I was in denial. And besides, I was too busy to worry. So I put it to the back of my mind and got on with the business of moving. By May, Simon and I were all set to join Alan in Wales. Corrinna said she was happy to travel up and down to school from Strabane.

None of us wanted to leave the house in Derry. It was a gorgeous family home and my pride and joy. I had taken to going to auctions. I loved viewing the furniture and got great pleasure from bidding and picking up bargains. Over time I had picked up a chaise longue, a couple of dressing tables and some side tables. I remember once I bought a fender from an auction at a hotel around the corner. We carried it home.

'Why do you want this old thing?' asked Corrinna. 'It's as black as boots.'

Which it was. But I found someone to dip it for me and it came up in this gorgeous brass.

I was worried about leaving Corrinna, particularly since she was having a tough time. She had fallen in love the previous autumn, with Richard Moore, a boy from Derry who was studying at Oxford University. They had seemed crazy about each other but he had recently called the relationship off. Corrinna was heartbroken. Yet, putting her feelings aside, she pulled out all the stops in her efforts to help me with the move. She was there on the day the removal vans came, helping us pack up the last bits and pieces and waving us off. I was crying as the car drew away from her. Simon was on my knee. I hugged him to me tightly.

We went on the ferry and moved into the house Alan had found. Seeing it was a shock. It was poky and dark, but it was the best he could do in the short time. It wasn't the ideal start, but Alan was finding his new job pretty pressurised.

I hated that house, but I assumed we wouldn't live there for long. This was 1988 and I had sold the house in Derry for £42,000. Everyone told me I could buy half of Wales for that kind of money. But the property market in Wales started to escalate, so finding a house to buy became another stress. We kept finding our dream home, then getting gazumped. It got me down. And I was pretty low anyway at that stage.

I had followed my GP's advice and got myself registered at a practice in Wales. And before I knew it, I had seen a neurologist and had been sent for an MRI scan. I had to go to Somerset for that because back then there were no MRI scanners in Wales. After the scan we drove on to Plymouth and stayed with Noeleen and Dave, who had moved back to Dave's roots. I didn't tell Noeleen about the scan. I didn't want to think about it until I had to, but of course I was worried.

A week later I went back to my neurologist for the result. He told me that I did, indeed, have multiple sclerosis. At thirty-four! I will never forget his next words.

'Whatever you do, don't *think* of contacting the MS society. If you do that at this early stage you'll get so burdened with information that you'll worry yourself into a wheelchair in a week.'

'What should I do?'

'Get on with your life. This could be a one-off attack; it may be years before you get another and you may *never* have another one. Don't put your life on hold.'

I am so grateful to him. I did worry about the MS. It was a *terrible* diagnosis but I tried hard to stop it from spoiling my life. Some would say I was in denial in those early days. Tom contends that I never fully accepted what MS could mean. He says that when we met he knew more about the trials to come than I did. But it was important to me to live my life fully. It's the only way I *could* live.

The worst part of it all was having to tell Corrinna. I wasn't going to give her news like that over the phone so I waited until she came over for the school summer holidays. We had a lovely welcome home dinner, then the next morning after breakfast I sat her down and said, 'Corrinna, I have something to tell you.'

'What?'

'I have MS.'

'What's that?'

'A condition called multiple sclerosis. And it's not good.'

Corrinna went deathly quiet. Later she told me that she had wanted to ask lots of questions but was frightened to. And she felt freaked out because she remembered a conversation we had had about MS years earlier. When we were living in Strabane, Corrinna and I loved watching *Top of the Pops* together. It was the time when those dancers, Pan's People, would be on the show every week.

We were talking, and Corrinna asked me if there was anything I was afraid of. And I said, 'Well, you see that lady there? That dancer? She's just been diagnosed with an illness called MS. And I'm really worried that I am going to get that.' She asked me why that worried me so much and I said, 'Because she is going to end up in a wheelchair.'

'I remember staring at the screen, horrified,' said Corrinna. 'The girl you had pointed out was the most pretty, angular, athletic-looking of all of those dancers. And I had thought, how could she *ever* be in a wheelchair?' When Corrinna reminded me of that – and it was years later, when I *did* start needing a wheelchair – I found it extraordinary that she could have remembered the conversation. She can't have been more than seven years old at the time. When I told her my news, she thought I must have had a ghastly premonition. And perhaps I had.

At the start there was no question of my using a wheelchair, and it was the first thing I said to Corrinna. I told her that the doctor had been reassuring. 'He said that my condition is remitting. I may get an occasional attack, but in between I will be quite okay.'

'So you won't lose the use of your legs?'

'No.' I shuddered, hoping it was true. 'Not unless the condition progresses. And even if it does, that won't be for years and years yet,' I said. Then I swore her to secrecy.

'But …'

'I mean it, Corrinna. Please, for me, keep this a secret.'

I was due to start a new job with the University of Wales in September. I was excited about it, but terrified that if my new employers found out about the MS they might renege on the offer. 'And I'm perfectly well now, as you can see.' I did a twirl to show her. 'I'll have no problems holding the job down.'

So she promised. But she didn't look very happy about it.

∞∞

The following September Corrinna rang me in a state of high excitement. 'I'm back with Richard,' she said, her words tumbling over each other. 'And I'm going to apply for Oxford University.'

She did that, taking the entrance exam in December. I was so proud of her. Nobody from her school had ever been to Oxford or Cambridge. When she heard she had been accepted, I don't know who was more thrilled – her, Richard or me. Corrinna has often said, 'It's just as well Richard was at Oxford. I wouldn't have followed him just anywhere.'

∞∞

I was enjoying being at the University of Wales, and I made a great success of my job there. My work was varied. One day I would be out, marketing short training courses to multinational organisations; another had me writing bids for European money to finance programmes for the unemployed. I was proud of the way I had climbed the academic ladder, and it helped that I could rely on total support from Alan. He never stopped saying he was proud of me.

I was reasonably well back in 1989. Life was good, and for once money was plentiful. While my work involved travel, Alan's didn't, so he was able to be around more for Simon. He was working for the council, managing leisure centres and parks. In the autumn we bought a plot at a little hamlet called Salem, just outside Llandeilo, twenty miles from Swansea. The guy selling it agreed to the price of £15,000 an acre, but just before we closed the deal, he realised that the market was picking up and he halved the size of the site.

I was furious. I can't bear situations like that where you feel out of control, and I hate it when people go back on their word. I loathe dishonesty. But we built a lovely house and moved in December. I had the greatest fun furnishing my new home. I went to a lot of auctions. By now I was getting quite skilled at bidding for good bargains. I spent every spare minute making curtains, determined to have the place looking good for Christmas. Corrinna was coming home and I wanted everything to be perfect.

Then, on 10 December, something happened that changed everything. My brother Shaun was found dead. He had jumped off a bridge when the tide was ebbing and he hit the bank. He was only thirty-one. It was the most terrible shock. Shaun had always been troubled, and in trouble too. Mammy leaving had affected him terribly; he seemed unable to sustain a good relationship afterwards. His second wife had just left him and he couldn't deal with it, especially because it meant he would be abandoning another child.

I did wonder if maybe his death had been a mistake. If there had been more water in the river he would have stood a chance, and I felt this could have been a cry for help. We were all devastated, and that Christmas we were steeped in the most terrible grief. I remember speaking to Brian on the telephone but both of us were sobbing so hard we could barely talk.

I hope we managed to hide the worst of our grief from Simon. We didn't tell him the whole truth; at five years of age he was too young to understand the concept of suicide so we told him that his Uncle Shaun had been run over by a car and killed. He accepted that without question.

I blamed myself for Shaun's death. Corrinna kept telling me I was being ridiculous. 'Nobody could have done more for Uncle Shaun than you did,' she said. 'If you hadn't been there to look after the family when your mother absconded, they could have ended up in care. Or in an orphanage, God forbid.'

I knew that, logically, she had a point, but I should have been more patient with Shaun. I should have let him cry. I should have talked to him more.

∞∞

The following two years were happy ones. We loved our new house, and Simon settled well into school. He had an amazing curiosity for a small child. He was always asking these impossible questions, like 'How does the sewage system work?' or 'What happens to the sun when the moon comes out?' I would be stumped but would promise to look it up in the encyclopaedia.

Corrinna used to joke that I was living the typical middle-class, green-welly lifestyle, and I suppose we were. It was certainly a step up from life back in Strabane in the council house. We had a Volvo estate car, and a springer spaniel to put in the back of it. Simon had been pleading for a dog, and we went to see the puppies one weekend when Corrinna was over. One of them had these sad hooded eyes. It was love at first sight. We called the puppy Ben. When he was tiny he would curl in around our legs.

On Saturdays we would walk Ben in the park, like any traditional family, but Sunday mornings were my time to bond with Simon. While the roast cooked in the Stanley range, Simon and I made queencakes. Simon adored baking. He helped weigh out the flour and the butter; he helped with the mixing, but his favourite part was licking out the bowl afterwards.

I would be playing jazz music very loudly, and when the cakes were safely in the oven Simon and I danced around the kitchen. I taught him how to jive. He would scream with laughter as we spun around. In the afternoons, after we had finished our Sunday dinner, we would take Ben for a quick walk, then Alan and I would relax with the Sunday papers in our good room while Simon played with his Lego at our feet. I loved having the time to put Simon to bed after my busy week. He would spend ages in the bath splashing around, then we would curl up together while I read him a story. I treasure those memories.

My work, meanwhile, grew increasingly exciting. I was flying all over Europe, lining up countries like Greece and Bulgaria to be attached to the University of Wales. I was so successful that all the department heads wanted me to work for them. I really enjoyed getting funding and running all these diverse programmes. The MS diagnosis was there but I put it firmly to the back of my mind. Perhaps I would never get another attack.

In the summer we went to Ireland on holiday. We stayed in Woodenbridge in County Wicklow and we loved the village. One day, driving along this tiny country road, we noticed a For Sale sign in front of a little cottage. It was very rundown but it was a bargain, and I absolutely loved it. We decided to buy it as a holiday home. I was so excited. It was miles from anywhere, and had a rambling garden.

Christmas that year was a happy one, marred only by the memory of Shaun's death. By then we felt well established in our house in Wales and we had made some good friends among the neighbours.

I didn't tell anyone about my MS, but the next year it began to have an impact on my life. I would get a mild attack; my limbs would be weak and I would feel woozy. When that happened I would ring in sick, saying I had the flu, and after a few days I would be well enough to return to work. Nobody ever doubted my word.

As time went on it became harder to hide the illness and carry on with my job regardless. One time my arms became severely weak during an MS attack. That was frightening. The job became more of a strain. Even between attacks I would get desperately fatigued. So tired that, a couple of times when I worked late and was driving home in the dark, I very nearly fell asleep at the wheel. My head would jerk me awake. That really scared me.

All I have ever really wanted in life is security for my family.

And I have always been determined not to rely on anyone else. I simply *had* to remain independent. As I saw it, working was the only way of controlling my own destiny. Not that I didn't rely on Alan. I loved him, and he was my solid emotional rock. He had rescued me, and transformed me from being a lone mother with no real prospects to a respectable married woman with a high-flying career. Between us we had created a stable family. I will always be grateful to Alan for that.

By the time Corrinna went into her third year at Oxford University, Alan and I were feeling settled and happy in our jobs. With our two salaries, money was plentiful. We decided to study together, taking a part-time MBA course. Life seemed complete.

I thought we were happy. Certainly I was. And if Alan seemed a bit remote at times, that was to be expected, when we led such busy lives.

Corrinna was home for Mother's Day that year, 1992. She was studying for part one of her finals in the kitchen one evening while Alan and I were in the snug, watching the ten o'clock news. Then Alan came out with a bombshell.

'Marie, I need a break,' he said.

'A break? A holiday, do you mean?'

'A break from the marriage.' He was mumbling, and couldn't meet my eye.

I felt numb. 'Oh, from *me*, you mean?'

'Just for a while.'

'Well, do you want to leave this minute, then?' I said, desperately trying to contain my panic; and at that moment Corrinna arrived carrying a tray with some cups of tea. Sensing the atmosphere, she began to retreat back to the kitchen, but I called her back in.

'You had better hear this, Corrinna,' I said, and I started to cry. 'Alan has just told me that he needs a break.'

'What? Why?' She sounded as stunned as I felt.

'Well, Alan?' I said. 'Can you tell my daughter why you want to leave? Because however you try and explain it, it doesn't make any sense to me.'

He looked uncomfortable and said, 'It's like I said to your Mum, Corrinna. I need a break. That's all.'

I was devastated. I'd always thought that our marriage was rock solid. I didn't get any sleep that night. I sobbed, and I raged at Alan. 'It's because of the MS, isn't it?' He denied it, but I knew he had found my diagnosis difficult to accept. I don't think he could face the thought of the future. 'You don't want to look after me when I'm in a wheelchair, do you? That's why you're leaving, you selfish bastard.'

'It's not that. How can you think that?' He sounded genuine. 'I'm not happy. I haven't been happy for some time.'

Well, that was news to me. It had come out of the blue. I would probably have accepted his explanation at face value, but the next day Alan's mobile rang, and after it had rung out I pressed the 'last call received' button. A woman answered, and she sounded all animated. Switching off the phone, I confronted Alan. Shamefaced, he packed a bag and left on the spot.

I was so glad Corrinna was with me. She was such a help, and looked after Simon for me while I struggled to hold myself together. And when she went back to Oxford she kept in daily contact. Every day there was something new to report. The woman, I discovered, was someone Alan had met through work. She was only twenty-four. They had been 'seeing one another' for some time.

It was hard to cope. When I had kept Corrinna, fighting my father and the power of the church, I was determined to stop the generational rot. I was *not* going to be like Gracie, and certainly not like Mammy. I had thought I could stay in control. And here I was, being abandoned again. It was like a carbon copy of what had happened to me, first with my mother and then with Jumbo. How much more of this was I expected to take?

After a few days, Alan came back and begged for my forgiveness. We completed the purchase of the cottage in Wicklow but the marriage was never the same again. Everything would seem fine; I would start to relax, and to believe Alan when he said that his affair was over, and then I would find a blonde hair on his coat and it would all erupt again.

Corrinna was busy gaining work experience that summer and I missed her sorely. But she came home for Christmas in 1992. I was determined to have a happy, harmonious day, and everything boded well. On Christmas Eve, as Corrinna helped me to make the stuffing and to bake mince pies, Simon was bright-eyed with anticipation.

I couldn't wait to see my son's face on Christmas morning. Alan and I had gone overboard. Corrinna teased me and said she felt jealous. 'It's like the *Late Late* toy show in there,' she said.

Simon was especially thrilled with his new bike and his games console. It warmed my heart to hear him say, 'This is the best Christmas *ever*.' Before lunch, Alan and I had a family drinks party for all the neighbours. The house was full of happy people.

We were all gathered in the good room, which was below our bedroom.

I was handing round some smoked salmon, and making small talk, when I noticed Alan leave the room. Something made me follow him. He was running up the stairs, and by intuition I ran into the kitchen and picked up the phone. Alan was whispering sweet nothings to that dreadful woman. I screamed. I couldn't help it. I just lost the plot, even though I knew all the neighbours were there. I simply could not control myself.

I don't know what Corrinna said to everyone but within minutes the house was cleared of our guests. Seeing them leave, I let rip. Alan denied that he had made the call and insisted that he loved me and had no intention of leaving me again.

I was too angry to listen to his excuses and protestations. Going into our bedroom, I started flinging Alan's clothes at him so he had no choice but to leave.

I tried to retrieve Christmas for Simon, who was eight, but from starting out so well it became the most miserable day ever. I cooked, and Corrinna kept Simon amused, playing techno Lego with him on the floor. Then we all ate Christmas dinner together, pulling crackers and trying our best to be jolly. Poor Simon. He tried to enjoy himself and he spent hours on his new games console, but it was his Daddy who had gone. He must have been feeling confused, if not bereft. He says now that though the memory is still there, he sees it in the third person, like a film.

Over the years I have worried about Simon. It can't have been easy living in a house where there were constant rows, especially when our fights were so noisy. After our most vicious arguments

I would find Simon curled up in a chair with Ben, burying his head in the dog's fur for comfort. I wish I could have saved him all that grief.

When I woke up the next day and found Corrinna asleep beside me I thought at first that everything was okay. Then I remembered Alan had gone and I got this sinking feeling. I was grief-stricken. I looked at Corrinna, sleeping so peacefully, and hoped that she would find the happiness in life that seemed to elude me.

Corrinna, as always, was a wonderful support to me. She cheered me up. On Christmas night she had rung Richard, who was at home in Derry, to tell him the latest episode in the saga of our lives, and when he'd put the phone down he turned to his mother and said, 'God, Corrinna really does have the most exciting life. And look at us. We're just going through the same old boring Christmas Day.'

Corrinna and Simon have always been extremely close, in spite, or perhaps because of, the large age gap. Simon often calls her his second mummy. It was good to have her there, giving him extra love when he needed it so badly.

Alan and I tried to revive our marriage. And we almost managed it. Corrinna, having got through her finals, secured a wonderful job with Unilever in London. Alan collected her, along with all the bits and pieces she had accumulated over the years. But almost immediately after her return I discovered that he had been with Sonia again.

That felt like the end, for me. I was so upset that I stormed out of the house. Corrinna ran after me, saying, 'You're in no fit state to drive.' I just panicked. I had no idea where to run to but I needed time to think.

Work was mad busy at the time. A delegation of Greeks and Bulgarians were coming over to take part in one of the programmes I had organised, and that evening a meeting was being held to arrange their welcome party. I drove there on automatic pilot but I have never felt so stressed. Corrinna said, 'Take it easy, Mum. You don't want a total breakdown.'

The stress wasn't the worst of it. Whether it was the situation with Alan that triggered it or just coincidence, I don't know, but my body decided to let me down. I had a really severe MS attack – so bad that I could barely move. Corrinna looked terrified. It wasn't the first severe attack I had experienced but it was by far the worst that she had seen.

Corrinna was quiet for a while. Then she said, 'Mum, you're going to have to talk to someone.'

'What do you mean?'

'You're going to have to tell someone that you have MS. How else can you explain your state of collapse?'

She was right. I had to tell someone, and I knew who that would be. Friendship has always been important to me, yet I find it very difficult to trust people. When I was growing up I had different friends for different occasions – some at school, some for playing in the street with, others who worked with me in the hotel. They were all different from each other, and yet there was one thing they had in common. Not one of them stayed in contact when they found out I was pregnant. The older I have become, the more carefully I have chosen my friends. But there was one friend at the university whom I knew would stick around.

I had met Sheila way back when I had my interview. She

worked for me, and her knowledge and implementation of funding from the European Economic Community was crucial. It was her accent that attracted me to her in the first place. I asked her which part of Wales she was from and she said, 'I'm a Swansea girl, born and bred. But my father was Irish.' That swung it for me.

Sheila and I often went to the theatre and the cinema together. We also enjoyed opera. Our favourite was *La Traviata*. When the heroine died of consumption, we cried. Sometimes Sheila accompanied me on my trips abroad. A Bulgarian professor liked her so much he tried to persuade her to become his office woman in Sofia. We really were good friends, and, although I knew she was trustworthy, I still didn't feel secure enough to tell her about the MS.

Corrinna sought her out and explained the situation. I think she was hurt that I told her only when I had no other choice, but she said that she understood my dilemma. Corrinna asked her first of all to find someone to cover for me, and she did that. Then she explained that we needed somewhere to sleep. We ended up in student accommodation. I will never forget that night. I was lying there unable to move, and Corrinna looked terrified because she had no idea what she could do to help me.

Once I had recovered enough to be moved, Corrinna and I went to stay with Noeleen and her husband Dave in Plymouth. They were shocked to hear all that had happened, and probably disappointed too. Noeleen and Dave had always liked Alan. They felt he was perfect for me. The four of us had gone on holidays together.

They were a great support to me. Dave was very sweet. He said, 'I know what will cheer you up, Marie.' Dave was really into his music. He riffled through his collection, and saying, 'Here we are. Listen to this,' he put on 'I'm Going To Wash That Man Right Out of My Hair'. He tried to get me to dance with him, and his enthusiasm made me smile. But I did wonder if he assumed this was just a tiff and that Alan and I would be back together soon.

As it turned out, even after all the drama, we gave the marriage one last try. It tottered along for a few months and then, after our most dramatic row ever, we split for good. This time Alan stormed out and he took Simon with him. I collapsed in a heap. I felt that my life, as well as my marriage, was over. I didn't know what to do.

Noeleen and Dave collected me from Wales and drove me to Plymouth. Corrinna, who was living with Richard in London, joined us there. I was distraught. The end of that marriage was just terrible. And the worst thing about it was that Simon was now with his father.

My instinct was to grab Simon back and take him with me to Plymouth, but I was a physical and emotional mess. I didn't feel I had the strength to deal with parenting him. It seemed best for him to remain where his school was, so that life would retain some normality. And to make sure that he would never ever feel abandoned in the way that my siblings and I had done, I arranged that he came to me every weekend without fail.

I lived with Noeleen from October until Christmas, then I went to London for a while and lived with Richard and Corrinna. I had taken sick leave from work. Simon, meanwhile, was living in our house in Wales with his Dad, Sonia and Sonia's children.

I lived for our weekends together. Alan would put Simon on a train, and Corrinna would pick him up and bring him to her house. And we had some good times there. But it wasn't easy. Not on Simon and not on me.

When I want to remember how vulnerable I felt at the end of my second marriage, all I have to do is look at a picture in our sitting room. It used to hang in that house Richard and Corrinna had rented. I was fond of it, and when Corrinna and Richard left that house they asked the landlord if he would sell it to them. He agreed, and they presented it to me.

The woman is sitting in a chair, bent over, with her head buried in her hands. She looks wounded and vulnerable. Back then I would gaze at that picture and say, 'That is exactly how I feel.'

When I was feeling better I found a house on an estate in Whitegates, near Swansea University College. One weekend, when Richard was away for work and we knew that Alan and Sonia were away, Corrinna and I hired two Bedford vans and cleared the house in Salem of everything I wanted for my new home. We did that with no help from anyone; looking back, I don't know where we found the strength.

If lumbering downstairs carrying wardrobes was physically tiring, the emotional toll was high too. It was hard seeing Corrinna's old room littered with Sonia's children's toys and clothes, and even worse seeing another woman's clothes in my wardrobe. I had worked so hard to make that house beautiful. I had sewn every curtain and painted every wall. But it was only bricks and mortar. I loved the house but it had never felt like home. The village only had a pub and a church. So I left the area without a smidgen of regret.

When we arrived at my new house, exhausted, and opened the garage doors to store my furniture, we found it was full of someone else's old furniture. It had been left there by the previous occupants. I was so tired I just cried. But we set to, cleared it, and put my furniture in.

I got sorted, and I lived there, went back to work, and finished my Master's in business. And any chance I got, I went to stay in the cottage in Woodenbridge. It was very run down, but I was really happy there. Richard and Corrinna joined Simon and me for some amazing holidays. It was always so restful. I started to plan my move back to Ireland.

When I look back at some of the experiences Corrinna and I have shared, they really are stranger than fiction. It makes me cry just to think about it. Whenever life has been particularly tough for me, Corrinna has always been there, happy to support me. I was so young when she was born. I loved being a mother to Corrinna, but I did so much of my growing up after her birth.

I know it has not always been easy for her. I remember one terrible time when my MS had just taken a turn for the worse. I rang Corrinna in tears and said, 'I just want a mother. I want someone to look after *me* for a change. I just want a mother.'

She got upset. And she said, 'It's okay. I'll be your mother. I'm here. I will do it. I will always be here.'

I was so touched, but saddened too. I'm emotionally close to my children. I am always there when they need to talk about a problem in their lives; I know they appreciate my input. But it struck me that my children must feel in need of a healthy mother. And if it was bad for Corrinna, it has, surely, been worse for Simon. I have had MS since he was small. He lived with my illness throughout his growing up, and there were many times when he had to look after me. It hurts me that, as my illness has progressed, it has prevented me from being a more physical presence for him and Corrinna.

CHAPTER TEN

LOVE AND NEIGHBOURS

∞❃∞

I knew that the University of Wales appreciated the contribution I had made. I, alone, brought in over £2 million in European Social Fund (ESF) grants to the college. This gave me a high profile. I was based in Swansea, but was invited to colleges all over Wales to impart knowledge about my ESF success. I was on first-name terms with the provost, who was thrilled with my efforts to donate such a large cash injection into the university coffers. In spite of my MS, I was flying high.

All that changed with the end of my marriage to Alan. It was becoming increasingly difficult to deal with everyday life. My marriage breakdown made me review and rethink the effect that the MS was having on me. I didn't regret my decision to hide my illness from my colleagues; and in fact even at this later stage I managed to keep it a secret from everyone except the family, because, while I felt I could cope with my symptoms, I realised that others would view the illness with more jaundiced eyes. But when it all spilt out into the open at work I was dealt with very fairly by all my colleagues. That was both surprising and gratifying.

Hywel Francis, my head of department, was accommodating. I could have stayed on working at the university for some time to come. All my friends there were willing to offer me support, but it was hard living in the same town as Alan when everyone knew that he was living with a woman who was so much younger than me.

Living without Simon was intolerable. It was necessary for his schooling, but it broke my heart to know he was living with his father's new woman and her family. He came to me for weekends, and he would bring Ben the spaniel along with him. Alan would drop him down. We had a good time together. Quite often Richard and Corrinna would come and stay too, and we would go for walks on the beach or in The Mumbles, the Victorian part of Swansea.

Sometimes we went to the cinema or to have a pizza. Or maybe we would go to Dunkin' Donuts. At nine years old, Simon loved that. We had a date every Wednesday too. I left work early, picked Simon up from school, and we would go for fish and chips. We both cherished that time together but I wanted a more normal life for him, and for myself. I felt a yearning to go and live in Ireland, in my lovely little cottage. Simon and I were already spending as much time as we could in County Wicklow. We had such happy times there. It felt like a refuge. I called the cottage Noddfa, which means 'haven' in Welsh.

A job came up at University College Dublin. I thought about applying for it. It was a difficult decision, so I wrote a list of all the pros and cons and I decided that I would apply. I had been happy in Wales but I always knew I wanted to return to Ireland because it felt more like home.

I applied, and I got an interview. Noeleen and her husband Dave came on the ferry with me. They thought I was making a terrible mistake leaving Wales, where life had been so good to me, but I felt very sure that I was making the right decision. I was delighted to be offered the job, and I moved into the cottage with Simon in July 1994. Simon was thrilled, and it was wonderful for us both to be together again. Corrinna helped me make the move; and she and Richard came to Woodenbridge from London as many weekends as they could to help me settle in.

I had waited until the end of term because I knew the summer would be the best time for Simon to settle into the village, before he had to face a change of school. I got him into the local national school. Simon didn't lose touch with his father. He went to Wales for weekends and sometimes he went on holiday with Alan and Sonia.

I felt immediately at home in Woodenbridge. It was a really close community and we had a wonderful welcome from the neighbours. Our next-door neighbours, Sean and Kitty Kilhoran, were especially helpful. I remember the first time I went down to their farm to see them, their eldest daughter Niamh came out to greet me, saying, 'Welcome home to you.' I really appreciated that. Having felt so displaced, it was exactly what I needed to hear. Kitty offered to look after Simon between school finishing time and my return from work. She would collect him from the school bus and take him down to the farm. Then she would send one of her capable sons to my cottage to get a fire going to welcome me back from work.

All the neighbours were friendly. I spent many happy evenings with them, eating supper in their various kitchens. We had a book club, though it was more about the wine and chat than the book, and there was always someone to attend art classes with. I got involved in the local amateur dramatics too. I wanted to make a fresh start, and I did *not* want anyone to know about the MS. I was still afraid of the way potential friends would view me if they knew about the condition. But one afternoon that first summer, Simon fell off the swing in the garden. He landed on his back and let out an ear-piercing scream. Corrinna was there at the time and, running faster than I could, she got to him first.

'Where does it hurt, Simon?' she asked.

'Everywhere,' he sobbed.

He was white and shaking. I was terrified he had broken his spine, and a future of both Simon and me in wheelchairs flashed before my eyes. I could see from her expression that Corrinna was scared too. 'Don't move, Simon,' she said. 'Don't move an inch.'

We called an ambulance and they put a neck brace on him. 'It's just a precaution,' said the elder of the two men. 'So don't go worrying now.' I got into the ambulance with Simon and he held tightly onto my hand. Corrinna followed behind us in her car.

The ambulance took us to Harcourt Street Children's Hospital, blaring its sirens to get us through the traffic. 'Listen, Simon, love,' I said. 'That nee naw is blaring out just for you.'

Luckily Simon hadn't come to any real harm, and once he had been examined and x-rayed we were allowed to bring him home. He was sore for a few days, and Kitty offered to look after him so that Corrinna and I could go shopping. When we got back I thought Kitty was looking at me with a new intensity, but she didn't say anything. The next time she saw Corrinna though she asked if she could have a word with her. And she said, 'Corrinna, is it true that your mother has MS?' Corrinna said nothing, but her blush of confusion said it all.

'I'm sorry if I've spoken out of turn, Corrinna, but Simon told me she had it. Is it true?'

'Yes, Kitty, I'm afraid it is,' said Corrinna, explaining that I had made her promise not to tell anybody. When Corrinna told me that Kitty knew, and that Simon had told her, I was furious. At first anyway, but Corrinna begged me not to take it out on him.

'But what if someone at UCD finds out? What will I do then?'

Corrinna said there was no way that would happen and that Kitty had realised she must keep it to herself, but even so I worried. Yet, another part of me found it something of a relief. At least now there was someone outside the family with whom I could let down my guard. Kitty quickly became more than a friend. A pillar of the community, she would visit with eggs or a jar of marmalade. Her most important role was as a lynchpin to her wonderful sons and daughters. When I needed something done around the cottage she would send her two very capable sons down to me. I could always rely on her to show kindness.

I enjoyed my job in University College Dublin, but in the end my mobility, or rather my lack of it, proved to be my downfall. The MS attacks increased both in frequency and severity. There was no doubt that the strain of the fifty-six-mile round-trip commute was having an impact on my health. And it wasn't just the commute that tired me. The job involved driving to the other national universities, so I had the long haul to Cork, Galway and Limerick to contend with too. It all became too much.

Add to that my continuing terror of someone at UCD finding out, and the desperate strain of trying to hide this worsening condition, and it was clear, even to me, that the best course of action was to give up the job and to try and find something less demanding. So that is what I did. I gave up the full-time job but continued in UCD on various projects. That suited me fine.

The great excitement of that year, 1995, was Corrinna's wedding to Richard. They had become engaged the previous summer and decided to marry from Woodenbridge. It seemed like a nice way to settle the family.

Happy as I was for Corrinna, I couldn't help thinking how, in contrast, I was a woman alone. I never expected that to be the case at forty-one. As if to emphasise that fact, my divorce papers came through just the day before the wedding. Talk about hammering it home. All I ever really wanted from life was stability, love and a lifelong partner. I kept dreaming about a passionate man who would lift me up and love me like I had never been loved before. Every time I heard Kate Bush singing the haunting 'Wuthering Heights', I'd fantasise about meeting Heathcliff's double.

Richard is Protestant, and the Protestant church, Castle Macadam in the Avoca Valley, is beautiful. Corrinna decided to marry there. The Reverend George Butler was to officiate. We all took to him, and were well pleased.

Corrinna's wedding day was perfect. It dawned warm and sunny, and all my family turned up. As I said to Noeleen's husband Dave, everyone scrubbed up pretty well. I had been over all the arrangements with a fine-tooth comb. I had checked and rechecked that the hotel was expecting us all. I had rechecked the menus, the flowers and the place settings but I was still nervous for me and for my precious girl. Noeleen propped me up wonderfully well. Helping me get ready, she handed me a glass of champagne to calm my nerves.

Jumbo came to the wedding. He had kept in touch with Corrinna over the years but she wanted me to walk her up the aisle. She was adamant about that, and I was, of course, delighted to. I thought it was a rather nice flouting of tradition, and Jumbo was happy to stand aside.

It was a lovely day. The 200-year-old church looked romantic as the sage green 1950s Jaguar pulled up in front of the heavy oak doors. The display of white chrysanthemums with trailing ivy welcomed us into the porch, but I still had butterflies as I supported my first-born up the aisle. Corrinna looked enchanting. It was obvious from the smiles and murmurs of appreciation from the guests that I wasn't the only one to think this. The white silk dress with its pearl-encrusted bodice suited Corrinna wonderfully. She had topped the dress with a hat – though a white one rather than the lilac I chose for my ill-fated wedding to her father twenty-three years earlier.

When I saw my tall, slim son Simon, dressed in his best man's outfit, wink at me from the altar steps, tears threatened the gold eye-shadow that Noeleen had painstakingly applied earlier. And when the Reverend George Butler stepped forward and asked, 'Who giveth this woman away?', a voice I didn't recognise as mine said, 'I do.'

Later, in my speech, I told our guests how emotional that moment had been for me. 'It was hard,' I said, 'giving Corrinna away. Because twenty-four years ago I had to fight tooth and nail to keep her.' Those words brought the house down. But they were nothing less than the truth. Corrinna made a speech too. I thought that was good. I have always felt that women should put themselves forward into the limelight. Why should such roles be reserved for men?

Seeing Jumbo again after all those years was strange, yet rather wonderful. He was still a charming rogue, and there was a definite connection between us. When we danced, everyone stood around and cheered and clapped. Watching us, Jumbo's sister said, 'Marie, you and Jumbo should be together. You are right for each other. You always were.'

⁔

In the autumn I was having problems setting up a new programme in UCD. I needed technical help, and I heard that an expert was coming in the following week to talk about upgrading the computer system. I asked could someone send him along to my office, and this small bearded man appeared and introduced himself as Tom Curran. I explained that there was nothing wrong with my system but I needed a little help to set up a programme, and he said, 'That will cost you a lunch.' I laughed at that but agreed, because although he wasn't my usual idea of a romantic hero, there was something distinctly attractive about the man.

We met the following week in a bistro near Trinity College in the centre of Dublin, and the conversation just flowed. We had a lot in common. He shared my thirst for knowledge, and he admitted he was lonely too. Like me, he had been married before and he was, I think, looking for a new partner. He had a teenage son called Dave, and we talked about our boys, agreeing that sometimes teenagers really can try your patience.

I felt that Tom was someone I would like to get to know better. There I was, in my forties, twice divorced. You could say I had been round the block a few times, but I felt chuffed to bits that Tom clearly fancied me. He told me that I was beautiful and sexy, and that he loved the way I talked, and the way I walked. He liked the way my head tilted when I listened to him. Damn it, he *liked* me. And if saying 'Marie, your sexiness shines like a beacon in the dark' was perhaps over-poetic, I admit his compliments thrilled me.

I liked his frankness too. We spoke about our marriage break-ups. Tom said, 'It takes two to ruin a marriage,' and I liked that in him. It showed fairness. After all my disparate experiences and disasters, I had told myself to be sure to check out potential partners for their prosperity. I reckoned material goods helped. But I didn't give a damn how much money Tom had, or what car he drove. I just wanted to know him better.

'I'd like to see you again,' he said, offering me a spoonful of crème brûlée.

'Okay,' I said, pretending to think it over. 'But that will have to be in County Wicklow, and you will have to let me bring Ben along to see how he likes you.'

'Ben? I thought you said your son was called Simon.'

'Ben,' I told him, 'is the love of my life.'

Tom raised an eyebrow. 'Let me guess. Does Ben have four legs?'

'Ay. He's a dog. But not just *any* dog. He's a springer spaniel, and he protects me against the world. If he doesn't like you, you're out.'

'Does he like the beach?'

'God, he loves it. I don't even have to throw a stick to get him into the water. He runs in anyway.'

'I like dogs,' said Tom. 'I can't own one with the travelling I do, but I walk them when I have the time.'

'You mean you borrow them?'

'Not exactly. A friend of mine rescues abandoned dogs. She might have seven or eight at any one time, so I help out when I can.'

'Jesus. How could anybody abandon a wee dog?'

Tom laughed. 'Some of them are not so wee. The last one I walked was an Irish wolfhound, and he was completely unmanageable. He spotted a cat and took off at a gallop. I hadn't the strength for him. He jumped over a wall and slammed me into it. The big brute.'

'Ah. Don't say that. It wasn't his fault nobody bothered to train him. And as for abandoning him – well – it's criminal.'

A couple of weeks passed before we met again. Tom was doing contract work in Thurles and he had to spend a lot of time there, so we would catch up with each other in Dublin for a coffee or a drink just now and then. But I kept to my threat of getting Ben's approval. Tom and I met in Arklow one day and we took him for a walk on the beach. Tom adored Ben, lavishing so much attention on him as he threw stick after stick that I almost became jealous. As for Ben, he looked up adoringly as Tom talked to him, pulling gently at his ears just the way he likes it. His tail, wagging so hard it went round in spirals, was the final nod of approval.

We kissed goodbye and drove away. And the minute I got back to the house the phone rang. It was Tom. He sounded flustered when he heard my voice and said he had meant to dial a different number. He told me later that he hadn't expected me to get home so fast. He had hoped to leave a romantic message on my answering machine. He had wanted to say how much he had enjoyed our 'date' and that he hoped we could meet again soon.

After that we met, and talked on the phone, as often as we could. The attraction between us was growing rapidly. One Saturday a few weeks later Tom suggested he could come to Woodenbridge and take me out to dinner in the Woodenbridge Hotel. That suited me. I agreed, and arranged for a babysitter for Simon.

'I'll meet you there,' I said. It meant I would have to drive, but I didn't want Tom and Simon coming face to face. Not yet. Not until and unless I felt the relationship had a future.

'And will I book a room?' asked Tom.

That took me aback. 'If you like.' I paused, then said softly, 'Yes. That would be lovely. I'll ask the babysitter to stay all night with Simon.'

I heard Tom's sharp intake of breath, and realised with

embarrassment that he hadn't been suggesting I stay there with him. He simply wanted to avoid driving home. But he was clearly very pleased that I had said I would.

Tom rang me on the Saturday morning, just to make sure I hadn't changed my mind. And it struck me, not for the first time, what a kind and considerate man he was. I dressed carefully that night. I normally wore quite long skirts and favoured loose clothes, but that night I wore a black fitted dress with a slit up the back and I had my nails and my hair done too. I felt breathless with nerves, or excitement, or a bit of both. I called into the living room to kiss Simon goodnight, telling the babysitter to be sure to send him to bed around ten o'clock. His eyes widened as he took in my finery. I had told him I was attending a business function and was being put up in a hotel. That was a common enough occurrence, but I could see he wondered why I had stepped up the glamour.

The car park at the hotel was packed, but as I searched around for a space for my grey Peugeot, Betsy, I spotted Tom's BMW. Good. He was early. I could make a confident entrance. Tom was sitting at the bar drinking a pint. He looked as nervous as I felt. It was strange. We had been so relaxed with each other at all our previous meetings, but the thought of what was to come had us both on edge. I still felt apprehensive, vulnerable even. I felt Tom could see into my soul.

I really fancied him, though, seen dispassionately, he was no Adonis. Six years my senior, his full head of hair was tinged with salt and pepper as it turned grey. He had a bit of a beer belly. But his green eyes were to die for. I found them intensely erotic.

The wine relaxed us both. By the time we had got on to the

second bottle we settled down. Tom loved to tell jokes, and he tells them well. But every time I laughed he would look at me in amazement, and sit upright as if in shock. Was it the volume of my belly laugh that got to him or was he not used to anyone finding his jokes amusing? I'm still not sure about that one.

By the time we had adjourned to the residents' lounge, sunk into a big squashy sofa and downed coffee and brandy we had progressed to more intimate banter. There was a lot of giggling too. 'I love your accent,' said Tom. He had already told me he loved my lips, my hair and my quiet sense of style, but I was enjoying this. What woman doesn't appreciate a smooth-tongued man?

'My accent? Not everyone likes the Donegal drawl.'

'They don't? It's those elongated vowels that get to me,' he said. 'I love the way you say, "Auch aaaye" and "Noooh".'

'Away or that wey ye.'

'Excuse me?'

'You know. Catch yeself on.'

'Jesus.' He ran his thumb gently along my arm, sending shivers right down to my toes. 'I didn't know Donegal had its own language.'

I punched him playfully on the arm. 'You'd better believe it. Donegal is a law unto itself. Not to be laughed at by Jaaack… eens.'

'Oh.' He closed his eyes in mock ecstasy. 'Say that again, will you? Oh … go on.'

'Jaaack…eens.'

And the night? Suffice it to say, it went well. We confessed to each other afterwards that we had worried at the thought of exposing our less-than-perfect, middle-aged bodies to each other, but there was no awkwardness, only deep, intense pleasure.

Tom said that he was first attracted to me because I was beautifu, but he said looks alone were not enough for him. He would never have considered being with me had he not found me intelligent. That made me smile. Richard had said the same thing to Corrinna when they first met.

With Tom and me it was also a matter of shared interests. We had a lot in common, because he'd had his struggles in life as well. His childhood was not as troubled as mine was but he was always made to feel inferior. He grew up with constant criticism from his father. He was born in 1948 and lived in Rathfarnham, County Dublin. He has always had curiosity about the world; he still has it, but it started back then. He wanted an education, but he came from a working-class background and that wasn't a given. He left school at twelve and went to a technical school. In one way, that made sense. He had always loved working with his hands, but his ambition was to go to university. He had assumed there would be a route into college from the technical school, but he had got that wrong. He took the Group Cert, which would have got him into an apprenticeship.

Tom was stubborn. Well, he still is. So he refused to give up on the idea. The only way for him to get to university in Ireland was to go back and study for the Leaving Certificate. But he made enquiries, and learned that if he went into the English system he could get some qualifications in a year. He took O-levels in a school in Dundrum, believing that they were the educational equivalent of the Leaving Certificate and would get him to college. It was only after he had passed them that someone informed him that A-levels were equivalent to the higher Leaving Certificate. That was a terrible kick in the teeth.

Tom didn't give up. He went to England and took A-levels at Barnet College. He took five subjects, including English, maths and applied maths, because nobody thought to tell him that he should really specialise in three. He worked like an eejit, planning to return to Ireland to attend university. Then someone pointed out that if he stayed in England, as an Irish citizen he would qualify for a grant. That obviously was attractive. So he went to Leicester University and studied electronics. He made himself a successful career and eventually had his own business in computers. I admired him so much.

His marriage had broken up a good few years before he and I met. He told me he had gone through a bad period but had straightened himself out. He hated living alone and had tried dating various women before we met, but he didn't meet anyone who ignited that essential spark.

Tom describes himself as a loner. He says he needs to have time by himself. But it is important to him that there is someone there at the end of the day. Living alone, he always felt lonely. His son Dave lived with his mother, but Tom did see a lot of him.

Tom says he has trouble talking about his feelings, but he made it clear from the start that he felt strongly about me. He was always saying, 'I could not believe my luck when I met you, Marie.'

Soon after that magical night in the Woodenbridge Hotel, Tom spent a weekend with me in my cottage. Simon was away for the weekend, staying with his father. Tom arrived on Friday evening and I cooked him dinner. He complimented my cooking, though I was soon to learn that he generally ate more exotic food. I have always favoured plain family food when I cook, because of all the years of looking after my family, but I appreciate exotic flavours too. That was something else that we share. It was a wonderful weekend, cold but frosty. We took my beloved spaniel Ben on long walks. Tom lit a fire and we curled up in front of it, drinking wine and talking. Always talking.

Relaxed though we were, there was one thing bothering me. Tom didn't know I had MS. He had no idea that one day I could need a full-time carer. I dreaded telling him. I had begun to realise that I did not want to lose him, but our relationship felt like a lie. It was an ever-increasing burden.

On Sunday morning we went to Clogga beach near Arklow. Tom was throwing sticks into the sea for Ben, and I thought, I must tell him now. I must let him leave before he gets in too deep. So I tugged his arm and said, 'I've got something to tell you.' He turned immediately, aware from the urgency of my tone that this was serious.

'What is it?'

I wrapped my scarf more tightly around my neck and said, 'This is hard.'

'I'm listening.'

I looked him straight in the eye. 'I've got MS.'

'You mean multiple sclerosis?'

'That's right. Do you know what that is?'

He nodded. 'Yes. That cellist, Jacqueline du Pré. She had that, didn't she?'

'And ended up in a wheelchair, alone and unloved. Yes. That's right.'

'Tell me,' he said.

'What, the technical stuff?'

'Yes, please.'

'Right.' I took a deep breath. 'I started getting sick when Simon was still a baby. An MRI scan confirmed it when I first lived in Wales. It showed that I had four exacerbations at the top of my spine, and that meant that it would affect my motor functions rather than anything else.'

'Motor functions?'

'That means walking, talking, lifting, swallowing and possibly feeding.'

I felt tears leak from my eyes. Noticing, he threw his arms around me and hugged me tightly. I felt safe, and buried my face in his chest. But then, extricating myself, I said, 'Let me finish.'

'Okay.'

'So far the results have been spot on.'

'Meaning?'

'At the moment I have relapsing-remitting MS. It started as general weakness. I'd get flu-like symptoms and have to take a day or two off work. That wasn't too much of a problem. Then I would get periods where I couldn't walk properly. I'd develop a limp, then it would suddenly go and I'd be fine for months. The problem is the future.'

'You mean the wheelchair thing?'

I was so scared back then of losing the ability to walk that just the word made me shake. I grimaced. 'They talk of that, but Tom, it won't happen to me. It just can't. I promise you, I'm going to fight it all the way.'

'But the worst-case scenario?'

'My functions could go, one by one. They tell me some people need full-time care.'

'That's okay.'

'What?' I assumed I'd misheard him.

'I said, "That's okay."'

I stared at him, wondering if he'd lost his reason. 'How is that okay?'

'We'll deal with it.'

This was mad. 'Tom, listen. You have absolutely no obligations here. We've just met. I'm only telling you this because it wouldn't be fair, on either of us, to get closer without you knowing.'

'I've said it's okay.'

'No.' I punched him on the arm, and he automatically rubbed the spot. 'Don't give me an answer now,' I said. 'You have to go away and think about this.'

'Okay.' He started to walk down the beach. I watched him, with a sense of resignation. Then, after just ten or so paces, he turned around and strode back towards me. He said, 'Right. I've thought about it. And I'm not going anywhere.'

I wept. He held me close, until Ben, who had been haring up and down the beach, started barking and, when that had no effect, jumped up at the two of us, breaking the tension and leaving damp, sandy paw marks all over our overcoats.

CHAPTER ELEVEN

HIGHS AND LOWS

ॐ

I was relatively well when Tom and I first met. I had the occasional relapse, where I would get some pain and have trouble moving, then everything would clear and there would be no sign of the MS. The condition didn't affect our burgeoning romance at all.

Even after Tom had assured me that he would never turn tail and run, I had trouble believing it. He had said it so lightly, as if I had said that I was ordering dessert. I should have trusted him more. His attitude continued to be, 'No problem. We'll deal with it.' He said he had always dealt with the difficulties life had thrown his way, and he didn't see that this should be any different. He has kept that attitude all the way through. Tom is the kindest, most honourable man you could ever hope to meet. Neither of us wanted another marriage – with our track record the idea seemed crazy – yet I sensed that the promise. 'Until death do us part' would not faze Tom at all.

I had planned a big family Christmas. Noeleen and Dave were coming, and Daddy was travelling from Donegal and staying over. I invited Tom to come for a couple of days before the lunacy kicked in. It was his turn to have his son Dave for Christmas that year. He planned to drive back to his house in Rathfarnham on Christmas Eve so that everything would be ready in the morning before Dave arrived. He hadn't told his family about meeting me as yet, though Simon obviously realised that something was up.

On Christmas Eve Tom offered to take Daddy to the pub for a pint or two and they stayed rather longer than planned. There was no way then that Tom could drive anywhere. So he stayed the extra night and left the house at dawn on Christmas Day. It was freezing that Christmas in 1995 and Tom's car refused to start. He then tried every taxi company but none of them even answered their phones. He had tried, and failed, to do a hill start, and was standing by the side of the road watching as the neighbours set off for church. In the end I took pity on him and went out and brought him back into the house.

He was frantic about letting Dave down, and when he rang to explain, his ex-wife sounded more than annoyed. But what could he do? Christmas was, I have to admit, chaotic that year. What had I been thinking when I had invited everyone? How did I expect it to be less than a nightmare when I squeezed seven adults and two teenagers into a two-bedroom cottage? There were arguments, mood swings, strained silences, and just to cap it all, the toilet blocked on Christmas morning. Were it not for the two Kilhoran boys, who came down and sorted it out, emptying the septic tank for us, I don't know what we would have done. Poor Tom was in the middle of all this family tension.

When, two days later, he managed to get the car repaired and set off to make it up to his son and his ex-wife, I was so tired I really didn't know how I would make it through until the New Year. Corrinna appeared in my bedroom carrying a tray with tea and a bacon sandwich. Thanking her, I said, 'I don't want to get up again. Not ever.'

'Another four days and we will all be gone,' she said.

'But why did you all come at the same time?'

She laughed. 'You asked us here. Remember? At my wedding? Nobody to blame but you and the vodka.'

It was thanks to Corrinna that worse warfare hadn't broken out in the Brolly clan. She had always been the peacemaker. Noeleen called her Henry Kissinger. She helped get us all through the next few days without killing each other. After the New Year Ball in Arklow, when she and Richard had returned to London and my family had dispersed in various directions, the house felt empty. When Tom rang to wish me happy new year and said that he was feeling lonely now that Dave had gone home, I asked him would he like to come back and stay. He jumped at the chance. Since then, he has never really left.

Settling down with Tom was like putting on my favourite cardigan; his love was reliable, soft and warm. And like that cardigan, he knew the contours of my body, while accepting its limitations.

Love at a mature age is different from that frenzied passion

I felt in my early life. There was a time I could not bear to be apart from Jumbo for more than five minutes. My love for Tom is less intense, but a great deal more relaxed. Tom and I didn't need that constant affirmation that we were the one and only. It wasn't all easy. Tom is a free spirit. Having lived on his own, he likes his own space, and wanted to set out our respective roles. I just wanted a loving relationship that included some laughs, and absolute trust.

Life soon settled into a happy enough routine. If we didn't exactly agree on everything, we enjoyed the arguments and debates that ensued when our opinions differed. Tom adored lamb, whereas I preferred chicken. I loved milk chocolate, he had a penchant for dark. We both enjoyed our garden, but whereas I planned, he planted. When things weren't going right, he paced, whereas I took to my bed. He loved cooking exotic meals for guests, and, while I loved eating them, when I cooked it tended to be more traditional family fare. We both loved wildlife programmes and made sure to keep up with current affairs.

We had heated debates over everything from the war in Iraq to decommissioning by the IRA, but Tom took such subjects to heart. I would be lying if I said that our debates didn't turn into rows or that our rows were always civilised. I have a tendency to take out my frustrations on my nearest and dearest. I always have, and I suspect I always will.

There's one story that became almost legendary around here. One of our neighbours, a farmer, was driving his tractor along the road one morning. It was a noisy old thing but he could hear me and Tom having a row above the din of the engine. When Tom next went down to the pub for a pint the farmer took one look at him and said, 'Jesus, your woman was giving you some going over.' Half the village heard him. Tom got a few free pints out of sympathy that night.

The problem, for me, is that Tom doesn't like an argument. He's stubborn. He will fight his corner but he won't scream and shout the way I will. He simply walks away mid-fight and there is *nothing* more irritating when there's something you want to say. After a few months of living together, the rows got worse. Tom accused me of going round in circles, throwing out the most hurtful abuse I could conjure up. He said I came up with things I didn't necessarily mean. It's true that I will dig up old hurts. Sometimes I will go back twenty years and tell someone how much their behaviour hurt me. It's the way I am. Corrinna says I am the matriarch. I like to be the boss. I need to be in charge. Over the years our rows have become part of our life together. They build up; we'll snipe at each other; I let rip; Tom sulks, and then we make up.

Tom's moving in wasn't easy for Simon. He was going through the usual teenage rebellion and resented having a new father figure around. The two had an uneasy relationship but now they have become extremely close.

By this time I had cut my ties with UCD and found a job nearer to home, in Arklow. I was working as a lecturer in women's studies on a back-to-school programme for adults. It suited me well. Driving even short distances was becoming a problem as my MS worsened. I found it almost impossible to use the brake, so Tom had my car fitted with hand controls.

There were bad days. Days when I could not control my limbs, and they jerked all over the place. It was embarrassing when that happened in public. People looked at me awkwardly. They probably thought I was drunk, even though it was ten o'clock in the morning. I hated being gawked at.

In the early spring of 1997 I became completely incapacitated from an MS attack. Tom was working in Thurles and would be away for two or three nights at a time. I woke up one morning and realised I could not get out of bed. I simply couldn't move. As luck would have it, this was a Friday and Tom was due home in the evening; he was staying for the weekend. Poor Tom. He got such a shock when he found me in bed. He rang work, telling them he would have to take a few days off, then he rang the doctor. She said I needed to get into hospital to have steroids administered intravenously, but the neurology department wasn't active over the weekend. On Monday I was taken into the neurology department of Saint Vincent's Hospital in Dublin and given a dose of steroids to boost my energy. I had to stay in for a few days.

While I got over the attack, for the first time since my diagnosis I did not make a complete recovery. My left leg started to drag a bit. I had a slight limp, but that impacted on my right leg too. I couldn't move it very well anymore. Everyone assured me that it wasn't noticeable, but it bothered me. Tom has told me since that he can spot someone who has MS immediately. He says there is just a slight dragging, something that the untrained eye can't see. My MS had reached the next stage. From there it was downhill all the way.

The following year I was bed-bound for six weeks with an acute attack of MS. To exacerbate it, I had fallen in the driveway when I was getting out of the car and had landed on a stone. It damaged my hip and was extremely painful. Being stuck upstairs with a commode and absolutely no view drove me quietly insane. Tom couldn't take all that time off work, so Corrinna flew over from France, where she and Richard were living, and she looked after me. Then when I felt better I flew back to France with her and stayed for a while to recuperate. After that episode Tom and I decided that we would have to extend our tiny cottage. If this was a glimpse of the future, I needed to have a downstairs bedroom, and one with a bathroom en suite.

Then one by one little things began to happen. My leg got very tired and I seemed to be dragging it, so the neurology department advised that I get a crutch. I didn't like the idea of that one bit, so I decided I would compromise and use a stick. Years earlier I had bought three sticks at an auction, never thinking I would have to use them, but I was grateful now. I managed with the stick for a few months but then I started to feel pain in my left leg. The hospital presented me with a Rollator – which is a Zimmer frame with wheels. It was a very practical piece of equipment; it had a seat attached, allowing me to walk a little way, then take a rest before continuing my walk.

I could see what a benefit the Rollator was, but I did *not* want to take it to work. Instead, I finally used the crutch I had been given originally. For a while I used it outside and the Rollator inside. But gradually I began to rely on the Rollator more. It was a great help when I got tired.

I struggled on with the crutch at work but I fell a few times. That was around the time that driving became a problem. When my walking deteriorated further I felt as if my whole world was collapsing. It would have made sense to take the Rollator to work but there was no way I was going to do that. I was teaching a group of FÁS students at the time and I imagined that if they saw me with the Rollator they would laugh at me, and I couldn't have borne that.

I struggled on with the crutch but then the college moved to new premises. I would have had to work upstairs, but by that time my left leg had become worse and I could not have managed the stairs. Leaving work broke my heart but there was no point dwelling on it. If I had to be at home all day, then I needed to find something to do. I took up painting and I began to write. I went to classes and started penning a memoir of my childhood.

I went to Kerry for a weekend workshop taught by the wonderful Irish writer Anne Enright. This was before she had won the Booker Prize. At the end of the weekend Anne took me to one side. She said I had talent and should try and get the memoir published. This was enormously encouraging to me, and though it would be some years before it would finally come to fruition, I never forgot her words.

I missed work, but there were benefits. I could go to London and see Corrinna, who had moved back from France to a small house in Chiswick. I stayed for a month or two at a time. It was a lifesaver when the cottage was being extended, and Tom would fly over for weekends. They were wonderful times. I would share the spare room with Simon and with my spaniel, Ben. Corrinna was working at the BBC, so Simon and I kept ourselves entertained, but in the evenings we would visit the theatre or the cinema. Often we ate out, and Richard would drive us round the sights of London in the dark. Simon adored that.

I still disliked using the Rollator. I thought of it as an old woman's walking aid; it made me feel like an invalid, and look like one too. There was no chance now of hiding my condition from friends, or even from strangers.

I took to wall-walking. Leaving the Rollator aside and using my hands against the wall, I could get as far as the bathroom. That way I could tell myself that I wasn't *really* disabled at all. I would think, tomorrow morning I will be as right as rain. That worked, so I started wall-walking to the kitchen and I managed to cook without using the frame.

I was congratulating myself on being independent again when the method began to fail me. I had to call Tom to fetch my frame in a hurry, and I had several falls. One time I fell behind my bedroom door and was unable to pull myself up. I tried to hang on to the end of the bed and pull myself forward but that didn't work. I tried to get up using the handle of the door but that didn't work either. I slid right down the door like a slug slides down your window pane. I ended up lying there for four hours until Tom arrived back from work. That incident marked the end of my wall-walking.

The main reason why I hated being reliant on the Rollator was that I knew the next stage in this progression, or rather regression, was a wheelchair. And that was something I found extremely hard to come to terms with. Tom knew that. He was, in retrospect, very clever. He introduced the idea gradually and made it seem fun.

In those years we had some wonderful holidays with Richard and Corrinna in France. The most memorable was a trip we took in 1997. It was to be a big family affair. Not only were

Richard and Corrinna joining Tom and Simon and me; Richard's parents were coming too. I was looking forward to it. We were driving over and staying in a big house. I was a little worried about how I would get around but I didn't share that with Tom. And as it turned out, he was several steps ahead of me.

We had taken the ferry to London and stayed a night with Richard and Corrinna; we were driving to France from there and Simon was holidaying with his father. I knew Tom was up to something. He spent hours and hours on the phone and then he disappeared, saying there was something he had to do. I heard him talking to Corrinna in hushed tones but when I asked her what was going on she was infuriatingly tight-lipped.

The journey to France was tiring. By the time we had endured the tunnel crossing, braved the worst that the French drivers could throw at us and found the house, I was flattened. We had plans to eat out that night and I didn't know how I would make it to the restaurant. I said as much to Tom and, smiling, he went out to the car, opened the boot and produced a wheelchair. 'Marie, meet the Gimpmobile,' he said. Encouraging me to sit in the thing, he danced me around the driveway as the others whooped their appreciation.

I blessed him. He knew how I had dreaded being so contained. The wheelchair had encapsulated all my worst fears about MS. I could see Corrinna's relief. She was well aware that I hated losing my mobility. Now though it was a case of, be imprisoned in the house while everyone else went out and enjoyed themselves or be part of this wonderful family holiday.

We had a lovely time. Tom and I share a love of France,

because we both appreciate good food and fine wine. Corrinna and Richard are the same. We all experiment. We make sure to order different things from the menu and then we will taste a morsel from each other's plates.

One day we had walked around the port and were about to go and find a restaurant for our lunch when Tom suddenly pushed the wheelchair up this steep slope. He went galloping up the hill and I had this wonderful sensation of speed. The wind was rushing through my hair. I felt amazing, and I was shrieking with laughter.

Corrinna and Richard were haring up behind us. And when Tom finally ran out of puff they were there to hang on to the Gimpmobile. 'Oh my God, Tom,' Corrinna said, catching her breath. 'I thought you were going to have a heart attack. Don't do that to us.' But she knew, as did I, that this was Tom's way of making me accept the restrictions of the life that was ahead.

Later that year I went to New York with Corrinna and Simon. We took the wheelchair, and had a wonderful week visiting the various sites. You name it, we saw it. One night we rushed to the Empire State Building just before closing time. To get to the top you had to take a series of elevators, and there were long queues. 'We'll never get there,' said Simon, his face falling. I thought he was right. It was almost midnight. Then this Amazonian concierge radioed someone and said, 'We've got a Hot Rod coming. I'll put her to the head of the queue.' Simon was falling about with laughter. My wheelchair has been called Hot Rod ever since.

Tom and I have always enjoyed going on holidays, whether with various members of our families or alone. It was good to get away as a couple, but very often those holidays would start with an almighty row.

For one of our earliest holidays we chose Corsica. We were both still working and had been eagerly anticipating some relaxing time together. I can't remember how the row started that time; maybe we had left home too late for comfort or perhaps one of us had forgotten some essential item. I am not sure, but with Tom and me, anything can spark an argument. I know that it erupted at the airport and that I was working myself into a lather.

When I get hold of something – an idea or a grudge – I have a problem letting go. Tom says I'm like a little terrier, that I don't know how to stop. He complains that I get to a point where I am saying things to be hurtful. I have a horrible feeling that he might be right. He complains that it's difficult to know whether I mean the things I'm saying or am just saying them to provoke a reaction or maybe release pent-up anger. Whichever, when we are at home and it gets to that stage where the row is going round in circles, Tom distances himself. He walks away. It drives me mad. But to my delight he couldn't walk away when we were on a three-hour flight. I had him trapped.

He couldn't walk away – but he did the next best thing, and ignored me. He wouldn't talk to me. He wouldn't even look at me. He hid behind his newspaper and buried his nose in a book, but I wasn't going to let the row go. I was in full flow, hurling insults and, Tom claimed, using some ripe language. I wouldn't let him ignore me. The more he tried, the louder I got. The flight attendant came up at one stage and asked Tom if he was all right. I glared at the attendant, furious that he would take Tom's side without knowing why we were rowing. I carried on shouting at Tom. I'm not proud of it. It's just how it was.

When we arrived and were getting our hand luggage out of the overhead lockers, a guy who was sitting with his wife a couple of rows back from us looked at Tom and said, 'I would *hate* to be going on your holiday.' I thought, what bloody cheek. How would he like it if his partner refused to engage with him? We sorted out the paperwork for the car, located it, and packed it up, and still Tom refused to engage with me. So I kept at him, trying to get my point across. And the next thing, Tom took a wrong turn and got lost. He started swearing, saying it was my fault.

'How do you make that out?' I asked. 'Am I driving? Did I tell you to turn right there?' He just continued to swear under his breath.

We settled in the villa we had rented but the row continued. By that stage we didn't know how to stop. Then I got a chest cold. The people who owned the villa lived on the land. They came around to see how we were getting on. They couldn't speak any English and we can't speak French, but we managed to communicate that I wasn't well. They brought round some lemons from a tree in their garden and indicated that we should use them to make a lemon drink to ease my throat.

The lemons were the size of footballs, but when you tried to peel them they turned out to be as small inside as the lemons we buy in Ireland. Tom made a drink for me. I took one sip and made a face. 'You've made this bitter just to get at me, haven't you?' I said. 'Typical.' Then I laughed, and hugged Tom. And that was it. The rest of the holiday passed off peacefully.

ഇന്റെ

Not all our holidays were quite as dramatic. Normally we all spend Christmas together, but one year Richard and Corrinna had planned to go to Scotland. It was the first year that Corrinna hadn't spent Christmas with me and I think Tom was worried how I would cope. So we decided we would get away too and have Christmas in the sun. We went to Florida, and it was certainly different.

I remember on Christmas morning we were on the beach, and Tom had a row with a policeman on a motorbike because he wouldn't let us park in the disabled space. We had a good day after that but I was tired and went to bed at around eleven o'clock. Tom went downstairs again to have a pint before bed and he got chatting to a couple at the bar. He explained that we were from Ireland and were there on holiday and they said, 'We'd like to meet your wife.' So he came upstairs and persuaded me to come down. I was still there at five in the morning.

The next day Corrinna rang from Scotland saying she was missing us. I was in the bathroom because I wasn't feeling too good and Tom brought the phone through to me.

'What's wrong, Mum?' Corrinna asked. 'Did you have a wonderful Christmas?'

And I said, 'You will never believe this, petal.'

'What? What's wrong, Mum?'

'I'm feeling sick.'

Corrinna panicked then. 'Is it the MS? Can Tom cope? Will you get home okay?'

I laughed. 'I'm hung-over, pet. I've had too many slippery nipples.'

෫๏෬

The best holiday of our lives proved also to be our last. I had always wanted to go to Australia. It appealed to Tom too, though he was keener still to see New Zealand. For years we had discussed which country we should go to, but with our work commitments we had never managed the trip. In 2003 we decided it was a question of now or never.

I was fifty that year and my health was deteriorating. My arms and hands still worked but my legs didn't. Since France I had become less anxious about using the wheelchair and I used it a lot when we were out. I could still walk a little, using the Rollator, but the wheelchair had become a necessary part of our lives. There was a real danger that if we didn't make the trip soon, the MS would prohibit it.

Our original plan was to go either to Australia or New Zealand for three weeks, but we couldn't agree which country to go to so we decided we had better take three weeks in each. The more we planned, deciding which parts of Australia to see, the longer the holiday became. In the end we were away for almost three months. Richard was an incredible help. He had been to Australia and he did all the research for us. He even got us upgraded into business class. Tom organised his work to make the trip possible. He made sure that he was finishing one project, and he didn't take on another one, to give me the time off.

We didn't travel light. When I looked at all the paraphernalia at the airport – the wheelchair, the Rollator, crutches and huge cases – I did wonder at the wisdom of this trip. But we had a wonderful time. And for perhaps the first time in our lives we managed the holiday without one single argument. Not one, in the whole three months. We both look back on it as an amazing, golden time. It truly was a trip of a lifetime.

We went to Sydney first and booked into a really upmarket hotel that overlooked the harbour. I had always dreamed of having my photo taken beside the Opera House and Sydney Harbour Bridge. Tom was able to grant both wishes from our bedroom, room number 2620. I was incredibly happy there. I loved simply gazing out the window.

We stayed in Sydney for three weeks. We heard an army band in the Opera House and we drove over the harbour bridge as often as we could to take in the view. From Sydney we drove down the coast road. We saw the Twelve Apostles stones that have come to life after their incarceration under the water for the past 200 years.

A highlight was our visit to the Blue Mountains. They were spectacular, with the blue haze rising from the acres and acres of eucalyptus trees. The smell of eucalyptus was tantalising. I will never forget the sight.

We went to Melbourne, and a lovely little fishing town called Port Fairy. Tom pushed me along the beach in my wheelchair and I dipped my feet into the water. We picked compost kelp for a woman who was gathering it up for her garden.

The food was sensational. We both love seafood, and we ate it from the moment we arrived until the day we left. There was barracuda, tuna and pollack. There was shark too. Tom enjoyed that but I refused to try it. 'You have to draw the line somewhere,' I said, humming the theme tune from the movie *Jaws*.

We met some wonderful people. We weren't too sure about

the woman running the hotel in Port Fairy at first – she had an exceedingly gruff manner – but once she realised we were from Ireland her attitude softened. She, it turned out, had once been a sister at a hospital in Cork. That affinity with Ireland made her particularly hospitable towards us.

Most of the holidays I've taken in my life have been marred by something going wrong – missing a connection, or the hotel being on a main road or on a building site – but on this trip all the significant arrangements worked like a dream.

There were some niggles. We had been planning this trip for months, checking carefully that all the hotels had wheelchair access, yet in the hotel in Sydney there was a flight of steps down to the road. We ended up going into the next-door hotel and taking a lift down to the road. It was an inconvenience, but didn't worry us.

The situation in the Blue Mountains was even more bizarre. We stayed in a beautiful hotel – it was a colonial house – but there were steps up to the front door and the only way to get my wheelchair in was to use an alleyway into a goods entrance at the rear of the hotel. That didn't matter during the day, but at night they locked the door from the inside. So when we arrived back from dinner Tom had to bring me around to the back entrance, leave me there sitting on my own, go round to the front door, make his way to the basement, open the door and let me in.

One night I said I would try the steps, and Tom helped me up. But it took the best part of twenty minutes for me to navigate them. We had ordered a room with wheelchair access. The bathroom had been fitted out to suit someone with a disability but there were two steps down from the corridor into the room.

It didn't matter. We were both so very happy on that holiday that it would have taken a lot more to upset either of us.

Used as I now was to being wheeled around, there were still times when I preferred to assert my independence. When we were in a restaurant in Auckland I decided to use the Rollator to get to the toilet rather than use the wheelchair. I had no problem navigating the dining room; I was managing fine. I got to the loo, but when I tried to stand up afterwards my legs just gave way and I crumpled to the floor. I couldn't think what to do.

I waited there for what felt like hours, wondering how I would ever get out. Then there was a knock on the door and I heard Tom call my name. It was such a relief.

'Jesus, this is a tight fit,' he said, trying, but failing, to get the cubicle door open. 'Shall I go for help?'

'No, please don't,' I said. 'That would be so embarrassing.'

It took half an hour and a lot of hilarious manoeuvring before Tom managed to get in there and get me on my feet and sorted out. Then we had to make our way back to the dining room. By then I was weak with laughter, and that didn't help. I couldn't imagine what the other diners were thinking we had been up to when Tom and I emerged together from the female toilets. It made us both giggle for days.

∞∞

In the following years my condition deteriorated further. The attacks became more frequent and the remissions less complete. Tom's IT consultancy business involved major projects and he was away a lot. He tried to organise things so that he could spend at least one midweek night at home, as well as the weekends, but that wasn't always possible. Sometimes he could not even get home at the weekends. I was virtually living alone.

One Friday in 2003 I collapsed on the floor in the bedroom. This was just after lunch and I couldn't move. I felt utterly helpless. I shouted out but of course there was no one to hear. I couldn't even crawl to the phone. I was lying there for four hours unable to move. When Tom finally came home he said, 'That's it, then.'

'That's what?'

'You can't be left alone anymore.'

I protested, but deep down I knew he was right. That, to me, was a defining moment.

We had long conversations examining our options. I could, technically, go into a home, but that was something we never considered. I couldn't bear that. I was in *my* home and I wanted to stay. We could get someone in but financially that wasn't practical.

'It's simple,' said Tom. 'I'll become your carer.'

'Are you sure?' I felt that was too much to ask of him.

'I love you,' he said. 'You're a beautiful person and I will regard it as a privilege to be your arms and legs. I am delighted that I can help you.'

I could see that he meant it. I thanked God, or fate, or providence, for putting Tom in my life. I wondered what I would ever do without him.

There were obviously financial implications. When we met we were both earning a reasonable amount of money. I had already given up my job, and if Tom gave up his, life could become a struggle. We mistakenly assumed that Tom would form a partnership with the state in caring for me. That was very naive of us. There are 160,000 carers in Ireland, and the amount of help they get is minuscule. We became dependent on the disability allowance and the carer's allowance. As an IT consultant, Tom had been charging more per day for his services than we were getting from the state in a month. Yet caring is a twenty-four-hour-a-day job. It was a huge adjustment to make.

Having Tom as my carer, as well as my partner and lover, meant that the relationship had to change. It could no longer be solely romantic, but I think it produces a more intense love. Tom swears that he gets as much, if not more, from the relationship than I do.

'I never think of you as somebody who depends on me,' he says. 'I look on you as my partner, my love.'

CHAPTER TWELVE

REJECTING DIGNITAS

❧❧❧

Using the wheelchair on holiday was one thing; relying on it all the time was quite another, so I continued using the Rollator for as long as I possibly could. But there came a time when I fell with that too. I fell in the garden; I fell getting out of the car; I fell trying to get out of the house. Tom pleaded with me to use the wheelchair that sat under the stairs, but I baulked at the very sight of it. It was not me. I was not designed to sit in a wheelchair. I was made to walk, to dance and to run. Then one day I could no longer push the Rollator. My arms were too weak. They just kept falling down to hang loosely at my side. That felt like the end of the world.

By 2005 I was using the wheelchair on a daily basis. I still hated the idea of it but Tom continued to fool around and make it feel like fun, and I definitely became less fatigued when I used it. There were other benefits, especially when my grandchildren were around; and by then the twins were three and Simon's son Evan was a year old. I was able to race them, and I became a carrier for them all too. They would be hanging off the back of the chair and they would stand on the footboards. It was a great plaything.

By that time I was in almost constant pain and it was hard to control it with the drugs the doctor prescribed for me. I read somewhere that cannabis is hugely beneficial to MS patients but I was reluctant to try it. I have always been horrified by the use of illegal drugs. But if it really *was* beneficial, not just for the pain but for the spasms too, surely it was worth a try. Indeed many people argue that it should be made legal for people like me.

The problem was that I have never smoked. We got hold of a small amount of cannabis and tried using it in tea. The first time we tried that, Kitty Kilhoran came to the door. Seeing her, I shouted at Tom to open all the windows. I was terrified Kitty would notice the fumes or, worse, get high on it herself. But it had absolutely no effect on her, or on me. Next I tried making cannabis cakes but they didn't work for me either.

'You will just *have* to smoke it,' said Tom. That was all very well, but I didn't know where to start. It wasn't just the smoking, it was the thought of making a roll-up with cannabis that would be quite beyond my capabilities. Tom couldn't help me and neither could Corrinna, because neither of them has ever smoked either. In the end I got a friend to help. I struggled. There was a lot of coughing and spluttering but I got there in the end, and once I had mastered the act of inhaling I *did* find relief from the drug; it was ten times more effective at controlling the pain than any of my prescribed medicine, and my body relaxed, so stopping the spasms.

Tom began to research how to get cannabis. The best thing, he decided, would be to grow it, so he bought some seeds online and planted a few boxes in the spare room. He researched into the best filters, and so I had my supply. The first year he wrapped the crop in newspaper and stored it in a bag in the bottom drawer of a chest in the spare room. When he went to collect the crop it had disappeared. Corrinna had been round tidying up, and when we rang her she said, 'Those bags of newspapers? I threw them away, of course.' She was horrified when she realised what she had done. But all was well. We found the bags at the bottom of the bin.

Although I knew, logically, it was a reasonable thing to do – and on one level I didn't differentiate between cannabis and legal drugs – there was a certain amount of shame, mystery and fear around it. I never smoked the cannabis in front of anyone. If a prescription drug doesn't work you can always attach some blame to the doctor and ask him to change it for another one. But what comeback do you have if you end up dead after smoking something akin to poison? It did play on my mind. But it helped me until my chest became bad and now I can no longer smoke it.

In 2004 I reached yet another phase in my deterioration; I started to lose the feeling in my hands. That, to me, was devastating. I began to look into the future and I didn't like what I saw. When you have MS you deteriorate bit by bit. Death can be prolonged, painful and undignified. I began to ask myself, 'Is that what I want?' The answer, I realised, was 'No.' I wanted a choice. I needed the right to take my life at a time of my choosing. I wanted to die when the time was right.

It wasn't a new idea. When Tom had given up work and become my carer, we had discussed the future and how we would cope when my MS became worse. And I had said then that maybe I could end my life. But we had not talked about it in any concrete way. Now, I realised, I had to tell Tom I was serious about the idea. It wasn't going to be the easiest conversation in the world. I felt that I was being selfish. I wanted to do this to save myself pain, but in doing so I would be inflicting emotional torture on those whom I loved. Now that Corrinna and Simon were parents, I worried even more. How would *they* feel when I told them my thoughts? There was a lot to consider.

The deterioration in my health had been rapid. When my mother died in 2002, I had been able to walk from the church to the graveside but it was a struggle. At the time I envied anyone who could walk for as long as they wanted to. Now I wished I had appreciated any strength I still had. I just thanked God that Tom, who is a planner, had gone ahead with the conversion of our cottage. We now had a beautiful bedroom downstairs for the two of us.

I told Tom, and I said I wanted to make plans so that it would be possible. He knew at once that this time I was serious. And he knew that as an intelligent woman I had considered the options and knew that this was what I wanted. I had stressed to him that wanting to die in my own time was *not* the same as suicide. Many people kill themselves – my brother Shaun, for instance – but generally for someone in emotional pain this is a spontaneous decision. And in that case it is devastating for everyone in the family. It was different for me. I was contemplating rational suicide; in other words, it was a decision I had taken time to make. A decision I knew was right for me.

Tom and I discussed all the implications of rational suicide for a few months, and then I realised it was time to tell my children. Corrinna was still living in London. In March she came over for the weekend, leaving Richard in charge of the two-year-old twins. After dinner Tom went down to the village for a pint. I had asked him to, so that Corrinna and I could have this most difficult conversation.

Corrinna and I are very close. We always have been. She is the perfect daughter. When she comes over – and back then she came every two months – we always cuddle up together on the settee. That night she was lying down with her head on my lap. My hand was running through her hair. I could still do that back then. And I said to her, 'Darling, I have something to say.' I could feel her body tense. I said I had been thinking of the future a lot. 'I want to die peacefully when my time comes.'

She sat up sharply and hid her head in her hands. 'No! Mum, no! Not now. You're too young.'

'Don't worry, pet. I don't mean that I want to die right now.'

'Then why ...?'

'It's something I want for the future. For when my illness becomes too much to bear.'

'But you're okay, Mum. You look well. I'm sure if you just think positively, the worst won't happen.'

I could understand her reaction, but I *had* to get her to understand. We talked and talked about it all weekend. We cried. We consoled each other. We hugged. She wasn't happy with my decision – how could she be? – but I brought her along with my beliefs. She understood.

It was even harder telling nineteen-year-old Simon. He had recently fallen head over heels for a lovely girl called Susan Hearne. They lived in Waterford. She had a son, whom Simon adored, and she was three months pregnant with Simon's baby. It was the best thing that ever happened to him. I will never forget the moment he told me. We were watching a Saturday-night drama and he sat beside me, his right leg twitching. I put my hand on his knee to stop the shaking and he told me I was to become a granny again.

'That's just wonderful.' I hugged him with delight and his body relaxed at once.

'You're pleased?' he said.

'Of course I am. It's the best possible news.'

'I thought you'd kill me,' he said. 'I was going to tell you last time I saw you but when it came to it I didn't have the nerve.'

I laughed. I could understand Simon's disquiet. Well, of course I could. Look how long it had taken me to tell anyone I was pregnant back in the day. He was just three years older than I had been, and he was only now starting out in life. I had told both my children to be careful not to get into parenthood too young. I didn't want them to compromise their lives the way I had.

Yet I really was happy for Simon. I felt it would be the making of him, and it was. It has all ended so well. His son Evan is such a joy. He paints nonstop. At eight he knew the difference between water colours, acrylics and oil-based paints. He is more studious than Simon ever was and Simon is now instilling all these wonderful qualities in him. So it was hard, just a few months later, to be giving him such sad news. I told him, and he could not get his head around the idea at all. He was desperately upset; but, like his sister, he was consoled to know that I had no intention of dying anytime soon.

The next step was to explore my options. None of us knew anything about assisted dying at the time, but Tom and I both assumed that it was available for anyone who wanted it. Tom thought that if he contacted a doctor, he could get it organised for me. But that was far from the truth.

Simon works with computers. He offered to investigate the issue for me and we realised for the first time that, like assisted euthanasia, it is illegal to help someone to end their life in most countries, including Ireland. Maybe we were all naive, but that came as a shock. The only real option was for me to go to Dignitas – the clinic in Switzerland where people with a terminal illness are helped to die. This is legal in Switzerland provided the person is of sound judgement.

Tom contacted the clinic and spoke to the founder, Ludwig Minelli. He found out what the trip would involve. We needed an in-depth medical report to say that my illness was terminal, and a psychiatrist's report to verify that I was of sound mind and had made the decision without duress. That meant that in the eyes of the Swiss courts everything was above board.

We had many conversations about it. We discovered that because in Ireland it is illegal to help someone to die, Tom would be breaking the law by taking me to Dignitas. He could be prosecuted and sent to jail. Even accessing the information was illegal. Would he be arrested when he came home? And what of my children? If they came to Switzerland with me, would they also be arrested?

There were other issues to face. Simon said that the clinic looked more like a factory. Did I really want to end my life in a country I didn't know? How was that going to feel? I couldn't imagine it. And Tom, Corrinna and Simon would then have to come back to Ireland without me. Yet I would *have* to rely on my family; I couldn't do it without them. Suddenly it didn't seem so simple.

We went ahead and planned it. Tom booked me a space in Dignitas for the following month. We couldn't delay because I had to go before my health became much worse. At that stage I was mobile. I could move my hands; I could shift around and walk a little. I could still swallow. To help someone perform rational suicide, they have to drink some liquid. As my illness progressed and my throat muscles weakened, the ability to swallow would go. Therefore the option of Dignitas would no longer be available. There seemed to be no choice.

We continued to discuss Dignitas; for a while we talked of nothing else. Tom said that it didn't worry *him* that it was illegal but we both worried about the effect prosecution could have on Corrinna and Simon. How could they risk going to prison when they had children of their own? We talked long and hard about the likely outcome and about whether the gardaí would take an interest in our actions. Tom felt that if ten people went to Dignitas with me, maybe they would be less likely to be prosecuted than if it was just one or two. We wondered about the doctors who provided the report and the travel agent who might organise the trip. Would they be liable to be prosecuted as well? And if the airline knows where you are going, are they breaking the law by helping that person onto the flight? Technically, I suppose they are.

Finally we bit the bullet. Tom booked me into Dignitas. We were going on a Tuesday to see them on the Wednesday but he had not yet got around to booking our flights. I could see that Tom didn't like the idea of it. He didn't say so but he became a little remote. That is his way of coping. Tom describes it as a wall he has to put up. He developed it earlier in his life when times were tough.

'I am on one side of the wall and everything else is on the other,' he says.

Sometimes when he uses that tactic he can come across as hard and unfeeling.

'I face the thing head on but my emotions are not involved,' he explains. 'Then when I am on my own I can feel the bricks falling off the wall, one by one.'

We had spent hours making the arrangements and discussing the emotions of it all. One afternoon we were talking about Corrinna and Simon. I asked Tom if he thought they would feel able to be there and, if they were, how would they cope with that? 'Would it be worse for them staying at home knowing it was happening, or being there seeing me die?' We hadn't yet told them of our definite plan; we had been putting that bit off. And we had never really teased that out with them. The more I thought about it, the more I worried.

I was brooding about it when Tom brought in a tray with tea and some biscuits. He put my mug down on the side table and took my hands in his.

'Marie,' he said, looking me in the eye, 'do you really want to die now?'

'No,' I said. 'Not really. Not in an ideal world. But, Tom, if I don't die now I'll have no option for a peaceful death.'

'Marie, there has to be another option.'

'But how? What? Tell me.'

He dropped my hands, stood up and turned away. 'I don't know.' He sighed, audibly. 'But I will find a way. If I do, Marie, will you cancel Dignitas?'

'You have a month.'

His body visibly relaxed. I don't know where he went for information but he came back to me within a couple of days.

'Well? *Have* you found an alternative?'

'I haven't found a method,' he said. 'But I have come across the organisation Dignity in Dying in England.'

'Who are they?'

'They are conservative, and exist to get the law changed.'

'What does that mean?'

'It means they don't provide information or help people to die but they told me that there are organisations that do help. And there are people out there who have helped themselves.'

'So what are you saying?'

'I'm saying I will help you. I promise. I promise that you *will* have a peaceful death, even if you don't go to Dignitas.'

'Can you guarantee that?'

'Yes. Absolutely.'

'You guarantee that I won't have to suffer and it won't be prolonged?'

'You have my absolute promise. If we don't go to Dignitas, I give you my assurance you can die at home, peacefully, when you choose.'

'Oh, Tom.' We hugged each other tightly. I cried, and I'm pretty sure Tom did too.

I knew it was a difficult promise for Tom to make. And I understood that he meant it sincerely, even though he didn't know how it was going to be achieved. He agreed because he loves me and would do anything for me.

'I never liked the idea of Dignitas,' he said.

I had known that. Poor Tom. I could sense his relief when I decided not to go. He says he wants me to be around forever. I think he would agree to anything to prevent me from dying too soon.

I slept well that night. I felt as light as air. For months and years I had been worrying about my death and if it would be a bad one. Once I got the assurance that I wouldn't have to die badly, I could get on with living.

With Dignitas fading into the background, I could live on. It was nothing but a relief for me but it made the situation more serious for Tom. Helping me to die was going to be a criminal offence, much more serious than helping me onto a plane for Switzerland. I asked him frequently if he was sure he was prepared to risk it.

'I've no choice,' he said. 'It's as simple as that. I know people find it hard to understand. I want you to stay alive irrespective of what suffering you have. But that is selfish. It is for my benefit and only for mine. It is your decision whether you want to stay or not, not mine. Of course your going will affect me. But your staying will affect *you*.'

In 2009 I heard on the radio that there was to be an Exit International meeting in Dublin. Exit International is a voluntary euthanasia, assisted suicide, information and advocacy organisation that was founded by the Australian physician Dr Philip Nitschke in 1997. Philip was over here to lead the meeting. There was a lot of controversy about it. Many people felt he should not be allowed to speak.

I was already aware of the organisation. Tom had found out about them when he was digging around but he hadn't got around to contacting them. I asked Tom to attend the meeting on my behalf and he agreed. He said, 'I had planned to go anyway.'

'Well, why didn't you say?'

'I wanted to wait until I had heard what he had to say. I didn't want to get your hopes up in case it was bad news.'

We both thought that it would be a small meeting. There was no debate in Ireland about assisted suicide back then. It is not a subject that Irish people tend to talk about. There was a lot of controversy in the media, and the organisers had problems finding a venue. It ended up in a community centre, but when Tom arrived, early, there were already fifty people there. That was the first shock. The second was that Corrinna was sitting in the second row. She was clearly as surprised to see Tom there as he was to see her. Tom said she was upset – but, then, so was he. He said that they held each other's hand for comfort.

By the time the meeting started, it was standing room only. Tom thought that maybe people were there to protest because in this Catholic country Philip Nitschke and his organisation are viewed with a great deal of suspicion, but when the meeting commenced it was clear that everyone in the audience was genuine and that they were looking for information for loved ones, just as we were. I had thought we were acting in a vacuum.

Tom wasn't altogether reassured by what he heard. From the questions people were asking, it was clear that helping someone to die in a peaceful, painless way is not an easy thing to do. And it is harder still if they are unable physically to help themselves. I was no longer a case for assisted suicide. We were now talking about assisted euthanasia; in other words, someone else, in this case Tom, would have to actually kill me. That, obviously, is a much more contentious issue.

By this time I was having problems with my swallow; I could manage my pills, although sometimes I would choke, and I ate slowly and with difficulty. I could never have managed the amount of fluid or tablets needed to end my life. Therefore Tom had to know whether there was an alternative method, suitable for someone like me. And it turned out that there was. I could be given an inert gas like helium or nitrogen. To work, these gases need an oxygen-free environment, so I would have to have a bag over my head. While it was reassuring to know that there was a method, we both hated the idea of it.

There were a few reporters at the meeting. Tom recognised Orla Barry from Newstalk, and when Philip Nitschke had wound up the meeting, the coordinator said, 'Is anyone prepared to talk to the media? They would love to hear your impressions of the meeting and to ask you why you are here.'

Tom checked with Corrinna and then approached Philip and

his girlfriend Fiona and said that he would be happy to talk. He assumed there would be a lot of people volunteering. He felt no hesitation since he had nothing. As it turned out he was the only person who came forward. He was to join Philip Nitschke on Orla Barry's show. He left the car where he had parked it near the meeting and shared a taxi to the Newstalk studio with Philip, Fiona and Orla.

Philip and Fiona were discussing their impressions of Ireland and of the meeting. It had been tricky to set it up. Three hotels had accepted the booking for the meeting, only to cancel when they realised what the subject matter was. 'That community centre was a joke,' said Philip. 'I'm amazed anyone could find it.' He had a point. It was down an alleyway off Mountjoy Square, not the most salubrious area of Dublin. 'It looked as if we were purposely hiding,' he said.

Fiona agreed. 'But the response was phenomenal,' she said. 'Far greater than we expected. We could really do with someone to organise things for us in Ireland.'

None of this was being directed at Tom; they were just chatting among themselves. But when they arrived at the studio in Digges Lane, in the centre of Dublin, and were waiting in the green room to be called into the studio, Tom found himself saying, 'I couldn't help overhearing your conversation in the taxi.' Philip looked puzzled. 'About the need for a contact person in Dublin?'

'Oh, that conversation.'

'I'll do it.'

'What?' Philip looked astounded. 'Are you serious?'

'Yes. I was surprised by the number of people who turned up

too,' Tom said. 'And by the number of people who are looking for information. I'd be happy to help.'

'That's fine then,' said Philip.

They did the show, and Tom talked about me and my case. I was listening at home with very mixed emotions. I was proud of Tom. He spoke well and fluently and put his point clearly, but it was the first time I had heard myself talked about on radio. I wasn't sure that I liked it.

When Tom gave that radio interview, it didn't occur to him, or to me, that assisted euthanasia was something he should keep quiet about. After the show the *Irish Daily Mail* called. This was the first time Tom had any contact with the media; he was an innocent. They rang Tom and talked to him and he chatted freely, but he never realised that his words would appear on the front page of the *Irish Mail on Sunday*. There was this huge headline. It said something like, 'I Am Prepared to End Marie's Life'.

Perhaps we should not have been surprised when the gardaí got in touch. But, innocents that we were, it was the last thing we were expecting. A detective sergeant from Wicklow called and said, 'You do realise that helping someone to die is breaking the law?'

'Well, technically ...'

'Mr Curran, we have to talk to you.'

'Do you?'

'There have been a lot of complaints about this. Can we arrange a suitable time, please?'

Tom was a bit taken aback. He expected this to be a forty-five minute chat at most but as it turned out he was in for two sessions of three hours each. I don't know how worried Tom was, but I was terrified the threats of prosecution would make him go back on his word. I should have known better.

First of all the gardaí reiterated that what Tom was suggesting meant that he was breaking the law. And that if he carried out his promise to help me to end my life, he could be imprisoned for murder. Serious though that was, the knowledge didn't make him change his mind. As he said to me afterwards, 'All I would be losing is my liberty. If I refused you, you would be losing much more than that. You would lose your right to choose to die when the time was right.'

The gardaí had to explore all possibilities and motivations including whether Tom had any additional agenda. They asked him about money and if he would benefit financially from my death. That is laughable. Anybody who knows us realises we have used up any resources we once had. There is no financial gain for Tom; there won't be any money for our children or grandchildren when Tom and I are gone. We were shocked that the Garda Síochána would think we had a motive like that.

Meanwhile, Philip Nitschke and Fiona had flown off and nothing happened for quite a while. Tom organised the Irish membership for them and got all the paperwork to the people who had attended the meeting and who had left addresses. That was the only involvement he had in Exit International back then.

Nine months later Philip and Fiona came back to Europe but not to Ireland. They had a meeting in London and in a few other cities around the UK. They asked Tom to fly to London and to travel around with them. He did that. They were formulating a plan for mainland Europe at the time but, with the language differences, that never really materialised.

The second time Philip came to Ireland was in March 2011. On that occasion Tom got a call from RTÉ's *Late Late Show*. They wanted to record a programme on Exit International and asked him to contact Philip Nitschke for them. He told them that Philip had already left Ireland and was now in Germany. They then asked him if he would go on the show as his spokesperson. He said he wouldn't; he didn't know enough about the organisation. So they agreed to fly Philip back from Germany.

They planned a panel with Philip, Tom and a barrister. Tom arranged to stay with Corrinna, but half an hour before he was due to leave for the show, he heard that the barrister had been removed from the panel. He found that strange.

When he arrived at the RTÉ television studio, Philip was already there. Tom told him that the format of the show had changed, and they took the researcher aside. He said, 'The producer has decided we want Dr Nitschke on the stage alone; you, Mr Curran, will be in the audience. We will call on you to tell your story.'

This worried them. They wondered if the show was trying to introduce some controversy. Tom and Philip were not due to appear until the very last section. Tom wasn't in the audience until then. He and Philip were in the wings looking in and he could pick out a dozen people who are well known for their right-wing views. He was worried and he told Philip so. Philip patted him on the shoulder. 'Don't worry, Tom,' he said. 'I can handle this. I'm well enough used to controversy.'

Tom got off lightly. Ryan Tubridy was nice, and most sympathetic to him, and the audience too were sympathetic to my story. But Philip was attacked from all sides. Tom felt that it was a set-up.

With Tom out fighting my cause, I got to spend some precious time alone with Corrinna. We talked for hours, and she has told me how emotional it is for her, watching each stage of my illness as it progresses. 'I've always felt so helpless,' she said. 'Simon and I were terrified when you had your first acute attack; we were terrified when you had to get the steroids, terrified when your mobility started to go.'

'Terrified? For yourselves?'

'No, for you. We couldn't bear to see the way it affected you.' She paused, obviously choosing her words. 'Though I suppose your reaction had an effect on us too. It did rather set the tone in the house. Do you remember, Mum, that time you arrived off a flight at Heathrow with Simon and Tom, and I was there to meet you? I was so worried that you would have been struggling with the walk from the aircraft. And the next thing, I looked and I gasped, because Tom was pushing you in a wheelchair with Simon walking beside you!'

I laughed. 'It was an airport wheelchair.'

'That's right. And I thought, Oh my God. I stopped breathing. I thought you would be really down. I thought you'd be thinking, this is the end.'

I *do* remember that incident. I remember that when Tom appeared with the wheelchair, I was about to protest. But he didn't give me a chance to. He made it seem like nothing at all. He treated it all as a matter of fact and so I just accepted it. It didn't feel like the end of the world.

'Simon and I would have been walking on eggshells,' said Corrinna. 'We would have been afraid to mention the elephant in the room. Whereas Tom said it as it was. "Your mobility is going. You need this to get your independence.'

'Has it been hard for you, pet? Watching my deterioration?'

She nodded. 'That's the problem with a chronic illness like MS, isn't it? We were all so busy worrying about new symptoms. If we had known what was to come, we would have focused more on the good times. And we never took that trip to Eastern Europe that I bought for your fortieth birthday.'

She was right. The idea was for us to go together. But I kept saying, 'Let's wait until I am better. Then we'll go.' But I only ever got worse. I wish I had focused on the relatively good health I was enjoying back then.

It is good to hear Corrinna talking so frankly. But it does make me feel a little guilty that I have relied on her so much. There was that terrible weekend in 2004 when my hands stopped working. Tom had had to feed me all weekend. I was so upset. Corrinna rang me that evening and I couldn't hide my tears. I said, 'I can't go on.' It was what I was feeling, but I scared Corrinna so much. I've made sure never to make that mistake again.

I hope Corrinna knows how much her support means to me. I have told her. I remember the conversation on that other sad weekend when we first discussed my exit plan. We had been reminiscing about Wales and I said, 'Corrinna, darling, you saved me. Without you I could have been dead a long time ago.' I meant that her being around helped me to carry on.

'I hated it when you talked about Dignitas,' she said.

'Yes. That was hard for us all.'

'I remember worrying about leaving you there. I couldn't imagine flying home without you after all that trauma.'

She said she'd felt happier when my plans changed. Until she attended the Exit International meeting and started worrying about methodologies. 'That meeting was horrible, Mum. I'm glad you didn't have to sit through it. Especially when I thought you might die with a bag over your head.' She shuddered.

'Until I went to that meeting, I didn't realise people had been prosecuted. I remember Philip Nitschke told the story of a woman who had helped her son, a heroin addict in England, and she was prosecuted. When we gave you our assurance, we thought it was a simple matter of helping someone you love. We didn't realise we could end up behind bars.'

'I wouldn't ever let that happen.'

'I realise that now.'

'It will be Tom and me doing this. You and Simon will not be involved. As parents, you can't be.'

Corrinna began to cry. Helping herself to a tissue, she dabbed at her eyes. 'I can't imagine what my life will be like without you, Mum. Ever since I was a baby there has always been you and me. You have always been there for me.'

'Careful, Corrinna, or you'll have me crying too.'

'But ever since your MS has got worse, I have felt a sense of grief.'

'I'm sorry, darling. So sorry.'

'You know how you usually start grieving when someone dies? I have a feeling that moment might be the beginning of the end of my grief.' She sobbed, and blew her nose. 'Because, Mum, I am grieving already for this lost life, this lost relationship.'

'You're still my darling daughter. My perfect daughter.'

'Oh, Mum. And you are still very much my mum. And very much a grandmother to my children, but …'

'There's an element of grief because of what I can't do. I know. It hurts me every day.'

'But you do you realise how important you are? And how much input you have into my parenting?'

'I'm glad, pet.'

'When I'm stressed about the children, you and Tom calm me down and talk me through the situation. Your advice is crucial. And you're constantly telling me what a good job Richard and I are doing. I really need that. Being a mother can be so difficult.'

I laughed. 'Especially when they are coming up to their teens.'

'You and Tom keep me buoyed up.'

'I'm glad you feel that way.'

It was a relief to hear her talk like that. It makes me feel that my legacy will live on through her parenting, and knowing that will make it easier for me when the time comes to end my life.

CHAPTER THIRTEEN
PREPARING A CASE

ഇൽ

Life has not always been kind to me, but in one way I am blessed. After two failed marriages I have the love of a good, caring man. Tom is such an integral part of my life. I wouldn't have a life without him. I am also blessed in my children. Corrinna has been a rock for me, someone who is always there, always rooting for me. I don't know how I would have managed my life without her.

Corrinna has taught me more over the years than anyone else. From her I have learned the meaning of unconditional love. She always showed such compassion, taking on a motherly role in looking after both me and Simon when care and comfort were needed. She and her husband Richard have helped me financially too. They have given me a dig-out when money was scarce. She is a beautiful human being, an unselfish daughter, wife and mother. She gives of herself relentlessly, regardless of cost, and believe me, there have been costs paid.

Corrinna is an inspiration. She gave up a fulfilling career to be with her babies full-time. I really admire her for that. 'I don't want to be dragging them out to a nursery at the crack of dawn so that someone else sees that first step,' she said. So she stayed at home nurturing and stimulating her five children. And she never forgot to give me some care too. She encouraged me in my painting and my writing. 'Mum, whatever you want to do, I'll be behind you all the way,' she said. And I know that's true. I was so pleased when she told me she was moving back to Ireland from London. She and Richard made sure to have the house in Dalkey fitted out with ramps so that I would be able to visit her there without a problem. The house has a granny flat too.

Simon is a constant support. He means so much to me, and my illness has perhaps been hardest of all on him. He has had to deal with my ups and downs since his childhood, and was forced to take responsibility so young. He is my golden boy, visiting me as often as he can and always making sure to stay in touch on the phone, checking that everything is ok. I am so proud of him, and only wish I could still make the trip to Waterford.

I have also been lucky in all my grandchildren. I've laughed with them, told them stories, given them the odd bit of forbidden chocolate and raced around the garden with them in Hot Rod.

Then there's Scruffy, our terrier-type mongrel who we never planned to own. He is now my constant companion. There's a story about that. When age began to catch up with my spaniel Ben, I told Tom that when he died I didn't want another dog. Nobody could take the place of my beloved Ben. But one day this strange little creature turned up in the garden. Ben was normally territorial but he didn't bark at the dog. He sniffed it and put up with it being on his patch. Tom thought that if he chased it the dog would go home, but he would creep back when Tom's back was turned, tail between his legs.

We asked around the neighbourhood to see if anyone had lost a dog but were told he had been spotted miles away. He was just a stray. Someone else claimed that they saw a car stop and someone throw the dog into the road and drive away. We never knew if that was true, but he kept coming to our garden and would not leave.

One morning Tom got up, went to the kitchen and shouted, 'I don't believe it. That scruffy fecker is *still* here.'

I felt sorry for the dog. He was dirty, with matted hair. I asked Tom to give him a wash and a brush. He looked a whole lot better afterwards and he licked Tom as if he was trying to say, 'Thank you.' We hadn't the heart to chase him away again. Ben seemed happy to have him around so we kept him, and the name Scruffy just stuck. Shortly after that Ben got sick and we had to put him down. It broke my heart. We would never have gone out to get a new dog, but having Scruffy around was a huge comfort. There is no doubt that the dog picked us.

಄಄಄

The deterioration in my health has accelerated in recent years. In 2006 when my father died I was too weak to go to his funeral. That upset me so much. I wrote a letter for Corrinna to read out but I grieved for months. I missed Daddy terribly – we had been so close – but it also made me look to the future, to my own death.

I gained great solace from the Reverend George Butler. George and I had become friends after he officiated at Corrinna's wedding. The twins and then Lorcan had been baptised in his church, and George had taken to visiting me. I told him that I was scared of the practicalities of my death now that I had broken with the Catholic Church. I realised I could not be buried near my father.

'Marie, you are always welcome in our church,' he said. 'You don't even have to ask.' That gave me the greatest reassurance. Now that I am too weak to go to church, George comes to the house now and then to give me communion.

It took twenty-four years for the MS, or creeping paralysis as I call it, to reach the stage where I am totally immobile in both my arms and legs. To the stage where everything had to be done for me, from washing, toileting, feeding and drinking. I feel like a trapped butterfly in a garden where there is no pollen. And we can't live forever without sustenance and freedom. I have no dignity. And sometimes I dissociate from real life.

There are times when I don't want to face the world. At those times I am difficult to be around. My carers are so good to me. They are patient and understanding always. And I would never dream of criticising them. But there are little things that annoy me. If they forget to rinse out my toothbrush, I will be upset for days and I take it out on Tom. He says, 'Why don't you just tell them that you are upset about it?' He says it's much worse if it comes from him because then they resent it. 'The trouble with you, Marie, is that you are a people pleaser.' He's always saying that. And maybe he's right.

Having MS isn't just a matter of losing your physical strength. The mental strength that I need for everyday living is becoming harder to find. I am told that I am one of the lucky ones because my brain is still active. And the last thing I want is to get to the stage of vegetating in front of a window all day. So I imagine myself running through fields or cycling for miles. I dance the night away. In my head I am the feisty woman I always was – determined, capable, with a great strength that others came to for advice. That's me. So I don't want sympathy. I was just the unfortunate person to get an illness early on in life. That's all.

In 2010 I nearly died. I was in bed with a severe kidney infection and my breathing was laboured and shallow. It got so bad that our doctor, Anne Marie, had to get me some oxygen. Without it I could barely breathe.

I've had infections since then. I had one a few weeks ago but nothing quite as bad as the one I'm talking about; I ended up with pneumonia, and for someone with MS that is one of the most dangerous things that can happen. It is the biggest killer.

One night my heart stopped and Tom had to revive me. I didn't know that until later, but something very strange happened. One minute I was in bed, in our room, and the next I was looking through this tunnel. At the very top of it was my father. He was standing with Ben, the spaniel I had loved so much. They were so clear. Behind Ben was this bright light, shining from the heavens. I thought: this is where the angels must be.

Everything was gentle. It was such a beautiful feeling after all the discomfort and pain. I wanted to stay there. Then Ben began to run towards me. I was so excited to see him, I bent down, ready to put my arms round him, but before he reached me he stopped and turned back. And I could hear Tom calling me from somewhere in the distance. Then I woke up and it was another day.

I have a strong faith. I've lost patience with the trappings of the Catholic Church but I still hold strong beliefs; I *know* there is a heaven. I always knew that. But since that night I have been convinced of it. And I am not now afraid of death. I know it will be beautiful and I will go to a better place.

I remember very little from that time but Tom has since filled me in on his side of the story. It always worries him when I am sick. As time goes on, the infections get worse and there is less time between them. He describes that illness in 2010 as a terrible time and a particular shock. He was convinced he would lose me.

'You were delirious for about three days. The one thing I kept asking you was, "Do you want to die?"'

'And I kept saying, '"No."'

'So I was determined to keep you alive.'

Some people don't see the logic in that. Tom has been asked many times why he didn't just let me die that night. It's very simple. I didn't want to. I don't have a death wish. I want to live, but I don't want to die painfully. That's the difference between what I would call irrational suicide and assisted suicide. And it's a big difference. That night, though, Tom almost lost me. I stopped breathing, and he gave me the kiss of life and massaged my heart for an hour. That happened twice. And he kept me breathing.

The following day, Tom called Corrinna and Simon. They had known that I was ill and they were already in a heightened state of worry. Tom told them that they had better come over quickly. They made the calls to my family in the North and within six hours everyone was here. They were all convinced that I was going to die. But I pulled through.

As Tom said, 'Thank God you pulled through, with our help.'

It was after that scare that the seeds were sown for me to take a case in the courts to allow me the right to die, in my own time, with Tom's help. To me, it is all about my rights.

A few days later, when I had got over the worst, I almost ran out of oxygen. It has always been a problem to get oxygen for home use. We have to rely on the goodness of our doctor; she gives us some from her supply at the surgery. But there is a limit to the amount she could give us. And the only way to get oxygen in a hurry is to phone an ambulance.

That was a problem. Tom couldn't just call 999, because if he did I would have been taken to hospital. And he knew that that was the very last thing I wanted. So he went to the ambulance station in Arklow, leaving me alone. He rang the bell but both ambulances were out. He then went to the gardaí and explained the situation, and then came home. The ambulance service had no obligation to give us oxygen, but fortunately they agreed. Shortly afterwards a fellow from the ambulance rang Tom asking for directions to our house. He came out, and they swapped the oxygen canisters. Tom was so relieved because there was very little oxygen left at that stage.

It is a constant struggle for Tom to keep me at home. All the medical people want to put me in hospital but I don't want that; it's simply not an option for me. It is a particular problem when I have a crisis in off-duty hours. That night, if Tom had rung Care Doc, the GP out-of-hours service, they would have wanted to call an ambulance. It's a mammoth problem.

When the crisis was over, Tom rang our GP, Anne Marie. He had not slept for three nights and three days at that stage. At the best of times, sleeping is difficult for him. He is scared to sleep in case I stop breathing. I tell him not to worry so much but he says, 'One day I will wake up and find that your breathing has stopped. And when you are sick it is ten times worse.' Anne Marie then organised for the palliative care team to come and sit with me. After a discussion, they changed the whole regime of my medicine.

During that time Tom had some stomach problems. He had a terrible pain but he was so worried about me that he ignored it. He assumed it was down to tension. But on a Sunday afternoon a couple of weeks after my illness, he was at a rehearsal for a play in Arklow. I had got him involved in the amateur company, Masquerade. He is in charge of sound effects. This was a week before the play was due to start.

He didn't feel well and suddenly vomited all over the place, which messed up the rehearsal. Everyone was concerned but, being Tom, he said he was fine. In fact he had a very severe pain in his stomach. The director, Kevin, realised there was a real problem and said, 'Tom, I'll get you home.' Tom insisted on driving, but Kevin drove behind him. They had to stop twice on the way so that Tom could vomit. He was sick again the minute they reached the house and Kevin said, 'I'm calling Care Doc.' He rang them and they told him to bring Tom in. By the time they had got there, Care Doc, worried about Tom's symptoms, had called an ambulance and Tom was taken to Loughlinstown Hospital.

He was on a trolley in Accident and Emergency for three days. The doctors were performing test after test but could find nothing. They were treating him with painkillers. On the second day a doctor came in and said, 'I'm going to test you for pancreatitis.' He had had it himself and thought he recognised the symptoms. And it turned out that he was right. When they tested Tom for elevated enzymes, he had a reading of over 600. The doctor was astonished.

'Is that high?' Tom asked.

'Normal is 40 to 50,' the doctor explained. 'When we see a reading of 120 we consider that a severe case. So yes, 600 is extremely high. You have obviously been ignoring your symptoms for some time, Mr Curran.'

Tom was immediately put onto treatment, which essentially was antibiotics, painkillers and no food.

Corrinna stayed with Tom all the time he was in Accident and Emergency. She knew that I was frantic with worry, so she stayed there until his condition stabilised. Then she spent her nights in the cottage with me, and visited Tom during the day. Meanwhile, she organised a rota of carers and neighbours to look after me. She assured me that Tom was all right. I knew that she would have said that anyway, to stop me from fretting.

I knew that Tom would be worried about me too so I told Corrinna to assure him that I was being looked after well. And I was. Even so, I knew he would fret. And he did. 'I worried about your tablets,' he said afterwards. He always gets my tablets ready in the morning and he was convinced that nobody else knew which ones I was supposed to take when. 'I remember lying on that trolley fretting about that,' he said.

And in truth I *did* miss Tom. I missed him more than I can say. Looking after me is second nature to him now and that gives me a great sense of security. When Tom goes away, for whatever reason, I feel insecure and vulnerable. And that time, worrying about him, it was so very much worse.

He came home with a wealth of stories. 'I was kept amused by the conversations going on around me,' he said. 'One man was concerned about his methadone. He was trying to arrange for a friend to collect it and deliver it to the hospital. Another was giving money to someone to buy heroin for him, to be brought in.'

After three days Tom was transferred to a ward. It was the coldest winter and he couldn't sleep. They gave him sleeping pills but he sat up all night worrying about me. 'I remember watching the dawn over the hills behind Loughlinstown and they were white with frost. People were coming in saying, "Jesus, the roads are bad."' That gave him another worry. Was I snowed in? He imagined me in a hospital somewhere. He didn't believe any of the people who assured him that I was not.

The consultant noticed that he was anxious. He said, 'I can't treat you when you are in this state.' He contacted the social worker and she phoned her colleague in Wicklow, who sent back a message that I was being cared for at home and was well.

Tom got home two weeks before Christmas. It was such a

relief to have him back with me. He was well again but he was weak, and had lost a phenomenal amount of weight. The minute he walked through the front door he noticed that my dressing needed attention. He got me up on the bed and changed it, and it was as if he had never been gone at all.

Two days afterwards we *were* snowed in. The roads was packed hard and at first only a tractor could get through. Danny Somers from down the road came to our rescue. He drove to Tesco on his tractor to do everyone's shopping. Even when it thawed, we were stranded. There was compacted ice on the road and we couldn't get out of either gate.

During that time RTÉ wanted Tom to go to the studio in Donnybrook for an interview. He told them that he couldn't get in there but they didn't believe him, because there had been a thaw in Dublin. Tom said, 'You come up to me, then.' And they said they would. They got as far as a mile outside Arklow and couldn't get any further. They reported the bad road conditions and it was mentioned on the news. Shortly afterwards we heard from the helicopter service. They wanted to know if we needed airlifting out. We said we were fine but they gave us the direct number of the crew in case of an emergency.

That was such a stressful time but it gave us time to reflect on our need for each other. In some strange way Tom being sick helped me to regain my strength. I had to get better so that he could recover his strength without the added burden that my infections bring.

I try not to think too much about the way my body has deteriorated; it makes me too sad. But it is hard, especially when I look at photographs of the way I used to look. One of my favourite photographs is of me and Tom walking Ben on the beach at Clogga. It was taken when we had first met, and the contrast between that photo and the 'me' of today is so great. Physically I look quite different to the way I looked when I walked darling Corrinna down the aisle. It's a combination of my ageing and the MS.

A lot of people don't realise how infirm I am. They think it is just my legs and my hands that don't work. I don't think they realise that I am like a dead weight. I can't do anything for myself. My head stays where it is put. It was brought home to me when my youngest grandchild, Cara, was born. I looked at her in wonder. I watched the way the newborn Cara was trying to hold up her head. I said, 'Isn't that amazing? Cara has more body ability and strength than I have. And she's only a few days old.'

Life is especially hard when I have an infection. I can't see Corrinna and Simon but we still need to speak. And the problem is that in those circumstances we can never have a private conversation. Someone has to hold the phone for me and we talk on speaker phone. I find that really hard.

Simon finds my illness especially hard to bear. He hates thinking about my death, and because I want to die in my own time, there's the constant focus on it. I hate to put the children through that.

When we are all together it doesn't hit us. The grandchildren are a distraction. I'll chat to them and they chat to me and the conversation is much more lighthearted. It is when it is just Corrinna or Simon and me that it is more difficult. We keep thinking about my passing and what we have to say to each other before I go. That's really hard.

When they have gone home, I sometimes have a good cry. I know that Corrinna does too. She says she has to process our conversation and the feelings it evokes before she can function as a mother. But we try hard not to break down in front of each other.

Since March 2013, when my health took a turn for the worse, I've been more aware that time is short. When I tell the children I love them, I do so with more intensity. When I am especially unwell it feels really important that they should remember me saying it. It's a kind of insurance. Just in case it is the last time I see them.

Until Tom became involved with Exit International, he had not realised how difficult helping me to die with dignity might be. When I had first told him that I wanted him to help me, he hoped we could call on a doctor to administer an injection, but that was not to be. It was going to be a difficult process both from both a physical and a legal point of view.

I remember early on, when Tom mentioned my wishes to a neurologist, he was told in no uncertain terms to leave his office. He said, 'The medical profession don't discuss things like that.' He was horrified. It seemed nobody ever talked about the issue. Tom and I felt that was wrong.

Tom was familiar with Article 40 of the Constitution, which concentrates on a person's rights, and he felt I should have the right to die. He has always been an activist and has been involved in civil rights worldwide. This started in college in Leicester when he noticed there was no counselling for students; he set up a group and got in volunteers to provide reduced-fee or free counselling for students. After his return to Ireland in 1966 he became involved in the Dublin Housing Action Committee, and he was a Samaritan for years. When I became ill and he realised the difficulties carers in Ireland were having, he became involved with The Carers Association too.

Once Tom was involved with Exit International, it was inevitable that my case would become public. One night he was interviewed by Miriam O'Callaghan on television and they showed pictures of me. I didn't like that. I hadn't wanted any campaign to be about me but I felt it was important that Tom should carry on with the right to die issue, so when he asked me if I was happy about it I said yes, I was more than happy.

That's when he began to research the right to die issue. He realised that in the Ward of Court case in 1996 it had been proven that a person had a right to refuse medical treatment even if the consequence was that they would die. In other words, the courts could not prevent you from refusing even if it meant in effect taking your own life. He wondered if refusing food and water could be considered in the same category as refusing medical treatment. Could a person legally die of starvation in a public institution?

He checked the Constitution and it seemed to him that in a particular section of Article 40, it specifically said that a person would not be discriminated against on grounds of race, being a member of a minority group or – and the bit that interested him – disability. In 1993 the law was changed and stated that a person has a legal right to commit suicide. That is a right, a legal entitlement. Yet if someone has a disability, that means they are unable to take their own life. So it seemed to him that those rights were in conflict.

Tom believed it would be a perfect case for the High Court.

He did all this research himself, in the background, and discussed it with people who are involved in human rights. Then he approached me and we talked about it. I urged him to go ahead. It was a way of legalising his helping me. He had made his promise to me and the last thing I wanted was for him to be prosecuted. Tom approached a couple of lawyers who had been involved in taking cases on issues of civil rights and liberties but they wouldn't consider it. They said nobody would take a case of assisted suicide. He approached people several times over a few years but the answer was always the same. He was told to go away.

The one person who was always supportive was Noeline Blackwell from FLAC (Free Legal Advice Centres). She explained that the organisation could not actively help Tom unless and until he had been prosecuted. If it came to that, they would be happy to assist him. Meanwhile, she said she was right behind our cause. She spoke to barristers on our behalf but she got the same feedback as Tom: nobody was prepared to take a case. 'It's all to do with the Catholic Church,' she said. 'While they are so strongly against assisted suicide, no lawyer will contemplate addressing the issue.'

In June 2012 Tom was asked to speak at the World Federation of Right to Die societies. They meet every two years and that year the event was in Zurich. He talked about our desire to have the law changed in Ireland and also of our conviction that the current Constitution in Ireland could be interpreted to mean that a disabled person already had a right to die and therefore a right to be assisted to die.

Among the delegates at the conference was a Canadian called Russell Ogden, head of the Farewell Foundation for the Right to Die. Tom had already been in contact with him by phone and email and they went out to dinner together. He told Tom that there was currently a case, similar to the one we wished to take, before the courts in British Columbia. Gloria Taylor, a 64-year-old woman with terminal ALS, or Lou Gehrig's disease, was seeking permission to the right to have a doctor to help her with an assisted suicide. They were waiting for the verdict. And while they were still at the conference, he heard that she had been granted a constitutional exemption and would be able to proceed. They had a huge celebration.

Russell knew that Tom had tried, and failed, to take a case in Ireland, so of course they discussed the issue. They compared the constitutions of Ireland and British Columbia and found that they were almost identical. The wording was slightly different but the concept was the same. That made Tom extremely angry. If they could take a case in Canada, why had they been so reluctant in Ireland? He came home ready to slate everybody.

The minute Tom returned to Ireland we decided to pursue the issue again. He asked around, and the barrister Simon Mills advised him to contact the solicitor Bernadette Parte. She had worked for Amnesty as a human rights campaigner both for and against the Health Service Executive. She and Tom met, and he liked her at once. He found her both helpful and sympathetic. Benedette said, 'I know you hit walls with this in the past but I feel this Canadian judgement will change things here.'

'How so?'

'The last constitutional change made in Ireland, which concerned search warrants, came from a result in Canada.'

'I didn't know that.'

'Canada has always been regarded as a very sensible place. The recent case there will give your proposal legitimacy. Especially as they ruled in favour.'

We were delighted. We had expected the process to take time but she got a team together much faster than we could ever have anticipated. It comprised Brian Murray and Ronan Murphy as the two senior counsel, with Simon Mills as the junior counsel.

CHAPTER FOURTEEN
THE HIGH COURT

಄಄ఙ

Since I first decided that I wanted the right to die, I have had problems knowing how to describe the process. I dislike the word euthanasia, but suicide is not the right word either. Suicide is more hurtful to families. I should know. I have never got over the suicide of my brother Shaun. A psychiatrist once told me that the reason I think about him so often is that I want him back in my life. I want to make better the hurt he suffered when my mother walked out of his life. I feel guilty to this day that I didn't recognise how troubled he was back then.

In my mind what I want to do is *not* suicide. When we had decided against going to Dignitas and Tom said he would help me to die at home when the time came, a weight lifted. A greater friend you could not meet. Since then we have had various ups and downs with my health. When I had pneumonia and nearly died, Tom asked me if I wanted to be saved or not. I chose to be saved. The time was not right. Therefore my submission to court is to save Tom and my children as best I can. I don't want them having to go to prison because they helped to grant me my wish.

I can't drink from either a cup or a glass and I cannot even scratch my own nose without help, so this other assistance is just a means to an end. It is a bit like blowing your own nose instead of being bunged up all day. I take 22 tablets a day, which is 154 a week, around 670 a month, and over 8,000 a year. And not one of those pills will cure my MS. They are all given to help me with the side-effects of my various MS symptoms.

I have intolerable pain but there are other side-effects too. There is my bladder defect, including spasms, and the spasms in my arms and legs. One of my shoulders has collapsed and the other one is starting to buckle. When the MS becomes worse, and it inevitably will, my swallow and my breathing will be even more restricted. According to my consultant at Saint Vincent's Hospital, Professor Tubridy, it is possible I could end up with a perforated lung. Bad as things seem today, there is a lot worse to come.

I have never had a voice. As a child, when I was trying to be a mother to my siblings and my father, I tried shouting for help, but nobody heard me. When I was pregnant, I took an overdose but nobody listened. I hope the court will give me that voice I have always craved.

In July 2012 Tom organised a meeting with a barrister and his team to talk about the possibility of my taking a case to get the law changed, so allowing me the right to have help to take my life. The three gentleman barristers and the lady solicitor, each a member of the Law Society, discussed with me all the aspects of the case. They said it might involve not just going to the High Court but appealing in the Supreme Court and eventually the European Court of Human Rights.

They contended that I was being discriminated against by the state under the Constitution; it does not allow me to opt for assisted suicide. They said that this was a very important case and one they would be more than happy to participate in. They asked me if I would like to proceed, and when I agreed that I would they explained the procedures that would follow. They would issue a notice to the High Court but, they said, the High Court would not be able to decide.

Then came the questions. How did my disability affect everyday living, including my day-to-day routines? Had I thought about the methodology by which I would like to die? I found all this difficult to talk about and extremely emotional. We discussed various methods. I said the most important thing for me would be to die in the arms of Tom with my family nearby. We arrived at three possible methods: taking the drug Nembutal, or one of the two methods using gases.

'Will you be able to attend the court?' the barrister Ronan Murphy asked.

'Not every day,' I said. 'That would be too tiring. But I will attend the first sitting.'

'That's good,' they said, explaining that it would undoubtedly help my case.

'When is the case likely to happen?' I asked. I thought, as did Tom, that it would take a year, if not longer.

But they said it was likely to be pushed through more quickly because I was classed as terminally ill. 'It could be heard as early as August. But we would be waiting longer for the outcome,' they said. They asked me how I felt about the media.

I shuddered. 'I'm not keen for my name and address to be in the public domain,' I said, and they agreed to apply for an injunction stopping the newspapers from identifying me.

'We will do our best, and we will pursue the issue of invasion of privacy,' one of them said. 'But we can't guarantee that some smart-alecky reporter won't turn up on your doorstep.'

'I would absolutely *hate* that to happen,' I said, imagining newspaper and TV reporters swarming all over my haven, my refuge. But I can't bear the idea of Tom suffering because he is prepared to help me die either. I *have* to secure Tom's innocence. I will do anything to make sure that he does not go to prison.

'Taking this case is my decision and mine only,' I stressed to everyone around the table. 'I don't want to have to worry that the minute I am dead my family have to deal with a garda invasion.'

'We understand,' said Ronan. 'And you do realise that this is a landmark case, a case in which history could be made.'

From the moment I met Ronan Murphy I felt happy about taking a case. We had such an open conversation and there was something special about him. He made me feel good. He made me feel as if my case was the most important one he had ever taken.

I felt like Eamon de Valera or Maud Gonne. I liked the idea of being able to leave a legacy, and for my life to have been worth something. It is important too to fight for other people who are in my situation. I *do* worry about my family in Donegal. I don't think they will like this case being in the public domain. But my first allegiance is to Tom, not to them.

When I was first diagnosed with MS I never imagined for a minute that it would ever come to this. But then I never *really* believed that, physically, it would get as bad as it has. I thought that if I told people often enough that I could overcome MS, then that is what would happen. And for the first ten years I really did believe I had got away with it. If only I had known what was ahead.

Now, in 2012, I needed an assessment before the case could proceed. In August I went to Dr Niall Pender, a neuropsychologist at UCD. He asked me to think of as many words as I could starting with an A, an S or a T. I had sixty seconds. Immediately my stomach clenched with nerves. 'Oh, shit,' I said.

'I will take that as your first word,' said Pender.

'Stress, suppository, stamina,' I began. But with ten seconds to go I stopped dead. The words left me, like water flowing downhill. Then I shouted, 'Armalite.' I don't know where that came from. I was bemused. I hadn't realised that my short-term memory was negligible compared to my long-term one.

At the start of September when Dr Pender called in to the house to carry out the second cognitive therapy test I was well prepared. I had practised my words so thoroughly you would have thought I had eaten the thesaurus. I couldn't wait to get started so that I could show him I was a woman of many words.

'We're doing numbers today,' he said, and a knot formed in the pit of my stomach. I couldn't even remember my own home telephone number. He gave me a list of numbers and asked me to recount them chronologically. At first I found this difficult. At five digits I felt angry. But I made myself focus and managed it, even when he got to ten digits. I felt so proud of myself.

There were more memory tests. I thought I had managed them all right, but I didn't expect the compliment that came afterwards. 'Marie, you are one of the most exciting people I have come across in ages,' he said with a smile. 'You are articulate, bright and very, very canny. Your short-term memory is impaired because of the MS but your long-term memory is clear and concise.'

I smiled at my new friend. My day was well and truly made.

ജോൽ

Three weeks later I met with Dr Paul Scully, head of the Department of Psychiatry at Beaumont Hospital. I didn't know what to expect, but he surprised me. He had barely said hello when he asked, 'Do you want to die today?'

That threw me. 'No.' I said. 'The time isn't right.'

'So, Marie, when *will* the time be right?'

'I just know it isn't now. But I will know when the time is right.'

In truth, that time has changed so much since I first made my intention clear. When I made the decision, I thought it would be the end when my hands stopped working. Then I thought it would be when I had to be showered and toileted. But those milestones passed and the time did *not* feel right.

Now I feel it will be when my brain goes, or my speech, or

my swallow, but I don't know which of those is likely to go first. Professor Tubridy cannot tell me that. I have made a contingency plan in my head. If my swallow goes, I will starve to death. I am *not* allowing any feeding tubes, or 'pegs' as they call them. I reckon that after three days the hunger pangs will stop and after ten days lack of water would kill me.

I liked Dr Scully. The minute I heard his Northern twang I felt he was one of my own, and it turned out that he was born twenty miles away from Lifford. Living in Wicklow, I don't meet many northerners, and I miss that.

I felt at home with Dr Scully but that didn't make the conversation any easier. He probed the parts of my life that I am not comfortable with: my childhood and my failed marriages. He was so skilled at this that I ended up telling him much more than I felt I should. His questions sharpened my mind and made me realise that my life could be summed up by one word: betrayal. I had been betrayed first by my mother, then by my two husbands. Hearing myself say this made me feel weak and teary. I asked Tom for a drink. He held the glass up and I sipped, then choked.

Alarmed, Dr Scully jumped to his feet. 'I didn't mean to upset you,' he said.

'It's not you,' I told him, and started to laugh. Our meeting finished in a light-hearted way. But first I had just one question for him. 'Am I mad, then?'

He laughed. 'Most definitely not.'

So I took it that I had nothing to fear from his report. That it would highlight that I am a sane individual.

Later in the week there was another big excitement: Tom was involved in a TV documentary. It talks of his response to my MS and the choices he has made in giving up work to look after me, and his response to my quest for him to help assist me to die should I choose to do it. It was shown in mid-November.

RTÉ came out to interview me. The producer, a beautiful young Norwegian woman, arrived in a fluster, with her driver in tow. She breezed into my living room, camera at the ready. Placing the microphone on top of the camera, she told me to talk freely and naturally. I nearly died.

'What the hell are we going to talk about?' I asked Tom. It terrified me that the microphone would pick up everything I said. In the end we settled on the weather. As we chatted mindlessly, the producer twirled around the living room like a ballet dancer. Then when we had settled, she started on her questions.

'Marie, what would you say to people who don't agree with your decision?'

That was easy. 'Just let them come and live my life for twelve hours and *then* tell me I should not be allowed to die when the time is right.' After that the interview flowed.

'Oh, well done. That was great,' she said, switching off the camera.

'Is that it?'

'For you, yes,' she said. 'I will edit it when I get back to the office.'

Then I began to worry. I knew this programme was sympathetic, but suppose my words were picked up and used by an unscrupulous producer in the future.

'Don't worry, Marie,' she said, seeing my unease. 'I won't let this out of my sight. And I'll make sure it doesn't find its way into the archives.'

I settled then. I liked her enormously. Her professionalism, clarity and empathy shone.

Before the case even began, it started to impact on my family. It was reported in the papers. When Corrinna called in, having seen the articles, she cried. She sat here and sobbed. 'It was seeing your photo in the paper,' she said. 'It brought it all home.'

Simon has been affected too. His boss had called him in and said, 'Is that your mother in the paper?' He rang me to tell me and said he was sad. He was finding it hard coming to terms with it all. Of course that worried me because there is nothing more important than taking care of my family. They didn't ask me to stop the case. They are fully behind me in my decision. But they worry, as do I, that the newspapers will sensationalise it.

∞∞∞

Around that time our solicitor, Bernadette Parte, came down to the house to take a statement from Tom and me about methodologies. 'We have to talk about the methods you plan to use that will end your life, Marie,' she said.

I explained the three methods Tom and I had agreed on, one being drinking of medication, but this presented a problem as it may not have been possible to swallow the volume required. The other two involved gas. I explained how in one method involving gas, you have to use a plastic bag to ensure it works, and in the other you inhale poison gas through tubes into your nose.

'Can you prove, theoretically, that this is a painless death?'

Obviously that was hard, since nobody can come back from the dead to tell us. But as the bag severs the oxygen flow to the brain, while the gases you inhale cut off the red blood cells that would take up the oxygen to the brain, a very peaceful death should follow. We gave Bernadette a book called *The Peaceful Pill* by Philip Nitschke, which outlines the methods, and shows you what you need to get and do, so that she could read up on the subject.

After our meeting I felt melancholic. All that talk of death made me think of those poor families whose loved ones have taken their lives through suicide. Especially now that suicide is on the increase in Ireland, in young men and in older people. It made me think more about my plan and how I must ensure that I leave behind good support for my loved ones. The last thing I want is for my death to haunt them when I decide to go.

Perhaps the best thing that happened that week, and indeed to have come out of the pending case, was the report from Dr Paul Scully. The eminent psychiatrist and at Beaumont Hospital stated that I suffer neither depression, psychosis nor madness of any kind. In fact he found me to be a very intelligent woman. Bless him. So to anyone who thought I was mad or selfish to take the case – and I am sure there are people out there who did – I can shout from the rooftops 'I am sane!'

The report was compiled for my legal team. They were afraid that the defence would put up a case questioning my sanity, possibly suggesting that I have psychosis. Dr Scully stated in the report that I was a truthful, independent woman who is very sure of the task she hopes to undertake and is in no way influenced by other people.

ೋಌ

In early October Simon became engaged to Susan Hearne, the mother of his child. This was quite wonderful news. He told me that he was thinking of changing his name to Hearne so that Evan and Susan's son Jordan could have the same name at school. He asked me would I mind. He said he hadn't seen his father for years and didn't want to continue carrying his name. I had no problem with him dropping it. Hearne is a good, solid Waterford name.

To celebrate, Simon organised a family lunch in a big local hotel. It was a gorgeous day. We gathered in the foyer beforehand and had some drinks. The grandchildren ran in and out of the garden, making a happy noise and playing well together. The air was filled with loving goodness. Then we went into the dining room for a beautiful lunch. On occasions like that we go round the table and ask everyone to tell us their news. We started with Tom's son Dave. I always think of Dave as an impoverished teenager, running around the students' union wearing jeans and a hat. It took my breath away to see him in trousers, a shirt, and shoes with a high polish on them. He looked the proper gent. I forget sometimes that he is now thirty and has started to work full time. He has a job with the trade union SIPTU.

The afternoon passed in a lovely haze, surrounded as I was by all the people I love. I felt empowered to remain strong to see to my future, and it made me realise how good that future could be. I enjoyed watching my grandchildren. I feel I can tell all their characteristics already – one strong, one gentle, one very vocal, another soft and gentle. One who will be spoilt and loved by everyone, and another two who will remain fiercely independent. In both families I can see the gentleness of their fathers combined with the strength of their mothers.

It was such a happy afternoon that nobody wanted to leave. We were looking at our watches but saying, 'Can't we stay just another bit?' Once we *did* move, the goodbyes and kisses lasted so long that the children, glued into their car seats, were getting fed up and were shouting, 'Please come.' So we left shouting 'Goodbye' and 'See you later.' It was my perfect day.

On a more frustrating note, my MS began to cause me a great deal of pain over the following days. I worried that it was a consequence of the day out on Sunday. My arms felt as if they were being pulled out of their sockets. My bottom felt flattened with all the sitting, and my spasms became uncontrollable. I lay down and my legs kicked out. I worried that one day my uncontrollable limbs would put out somebody's eye.

Other than that, I felt great. I thanked God for the spirit that I have and for the jokes and stories my carers told me to keep me amused. I don't have time or want time to think about anything else. I just live for the moment, and with God's help that will continue.

Talking of God, I watched a programme during that week discussing creationism versus Darwinism, and I believe in both. The fascinating programme concluded that God created the world and Darwinism filled it, and that theory sits well with me. I want to believe that I am going to meet each and every one of my relations in the next life. That is why I have no fear of dying. I believe dying is like going into a different room and shutting the door behind you.

Around that time a director approached Tom. He wanted to interview me about end of life issues but I am against having a production team involved. My views are private. After death is not a problem to me – it is the thoughts of pre-death that worry me: the sorting out of legal issues, such as making a will, leaving my home in the hands of someone who will love it as much as I do and, most important of all, making Tom feel as secure as possible and *not* making him a criminal. He deserves it and I owe it to him.

Tom has looked after me for the last eighteen years. He danced me around the room when I could dance, he wheeled me across Europe on holidays when my legs felt iffy, and he put up with me wetting myself everywhere we went. In Australia, on day two, I had him parked outside a hardware store trying to get granny pads that I could use. He put up with all that, and now to have to get me up, dressed and positioned in my chair for *Strictly Come Dancing* is a real endurance for him. Not to mention feeding me, giving me numerous drinks of water and turning the telly up or down as my hearing lets me down. So what if he escapes during the week to have a quiet coffee or a chat in peace on his mobile phone? Small deeds in payment for a lifetime of care, of the care of someone else.

Towards the end of October I had an appointment with my neurologist guru Professor Niall Tubridy, or Prof. Tubs as they call him in Vincent's. We needed him to write a report for the High Court. He was in a good mood and he laughed and joked.

Meanwhile, the papers were served on the Director of Public Prosecutions and the Attorney General. They each had ten days to respond to the preliminary hearing. Once a date is allocated for a court case, then, and only then, is the full documentation presented to the High Court. Our solicitor had sent us a copy of everything she presented. Meanwhile, the Irish Human Rights Commission decided to join the case on our side.

The legal eagles presented the papers to the High Court and they were accepted. The hearing was to be on 4 December. In the public interest there were to be three judges presiding over the case instead of the normal one. My legal team were pleased with that. It meant that the case would be fought on points of law rather than on witness statements. And there was more good news. The International Committee for Human Rights wanted to become involved. Tom had a call from them.

As the case drew closer we had to discuss all the specific details. I didn't want to read out a prepared statement to the judge for my presentation on 4 December 2012 as *I am* that statement. I live my life every day of the week, sometimes in great pain, but I always try to have a smile on my face. My carers and helpers don't want to come into an unhappy house, and I like to be able to lift their spirits, and when I do that they invariably lift mine. Above all, I am an independent woman. As part of that, I wanted to write my statement myself.

In the last few days before the case I had too much time to think and I was filled with anxiety and apprehension. I went over in my mind what questions the legal eagles would ask me. Then I began to worry that the judge might not understand me now that my voice had become so weak. Or perhaps they would not understand the Donegal accent I am so proud of.

It was an early start for me on the Tuesday when the case

began. I was woken at seven and hauled out of bed at eight. I went through my tedious morning routine of getting showered, toileted and then dressed. Then my carer of the day made me some breakfast. By the time ten o'clock came, I was all ready to go. Three hours in total to get me out of the house.

Tom loaded me into the car. We bumped our way on the terrible road into Woodenbridge; Tom had to stop a few times to reposition me. We've been trying to get the council to mend the crevices of potholes for years but nothing ever happens. We called at Corrinna's house in Dalkey and had a cup of coffee there while Corrinna gave instructions to Cara's childminder. Simon arrived soon after us; he had driven from Waterford. Tom drove all four of us into town from there and we picked up his son Dave on the way. We felt it was important to arrive as a family.

It felt so strange to be going to the High Court for the first time since I was sixteen.

Simon was fascinated when I said how poignant it felt, going there in such different circumstances. We arrived at the court at about a quarter past one. We rounded the corner, heading for the car park, and a swarm of photographers jumped at us, appearing from every angle, flashing and clicking, even scratching the window with their cameras in the hope that you would turn your head and look their way. We stared straight ahead and hoped that the Wicklow mud on the windows blurred their view.

I was sitting there, strapped in, and with my neck brace on, with Corrinna and Simon each side of me clutching on to my hands. It wasn't the most glamorous pose; I felt like a tiger at the zoo. Simon told me later that he was quite sure that the press would print that picture. The image of it stayed with him all day but the journalists were more sensitive than he feared and not one of the papers stooped to that.

They had kept a space for us in the car park, away from prying eyes. That was a relief. Once we had parked, my legal team came out and sat in the car with me. They went through all the questions they were going to ask me; they wanted to make everything as easy as possible. That was wonderfully reassuring.

When we entered the court I was instructed to sit by the journalists' entrance. This was because the three High Court judges had decided they would come and sit close beside me to question me, rather than sit on their thrones a mile away. I smiled to think of them coming down to earth for the first time in a wee while.

Both Tom and Bernadette Parte had visited the court beforehand and had gone through all my needs. The court could not have been more accommodating. Benches had been moved and an entrance blocked off to make way for my wheelchair. The press gallery had been cleared to make way for the judges. The journalists had to sit where a jury would normally go.

They gave me a radio microphone; apparently that is rarely heard of in the court. Tom was very impressed. They asked him to place the microphone on me. He was in his element. He asked jokingly if we could keep the microphone. He would have liked it for Masquerade, the theatre group in Arklow, for his sounds and sound effects.

Nicholas Kearns, the President of the High Court, asked me how I would like to be addressed. Could they call me Marie or would I prefer to be referred to as Mrs Fleming? I thought that was so considerate.

The court, it seemed, had done everything in their power to make me feel comfortable. Tom had told them about my difficulties in swallowing. I found that warm water eased my throat the best, so when the clerk of the court, bringing over a glass of water, with a straw, assured me the water was warm, I was touched.

I looked around me. Why was everyone in black? Nobody was wearing any kind of colour; even those in the public gallery were dressed as if they were going to a wake. My wake, I presume? I was distinctive, and not just because I sat in my wheelchair. I was wearing a bright red jacket.

I swore on the bible, feeling that today was a good day for my voice. I felt I could talk without stopping. So when my barrister introduced himself to me in court – like an act, pretending he was a stranger to me – I was ready to answer any question he could throw my way.

'Tell me, Mrs Fleming, why are you here today?'

That was easy. Concentrating on speaking clearly, I said, 'I came today while my voice is still working, to tell the court, and anyone else who is listening, that I want to die peacefully, but to die peacefully I need assistance, and Tom Curran, my partner of eighteen years, is willing to do that for me. Unfortunately, this could mean that he is prosecuted and jailed for up to fourteen years. And if my children are in the house at the time, they could be charged too. That is not a legacy I am willing to leave behind.' My voice was growing weak, so Tom helped me to have a sip of water.

'And what about palliative care? Have you thought of going into a hospice to die?'

'That is not acceptable to me.'

'Mrs Fleming, how do your children react to you coming here today?'

'My children have been grieving for me for over twenty years. They thought they might lose me two years ago during a bad bout of pneumonia. When I told them what I proposed to do they said that whatever decision I came to, they would support me fully. My children love me and know exactly how difficult it is for me on a day-to-day basis. They don't want to lose me or all the good times we have had together. We are a family that spends holidays and Christmas in each other's company. We are together in court today. This family is one for all and all for one. We are the best of friends and the worst of friends at times but I have made peace with the world and the world has made peace with me. So I have no regrets, just celebrations.'

'Have you thought of the actual process of dying?'

'Yes. I have thought of the methodologies, and about my funeral. So the methodologies would have to be some gas intake or some injection intake. I would need assistance with those. I want a wicker coffin and I want jazz music played. I don't want any expensive cars to take me to the crematorium. I would be happy in the back of my own car.' That was telling them, I thought. Nobody could say that I had not been thinking about this.

Then they repeated the first question. 'What did you come here for?'

'I only had one reason. I was looking for the court's help.' That was it. The questioning was done for the day.

Neither the human rights defending barrister nor the state barrister had questions, so I was free to go. It was back into the media flashbulbs. It was strange, later, watching ourselves on RTÉ television news. And when Corrinna texted to say we had gone global, I laughed. 'It's about time the world heard me,' I said to Tom.

Chapter Fifteen

Results and Reactions

Tom was proud of me after my day in court. 'You were
incredible,' he said. 'I was so worried that you wouldn't
make it. I was worried that you would not have the strength for
it. But your voice was strong and clear.'

I shrugged off his compliments but of course I was pleased.
And I had been worried too. I had fully expected that my voice
would give out before I had said all that I wanted to say. 'You
came across so well,' Tom said, and I saw tears in his eyes. 'Truly,
Marie, you were unbelievable.'

We had both been anxious that the defence team would
cross-examine me. As it turned out, they did not. We realised

afterwards that there was no way they would have done that. 'They were so impressed that you were prepared to attend the court that they were going to make everything as easy for you as they possibly could,' said Tom. 'You were there to say your piece and that was it.'

In legal terms we were challenging the constitutionality of the ban on assisted suicide contained in the Criminal Law (Suicide) Act of 1993. We were saying it was incompatible with the European Convention on Human Rights Act 2003.

The case lasted for six more days. Tom attended every day but I stayed at home. And with me no longer present, the court got down to fighting a legal case, and in Tom's eyes I turned from being regarded as a person to being merely a commodity. I know that is how the courts work but Tom found it very upsetting. When he heard the dispassionate way they spoke about me and about 'Mr Curran', he felt like sticking up his hand and saying, 'I am here. I am a person.'

Our legal team were keen to keep Tom off the stand. They felt that his presence would not help the case because he had openly stated that he would help me to die, whatever the law said. They also felt that with his involvement in Exit International it might come across as a campaigning case and not a personal case. They felt it would seem as if Exit was using me, but of course that was not true. Tom would never have become involved in Exit International were it not for me. It felt to him as if there was a gagging order on him.

'It annoyed me too when the defence brought forward two witnesses representing palliative care,' he said. 'One of them said that he felt palliative care would help you and he claimed that we had refused to contemplate it.' That wasn't true. And Tom wanted to jump onto the stand and say so.

'So what happened?' I asked.

'I got into a huddle with our team. They agreed that in this case it would be good to let me give evidence and to knock that accusation on the head. I felt I could have handled it.'

'Yes, I agree. You're always good at stating your case.'

'But the team worried that if I was questioned, the defence could twist my words and make it sound as if I was driving *you* to take the case.'

'But that simply isn't true.'

'We know that. But you know lawyers,' said Tom.

The truth was that he *had* applied for palliative care. He had met the team at Saint Vincent's Hospital but because I was not an in-patient they could not be involved. They referred us to the Blackrock Clinic and he tried to get them drawn in to help me but he failed miserably. They said they could review my case if I went into hospital for a while but I was adamant that I did not want to go in. I am scared that in hospital I might pick up an infection. I want only to stay at home. And Tom wants what I want.

It was so hard for me to be sitting at home waiting anxiously for news. But it wasn't easy for Tom either. He said it felt odd having to come home and report the case to me, the person the case was all about. He found it a strain going through all the legal details with me. We were of course anxious to hear the outcome but the three judges reserved judgement.

The case was taking all our energy. And I was worried about the effect it could have on the rest of the family. Before the case began, I rang Corrinna and Simon and told them to be sure to tell the older children about the case before they heard it from someone else.

'Explain it all to them before the case starts,' I had said. 'Because if you don't, they are bound to hear about it at school. They might even learn about their granny's case in class.'

Richard and Corrinna sat Cormac and Aran down and told them together. It was difficult, because they had to explain the complexities of the case. First they needed to tell them what suicide was and then they went on to explain the concept of assisted suicide. My grandchildren were shocked, obviously, and really upset, but it was Aran who took it worst. Cormac understood why I was doing it. 'This is about Granny having the same choices as everyone else,' he had said to Aran.

'Cormac really surprised me,' Corrinna told me later. 'He came up with a comment that showed he knows me almost better than I know myself.'

'What was that?'

'You know how, when I am angry or upset, I tend to withdraw inside myself? I will maybe sit and think but not speak?'

'Oh, yes. Yes, Corrinna, you were always like that.'

'Was I? Well, I'm barely aware that I do this, but Cormac turned to me and said, "Mummy, when Granny *does* die are you going to sit at the table and not talk for about six months?"'

I laughed. 'And how did you reply?' I was intrigued.

'I couldn't think what he meant at first. Then I realised this was his way of asking me how I was going to grieve. I was trying to come up with an answer when Richard piped up. "Boys," he said. "It's only ever really been Mummy and Granny. Mummy's mum and dad split up and Granny split up with Uncle Simon's dad as well. A few years later Granda Tom came but it was just Mummy and Granny for a long time. Because of that, Granny means everything to Mummy."'

'Well, that *was* perceptive of Richard,' I said. And I wished I could put my arms around my darling daughter.

'I know. Then he said, "Mummy is going to find it really, really hard when Granny dies. And we are just going to have to be there for her. And however Mummy reacts, whether she's quiet at the kitchen table, whether she cries, we are just going to have to accept it. It's part of us all learning what it is like to lose a parent."'

'Well, that was profound.' I was pleased for Corrinna. I worry about her. It's good to be reminded of how good Richard is. How he is a silent strength and support.

'You must hate me sometimes, Corrinna, for putting you all through this.'

'No, but I do have to argue with people who think you should not be fighting in the courts.'

'What do you say to them?'

'That you are doing the ultimate thing for me and for Simon.'

'How do you work that one out?'

'I believe your role as a parent is to prepare your children for things you will come across in life. And by going to court you are preparing me and Simon for your death. And very few parents have the courage to do that. And though sometimes it is all terribly hard, you are holding our hands through the most difficult thing we will ever have to face, which is losing you.'

Corrinna found the court case difficult to sit through. But she was impressed with the reaction to me. 'It was so emotive when you gave your testimony,' she said. 'There was utter silence in the court. Even the journalists had tears in their eyes.'

After the case, some barristers that Corrinna knew went over to her to say how extraordinary they had found it. They said, 'I've never seen judges come down to talk to a witness like that.'

'I know they meant well, Mum,' said Corrinna, 'but it annoyed me that they felt the law was doing you a favour. Surely the law is there to serve people, not the other way round. They seem to think it's okay that the pomp and ceremony should take precedence over the people.'

After the case, Tom and I went straight home but Corrinna and Simon decided to go for a coffee with Tom's son Dave. It was the first time ever that the three of them had sat down to talk without anyone else around. That might seem strange, but when Tom and I met, Dave and Simon were just teenagers. Corrinna had recently got married and was living in London and working. The boys were still at school, so the three of them had a very different kind of relationship back then. They had never really discussed my MS.

Corrinna asked Dave what he felt about the case. Did he mind his daddy being involved? It was something that worried her. She said, 'We know how *we* feel about it because it's all about our mum, but it must be more difficult for you.'

Dave reassured Corrinna that he supported what Tom and I were doing 100 per cent. Then she felt she should address the impact Tom's relationship with me might have on him. That was something else they had never talked about. So she said, 'Dave,

I don't know if you realise the impact Mummy meeting Tom has had on my life and on Simon's. If it wasn't for Tom, we wouldn't have a life. And neither would Mum.

'Your dad is amazing. He has been there for Mum at every single stage. He helped her accept the Rollator, then the wheelchair, and he made her realise these devices were designed to help her to be independent. Whereas before, she looked at them negatively, as signs of her increasing disability, he showed her all the benefits and he did that in a fun way. Dave, you could be thinking, Who *are* these people? Are they just taking advantage of my dad? Why should he risk being imprisoned for someone who was already sick when he met her?'

Dave had been reassuring. He pointed out that I had had an incredible impact on his father too. 'She has been vital to him,' he said. Dave had worried about Tom before we met. He had been lonely. 'Look at him now,' Dave had said. 'He's so happy and fulfilled.'

It was really good to hear that. I wouldn't expect anything less of Dave, and Corrinna hadn't *really* expected him to object. Dave is a lovely, charismatic man – he is very like Tom. My grandchildren call him Lego man because when he spends time with them, he is always on his hands and knees constructing things.

ℝ℞

It was difficult getting through Christmas without knowing the result of the court case. Judgement finally came in January; thankfully I was well enough to attend. We drove up with

Corrinna and met Simon and Dave in the court. Once again benches had been cleared so that we could get the wheelchair in. We sat where the counsel usually sit. We all hoped it would go our way but the outcome was an emphatic 'No!' While we were very disappointed, we were not surprised; we had not really expected anything else. Tom was holding on to my hand, and when the judgement came he raised it to his lips and kissed it. One of the papers picked up on that.

The court did not agree that my rights under the Constitution negated the ban on assisted suicide. The judgement said, 'While a competent adult patient has the right to refuse medical treatment, even if this leads to death, the taking of active steps by a third party to bring about the death of another is an entirely different matter, even if the difference in some cases between the two types of decision may be nuanced and blurred.'

The court showed some sympathy for my case. The judgement went on to say, 'If this court could tailor-make a solution which would suit Ms Fleming alone, without any implications for third parties or society at large, there might be a good deal to be said for her Article 40.3.2. case. But this court cannot be so satisfied.'

We had thought that the decision made in British Columbia might sway the case in our favour. There the court concluded that in jurisdictions which allowed assisted suicide there was no abuse of the right, but quoting that judgement the Irish court said that having looked at the same evidence, they had come to the opposite conclusion. They said that examples of abuse of the law were deeply disturbing.

'At least the court was impressed with you, Marie,' said Tom.

'But after the strength you had shown giving judgement, that didn't surprise me. I *know* that you are a remarkable woman.'

Delivering his verdict, the judge, Justice Kearns, said that in the seventy-five years since the Constitution has been enacted, few cases had emerged which were more tragic, or presented more difficult or profound questions, than my case.

I admit his words pleased me. He said that the court had been both humbled and inspired by my courage and mental clarity in giving evidence. How could that not make me feel good?

Tom wonders if we would have been successful had we approached the court case differently. Our legal team decided to put emphasis on the autonomy side – that is, that a person has a right to make a decision for themselves. That had been tried before in England and elsewhere and had failed. He felt we could have had more success if we concentrated on my being discriminated against because of my disability.

It was cold on the day of the decision and the court knew the press would need photographs. They allowed the cameras into court so that I wouldn't get cold waiting around. They allocated a place near the Law Library. That was thoughtful of them but there were so many cameras in court that day, and a barrage of press, that we felt crowded and pushed around.

Bernadette Parte read out our prepared statements. Tom was itching to comment and to talk about the disappointment he felt but our legal team said he must not, because if he did he would inevitably be asked questions. They were worried because of the possibility that we might challenge the decision in the Supreme Court. That was frustrating for him.

After we had left the court, the five of us, all the family, drove out to Dún Laoghaire and had a lovely relaxing meal in The Hen House. It's a place we go to often. We love it, and sometimes take the grandchildren. It was a good way to get over the stress of the day.

When the news broke, Tom's telephone buzzed all day. Texts poured in from people saying how saddened they were to hear the verdict. It was heartening to learn how much goodwill there was towards us.

✎✎

On Tuesday 26 February 2013 the Supreme Court with its seven judges began discussions on the three submissions made to the court – one by my team, one by the state and one by the Irish Human Rights Commission. To sum it up, my submission stated that I had a right to choose whether to die or not, that it was my right. The state declared that it had not been proven that I have any rights. The Irish Human Rights Commission disagreed with the state; they said that I *did* have a right and that this right was being invalidated by the state. That was the starting point for a discussion on a 120-page document. The court stated that no decision would be formulated until at least Easter.

One of the difficulties had been finding seven judges to conduct the trial, never mind getting them all to sit down and agree an outcome. Just before the case began, our solicitor, Bernadette Parte, rang to say that one of the judges was on the board of a palliative care unit. She asked us if we wanted him taken off the case but we felt he should stay. We accepted all seven judges with a good heart. At eight o'clock on that

Tuesday morning Tom's phone was buzzing with text messages. Most of them were from family and friends wishing him well. Nine were from journalists.

Since I wouldn't be attending the court, I felt somewhat detached from the case. Poor Tom spent his Sunday reading all the submissions to me, and to be honest it left me with a sore head and the ability to think that it was all happening to someone else. It was easier that way.

The first day of the court hearing was a tough one on Tom. In the morning the court discussed whether or not I had a right to die. Tom phoned at midday and said that Brian Murray, our senior counsel, had certainly earned his wages. He had all seven judges firing questions at him and he didn't falter once. Brian Murray had the floor for one and a half days, then the lawyers representing the Irish Human Rights Commission would be allocated a half day. The state would speak on the third day, and Friday was apparently a day of rest.

The afternoon, according to Tom, was less vigorous; it was all about point-scoring. Tom said that the power of suggestion was unbelievable. Brian Murray took every opportunity to talk about my rights. On Wednesday morning he conducted a question and answer session and Tom felt that his questions were extremely insightful. He felt sure that two judges were on our side; unfortunately, we needed at least four.

In the afternoon a lawyer for the Irish Human Rights Commission stated that body's case, but of course it all depended on the state. They took the floor on the second day and we were in limbo until we heard what they had to say. It was so hard for me waiting that day for Tom to come home. And when he did, it was clear that we were going to have to wait until after Easter for a decision on the case.

I wished I could have attended the Supreme Court but Tom said it was a good thing that I wasn't there. He said that we were nothing more than tools for legal argument.

We both know that this is what the Supreme Court is about. In effect we *are* only there so that a legal argument can be implemented but Tom wanted to highlight to them that it is people they are talking about. 'The legal profession is supposed to be there on behalf of people, not on behalf of the court,' he said. 'The court is there for people but they act as if they are above people, that they are in this higher position. I think they should appreciate this and show more sensitivity.'

I have rarely seen Tom as upset as he was after Judge Susan Denham's summing up on the last day. He talked about nothing else for days.

Soon after the case I became ill again. Instead of celebrating Saint Patrick's Day on 17 March, Tom was up day and night caring for me, convinced that this time I would die. One day I was so ill that he feared my speech had gone. He worried that the MS had taken a firmer hold but, thank God, when the infection eased, my speech returned.

Because of my deterioration, my routine changed. My morning now started at 11 am instead of 9 am. I rarely ventured out. So although Tom visited the Supreme Court to check the building for wheelchair access for me, neither of us thought I would be well enough to attend the judgement. And so it proved.

My health continued to worry Tom. I would recover from one infection, he would start to relax, and then I would go down with another one. That was the pattern during the spring. When a date finally arrived for the Supreme Court judgement I was unable to attend the court. Tom left me at home, promising to ring through the result, and he attended on 28 April with Corrinna and Simon.

The seven-judge Supreme Court ruled that there was no constitutional right – which the state, including the courts, must protect and vindicate – either to die by suicide or to arrange for the termination of one's own life at a time of one's choosing. Neither did the principle of equal treatment apply. As a disabled person I did not have the right to be assisted in taking my own life.

Justice Susan Denham did say, and I quote, that 'nothing in the court's judgement should be taken as necessarily implying it would not be open to the state, in the event the Oireachtas were satisfied that measures with appropriate safeguards could be introduced, to deal with a case such as that of Ms Fleming's.' I didn't find much comfort in that.

It wasn't just that we had lost the case. As Tom said, we had expected that, but it was the words that were used. We were 'dismissed'. That word repeats in Tom's memory over and over again. We were dismissed. We might as well have been told, 'Go away. Stop bothering us.'

Tom's first thought was to ring me. He found that hard but he knew it was important that I hear the news from him. He knew I would be disappointed. We expected the result, yet there was always that glimmer of hope, hope that had now been dashed. It was a short conversation.

There was one good thing. Now that the Supreme Court

case was over, our lawyers could not object to his speaking in public. At last their gagging order was off him and he could speak his mind. Knowing that there were cameras and press interviewers waiting for the family outside the court, he worked out in his head what he would say to them. The minute he stepped outside, this sea of journalists rushed forward, asking him if he had any comment to make. He had made a few notes but in the event he didn't even look at them. He started talking and all these words poured out. He just said it exactly as he was feeling it at the time.

He said that he and I were very disappointed by the Supreme Court's verdict. 'It's very difficult to understand how a person with a disability can be deprived of something that's legally available to everybody else, every able-bodied person, and for that not to be discriminatory under the Constitution. That is something we fail to understand,' he said.

'The Constitution is there to protect people like Marie and to give them solace that they will be looked after. The court has ruled on Marie's future, as far as they're concerned, and we will now go back to Wicklow and live our lives until such time as Marie makes up her mind that she has had enough. And in that case the court will have an opportunity to decide on my future.'

'Does that mean you will help Marie to die?' This from a journalist.

'That will only come up if Marie makes the decision herself.'

One of them asked why Marie was not there to hear the decision.

'Marie was very disappointed that she could not attend. She is suffering from what could have been a fatal chest infection. As you probably know, it has been a very difficult situation, both emotionally and physically, for Marie to bring this case here, to ask for help to die.'

With that Tom walked off, pleased to have got it all off his chest.

All week Tom's phone rang with journalists wanting to interview him for newspapers, for the radio and for television. That week's edition of the *Sunday Independent* used the part of his statement starting *The court has ruled on Marie's future, as far as they're concerned, and we will now go back to Wicklow and live our lives until such time as Marie makes up her mind that she has had enough. And in that case the court will have an opportunity to decide on my future* as their quote of the week. And later we discovered that Tom's fame had spread further. The same quote was picked up by a New York newspaper and became its European quote of the week.

Miriam O'Callaghan wanted Tom to go on *Prime Time*. He liked her interviewing style but he had the choice of doing that or going on *The Late Late Show*. Miriam felt the issue was best dealt with on a current affairs programme but Tom and I disagreed. We think the people who tune in to programmes like *Prime Time* are already politically aware. You are not telling them anything that they do not already know. *The Late Late* has a different audience and a bigger one.

I was impressed with Ryan Tubridy. He rang Tom before his appearance on the show and said, 'We're going to be talking about Marie. You know her, but I don't. Can I come and meet her?' He came out to the cottage one morning. We both liked him, and he and I were drawn to each other.

At one stage he asked me if he could be very forward and touch on a difficult subject. He said, 'If you were my mother or my wife or my sister I wouldn't want you to go anywhere. Am I being selfish?'

And I said, 'Yes, you are being selfish. You're only thinking of yourself.'

Tom thinks he was very moved by me. And I really appreciated his visit. It gave me a voice.

The next morning Tom got a call from Ryan. It was early and he was on his way into work. He thanked Tom and said, 'It was lovely to meet you both.' He asked Tom if he could talk about his visit on his radio show. 'I want your permission,' he said. I was really impressed. He said he needed our permission because he had come to see us for a different purpose.

I listened to his show on RTÉ 2fm. He told all his listeners not only what an impressive person I was but what an intellectual, and how nice I was. He said you could feel the love between Tom and me in the room. I liked that.

When Tom was setting up for his appearance on the *Late Late Show*, he told the researcher that he didn't want to answer adverse questions from the audience. He had a story to tell. He knew it would be hard, and emotional. The researcher said, 'But there are so many people who will be empathetic to you.'

'That may be so,' said Tom. 'But there may be others who don't agree with what I'm doing. I don't feel strong enough to deal with arguments tonight. I can't face the risk. So if I see that boom microphone coming out, I'm leaving.'

'You wouldn't.'

'Watch me.'

He said it lightly, but the researcher knew he was serious.

Tom gets nervous when he appears on television. He doesn't want to see anyone before the show because being with people creates more tension for him. It has become a thing for him to go to Dalkey and have a meal by himself in Ouzo's restaurant. It calms his nerves. Then he goes across the road to the Kings Inn for a pint. The RTÉ cab picks him up from there.

The other times he had appeared on television hadn't been so important. But this appearance was different. He knew he was going to be talking about me for a long period and there was nobody else to help him out. I had deteriorated a lot since the last time he had been on television and he knew it was going to be emotional.

When he went into the green room a few people came up to him and said, 'I know who you are.' He was so nervous that he couldn't talk to them. He saw the researcher and said, 'I have one request.'

'You don't want audience questions, I know,' he said.

'One more request then. I'm not a bloody film star and I don't want the TV audience to see me walking onto the set. I want to be sitting there already.'

He didn't necessarily like Tom's suggestion but he agreed to it.

Simon was in the audience with Susan. Dave was there too, as was Tom's sister Ann, with her daughter. One of my carers went with her sister, as did Anne Walsh, who writes down my diary. So he had a lot of support. Corrinna was spending the evening with me.

We had decided to have a girlie night. She had promised to

bring Aoife and Cara to stay, and Richard was to look after the boys. But poor Aoife wasn't well that night.

We missed her. She is the sweetest child, and will always jump up and give me a sip of water. Cara tried to do that, and when she could not manage it she popped a grape into my mouth. We had a lovely time. A friend of mine, Mary Graham, came over too and we had a Chinese takeaway for tea. When it was time for the show to begin, we were lying on the bed. Tom kept ringing, telling us what time he was to appear. He sounded more and more nervous. I worried for him. When at last he came on, Corrinna and I held hands. As he spoke, I kept saying, 'Oh, no!' It was very hard to listen to him talking about me.

Tom looked nervous sitting beside Ryan Tubridy. He had dressed up for the occasion and was wearing a blue jacket with a mauve shirt. Ryan, I noticed, had on a suit and a red tie, but that is his usual TV style. I saw Tom take a few deep breaths as the cameras turned towards him.

Ryan started off talking about the judgement. Tom told him how cold the whole experience had been and they discussed the way the law works. Then he asked Tom how he met me and how he felt when I told him about my diagnosis. He explained, and they talked about the need for Tom to give up work to care for me.

He asked Tom to describe a typical day, then he asked if we ever had rows. Tom said, 'Yes. And one of the problems is that Marie can't shout as loudly as she used to be able to.'

Ryan laughed. 'Is that an advantage?'

'Uh-oh,' said Corrinna. 'I wonder what's coming next.'

'Certainly it's an advantage to me,' Tom said. 'But the other advantage to me is, when we used to have rows … I tend to get to a point where I realise there is little point in carrying on. And I walk away. She used to walk after me. She can't do that now.'

Ryan said, 'Now I know she is watching, from her bed.'

'Yes. I'm going to get it in the neck.'

And how right he was. 'Too right, you bastard,' I said, and Corrinna laughed.

After that the conversation turned serious. They talked through my decision, and Dignitas, and everything leading up to the court case. Then his questions became more probing. He said, 'Tom, are you still willing to help Marie end her life?'

'I gave her a promise and she has no other option. There is no legal option available to Marie. At this stage. When we realised it was illegal, we did everything in our power. That is the reason we took the case. The case was not to give Marie an option but it was to make sure that Marie had that option legally.'

'She doesn't.'

'She doesn't have that option legally now, no. But there is nothing stopping us from taking on the task and changing the law.'

'And in the event of that not happening in the near future?'

'I've given Marie an assurance.'

'You are going to do it if it has to happen?'

'But the decision will be Marie's, not mine.'

'When might that happen?'

'Again that's a decision for Marie, and I hope it is a long time in the future. Because selfishly I want Marie to be around forever.'

After recounting the conversation he had had with me when he visited, Ryan asked Tom to explain what he meant.

Tom said, 'You are wanting that person to stay, irrespective of what suffering they have. But it's for your benefit, and only for yours. And surely it is *their* decision whether they want to stay or not. Not yours. Of course their going will affect you. But their staying will affect *them*.'

Ryan then turned to points of law and the rights and wrongs of it. They talked of my health, and the interview ended with my words. This was the part Tom had most dreaded. He was to read out a letter he and I had prepared together. And he didn't know if he could do so with dry eyes.

The studio was silent. It was as if everyone, the whole studio audience, was holding its collective breath. Tom started off by saying, 'This may not be easy for me.' And then he read it:

Thank you for listening to what I have to say. This is what was missing from the court. While I feel let down by the judgement, it is more upsetting that it feels I wasn't listened to. It seems the state doesn't want me to die, but all the time it chips away at my quality of life, one cut after another, the latest being the mobility scheme, and carbon tax increasing heating and transport. Shame on Enda Kenny for what he is doing to people like me.

If the people who make the decision won't listen to me, I would ask them to come and live with my life for just one day or even one hour. And tell me how enthusiastic they would be about living. It seems they will not give me permission to die, but they will not help me to live either.

On a positive note I want to say how grateful I am to Tom, my family and all my carers for what they do for me. They do all the things I would love to be able to do for myself, like showering, dressing, feeding, and even scratching my nose when it itches.

I tolerate a lot and I don't ask much. All I ask is to be allowed make my decision about death and to be given that help that I need to carry out my wishes.

Through no fault of my own, I cannot carry out my wishes myself. I am not asking to find someone to help me. I have that person already. All I ask is that I can carry out my wishes without getting him into trouble. Is that too much to ask?

Tom had helped me to put those words together and I think they had some power. I was so grateful to him for reading them out and told him later that it was no harm that he had to stop and compose himself. It meant that everyone could see how sincere he was. It meant so much to me that, even though I could not attend the studio that night, the nation would know my thoughts on the court case.

And, reading my words, he did falter. Tears came. But he did get through it – if only just. When he finished, Ryan thanked him and the show ended.

After the show, Tom rang. And he was so upset. He said that normally when you are the last guest on the *Late Late Show* you are taken down from the podium to mix with your family and friends. There's a chance for members of the audience to talk to you before you and your connections go to the green room. That night Ryan could see that Tom was in a state so they took him backstage to a dressing room. He went in there and he cried for twenty minutes before he could face going to the green room.

The following day the case was all over the papers, and in the following weeks Tom was in demand on radio shows nationwide. To my relief, and that of the family, the response to my case was sympathetic. People stopped Tom on the street and in the supermarket to congratulate him and give us their support. The producer from *The Late Late Show* rang and said the ratings for the show had been the second highest ever, beaten only by the special programme they produced when the original presenter Gay Byrne left the show.

My story touched everyone, but as Tom says, so it should. I am still only fifty-nine. Tom and I should be enjoying life now that neither of us is working. We should be able to say, 'Let's go to Clare this weekend.' We should be travelling, and eating out together. We should be going abroad.

Nobody has said to us that we were wrong to take the case. Not one person. No one has come to Tom or to me and said it was wrong. But we are talking about a real case and nobody is prepared to argue against that. They will argue, for instance, when they debate a lot of hypothetical cases. Like the palliative care witnesses in the High Court. They will argue that the law change would open the floodgates, but that was all conjecture rather than fact. And they did not mention me at all. Nobody who has heard my story has come along and said, 'Marie, you should suffer through your pain and indignity, and it is wrong to allow you the right to die when you feel the time is right.'

Now that the court cases are behind me, with both the High Court and the Supreme Court dismissing my case, I am left with a legal right to live but not to die. That makes me feel as if I have no rights at all. I have lived for fifty-nine years as well as I could, but now that I am in a stage of terminal illness I have no right to an easy death. They have been discussing assisted suicide in England for the last few days. They now believe that a doctor should be able to give a terminally ill patient tablets to hasten their death; it will probably take us another twenty years in Ireland before this issue comes to the fore again.

Tom has been pursued by TV and radio pundits such as Pat Kenny, Miriam O'Callaghan, Ryan Tubridy and a cohort of journalists all looking for an exclusive interview. He has protected me by being the one to conduct any interviews that he deems important. The papers have sensationalised everything, from me going to ask him to kill me down to the method by which he might assist me to die. This has been going on now for weeks. The one good thing to have come out of the media coverage is the number of cards and letters of support that have been sent to me by people in Ireland and from as far away as Canada and Australia. Not one has been derogatory towards me.

People ask me what it feels like to be so famous. I don't think about that, not for one minute, not even for a second. Tom and I have gone public because we want people to learn more about the right to die movement. That is the only reason. We don't want to be celebrities.

Tom has become known as a campaigner for the right to die movement and some people assume that he would like to bump everyone off. I would like everyone to know that is not the case. He is in favour of people having the right to die, and the right to live. If they want to live, they should be given all the help in the world so that they can live well. They should be kept as comfortable as possible. Equally, if they don't want to live, they should be given that right as well.

Tom feels so passionately about this that he is starting an initiative of mentoring for people who are caring for someone who is at the end of their life. Carers of patients with MS, for example, need to know how to handle it and what to do, and many carers do not know. He is talking to the Irish Hospice Foundation, to MS Ireland, The Carers Association and has also engaged with the forum on End of Life in Ireland. He would like the Irish Hospice Foundation to train people to mentor others. He feels this would be of tremendous benefit and so do I. I am so proud of him.

Tom speaks so well, but he is naturally shy. He finds the right words because he is so passionate about the issues he talks about. If it were something trivial he would not feel able to speak. He describes himself as a backroom person. And he is doing a lot behind the scenes too.

When Enda Kenny dismissed John Halligan's question in the Dáil, he gave the impression that he was unable to change the law. That isn't the case, and Tom spoke out, saying he was mistaken. Enda Kenny then agreed, publicly, that theoretically the Dáil could change the law. Tom has been lobbying for a change in the law ever since. He has set up meetings with Enda Kenny and with the other political parties too. He will not let our case be forgotten.

The court case was not easy to live through and the result was disappointing. I feel bad that the court didn't listen but I don't regret taking it. It has achieved awareness that there are people like myself living with the fear of a bad death. There are also people – older people – living in institutions who have lost their dignity. My case has raised awareness of them too.

I am so grateful to Tom for enabling me to live at home. I would never have been able to cope living in a hospital or another institution. It would be total anathema to me. It would be lacklustre. I have a head. I have a brain. I need stimulation and I can get that from listening to the radio and from dictating my writing. I am a woman with a mind, and at home I can make decisions. I need to be dressed, but I can decide what to wear. I decide whether to have a shower or not, albeit that it has to be done by somebody else.

I am lucky to have known all my grandchildren. I feel proud of the role I have had in their lives. They are all such wonderful individuals, and if I have taught their parents anything, it is to accept their children for who they are and never try to mould them into a lesser version of themselves.

After all the infections I have suffered this year I am currently well. My doctor says my recovery has been miraculous. She has said the same thing maybe five times in the past but this time she is very impressed and amazed by my recovery. I am better than I have been since March 2013.

But things have changed since then. I have stopped going out. I'm annoyed about that but I feel unsafe outside my home. I can't control my wheelchair and I worry that someone will move me. I hate feeling helpless. I never feel helpless at home; nobody can get to me here. I feel wonderful. I know every crack in the walls, and every piece of wood, because I went and bought it and decided on it.

I have so much time now to think and to reflect on my life. I have some regrets. I wish my two marriages hadn't failed. But there is much I am proud of. I had a difficult start in life but it did not stop me from getting an education. I am proud of all that I achieved.

I've always said that I wanted to stop the rot of previous generations. The lie of my mother's parenthood, her being raised by her grandparents, unbeknownst to her until she was much older, her own mother little more than a child when she had her. Then her own early initiation into motherhood at just sixteen, the consequences of which bore out on all her children's lives as we struggled to stay together as a family in the aftermath of her departure. Too soon I was a mother myself but I was determined to do it differently. I am proud that I fought for my rights. But my greatest achievement, the best thing I did in my whole life, was to fight the church to keep Corrinna, and to fight tooth and nail to keep a sense of family for Simon.

EPILOGUE

⊰⊱

I have always said that if my brain goes, I go too. At the minute I am a rational human being with a great longing for knowledge. I am still interested in general knowledge, in current affairs, and in anything to do with space. I retain my love of books, even though I now have to listen to the audio versions. I often fall asleep while I listen to them, but even so, it helps to stretch my vocabulary and my thinking process.

If I were to lose that function, I would no longer be me. I would be an entity, an energy, or whatever word you would ascribe, but I would not be me. Therefore, choosing a time of death is my last privilege.

Before Tom's promise, I worried about the way I would die, but placing my trust in Tom has changed everything. I know

I will be all right. His promise has made all the difference in the world to me. It will be hard saying to Tom, 'I am ready.' I don't know how he will cope. But death holds no fear for me. I know that my father will come for me and he will bring Ben, my dog.

I have said to Tom I will know when the right time is, and that is not just to do with when my body gives out. I will have done in life all that I have intended to do. Earlier this year my aim was to attend my son Simon's wedding to Susan Hearne in August. I have done that. I was there. Now I want to get this book published, as a way of saying that I lived and I had a life. It has been a life of love. Love for my father, for the siblings I looked after; love for my children, my adorable grandchildren and my friends; love for Tom. All people see now is a woman in a wheelchair who can't speak very well, who can't move at all. But I lived. I loved. I am somebody.

MARIE'S LAST LETTER

READ BY HER DAUGHTER CORRINNA MOORE AT MARIE'S FUNERAL

൭൦ൻ൪

Dear friends, I lie here before you today on my final journey. I am not frightened, as rest assured my beloved daddy Danny will have come for me, to ease the way over to those that love me on the other side.

There has always been so much to say and so little time to say it. But before I leave, there are people I must thank.

George, thank you for inviting me into this beautiful church where I have such happy memories. It has given me such solace over these past years to know that I will rest in peace here.

My beautiful sister Noeleen and strong brothers Brian and Don. We went through so much so young, but think of the bond we have, and take strength from that. I'm with Shaun now and wait for you here. I love you and know how much you love me.

My friends and colleagues in Derry, Wales and Dublin. You helped me accomplish my dream: to educate myself and then in turn to impart that knowledge and wisdom to others

To my wonderful friends in Arklow and Killahurler, you welcomed me in, gave me a home and a new life. For that I thank you.

To my beautiful carers and friends, you know who you are. Thank you for the life and the joy you have brought to my home, and for helping enable me to stay there.

To my legal team, who helped me fight for what I believe in, the right to avoid a protracted, painful and undignified death. It is better to have fought and lost than not to have fought at all.

To my co-authors, my final accomplishment, a published writer. A dream come true thanks to you.

To my beautiful Simon and Corrinna, you are my finest achievement. You have given me the most wonderful gift in life: love, the reason to live. My legacy is in your hands. Now, take what I have taught you and guide these seven beautiful stars through life. Remind them of their granny Marie, and how much I love them, and tell them the delight they brought to me.

Finally, to my Anam Cara, my soul mate, weren't we lucky to have found each other? Tom, words cannot express how much you mean to me. My partner in life and love. Thank you for loving me, for carrying me, for caring for me. For fighting my corner and making sure my voice was heard. I love you and am with you. Find strength and carry on in my name. And if you waiver, know that I am in your heart. And if you miss me, walk around the beautiful garden we created together and know that my spirit is there in the gentle breeze.

Marie

ACKNOWLEDGEMENTS

೧ഇൽ

On Marie's behalf, Tom Curran, Corrinna Moore and Simon Fleming would like to thank the following people for helping this book come to fruition:

Anne Walsh, Anne Reid, Miriam Donohoe; Sue Leonard and Jonathan Williams; Ciara Considine, Breda Purdue and all at Hachette Ireland; Anne Enright and Dermot Bolger.

೧ഇൽ

Sue Leonard would like to thank:

My agent Jonathan Williams for getting me involved; Tom Curran, Corrinna Moore and Simon Fleming for endless hours of meetings; Breda Purdue and all at Hachette Ireland, especially my editor Ciara Considine, whose care and suggestions made the book so much better; the late Marie Fleming for writing her extraordinary memoir, and for allowing me to help her complete it.